DEEP, DARK, BLACK HOLE

DEEP, DARK, BLACK HOLE

*A Christian Pastor's
Story of Mental-Emotional
Collapse and Survival*

Mitchell Wayne Flora

FloraWorks Publications

Grimesland, North Carolina

FloraWorks Publications
Grimesland, North Carolina 27837
floraworkspublications.com
author@floraworkspublications.com *or* m.wayne.flora99@gmail.com

First Edition
Printed in the United States of America
ISBN 978-1-7349164-0-9 (paperback)
ISBN 978-1-7349164-2-3 (hardcover)
ISBN 978-1-7349164-1-6 (ebook)
Library of Congress Control Number: 2020906714
Cover design by Byron Eugene Gill
Editorial and Proofing by Rhapsody Flora Smith

Publisher's Cataloging-in-Publication Data

Names: Flora, Mitchell Wayne, author.
Title: Deep , dark , black hole : a Christian pastor's story of mental-emotional collapse and survival / Mitchell Wayne Flora.
Description: Includes bibliographical references. | Grimesland, NC: FloraWorks Publications, 2020.
Identifiers: LCCN: 2020906714 | ISBN: 978-1-7349164-0-9 (pbk.) | 978-1-7349164-1-6 (ebook)
Subjects: LCSH Flora, Mitchell Wayne. | Church of God (Cleveland, Tenn.)--Clergy--Biography. | Depressed persons--United States--Biography. | Clergy--Mental Health. | Clergy--Job Stress. | Burnout (Psychology)--Religious Aspects | BISAC BIOGRAPHY & AUTOBIOGRAPHY / Religious | BIOGRAPHY & AUTOBIOGRAPHY / Personal Memoirs | RELIGION / Christian Living / Personal Memoirs | SELF-HELP / Mood Disorders / General | SELF-HELP / Self-Management / Stress Management
Classification: LCC BV4398 .F56 2020| DDC 248.8/92--dc23

Dedication

"A good   woman is
hard to find, And   worth far more than
diamonds. Her husband   trusts her without reserve,
And never has reason to   regret it. Never spiteful, she
treats him generously all her life long" (Prov. 31:10-12;
MSG)

I found one!
I dedicate this book to you, Lou.

My wife, my friend, my inspiration.
God's gift to me to save me from
despair in the darkest days
of my whole life.

I love
you
!

Contents

In Praise of Deep, Dark, Black Hole

"Rarely will you find someone in religious leadership willing to make themselves so vulnerable and transparent as to the realities of their *own human suffering,* especially in matters of mental and emotional health. This is a masterful work that helps us understand how to place such crises into the framework of faith. Pastor Wayne has truly reflected his servant's heart, bearing his soul in hope of blessing those in need. I know you will be encouraged by his story! I assure you that what God has done for him, He will do for you!"
– *Pastor Steve Evans, Faith Assembly Church, Winterville, NC*

"I admire Dr. Flora telling his story of the deep emotional trauma that challenged him personally and spiritually, and particularly his image as a Wesleyan Pentecostal pastor. His transparency dealing with the trauma and tests of this harrowing experience will hopefully encourage other ministers from his tradition *and beyond* to embrace the challenges *they* incur and still continue in their walk with God." – *Donald G. Bennett, DMin, USA Coordinator, Division of Education, Church of God, Cleveland, TN*

"Throughout my many years in the church, I have seen numerous pastors, church leaders and parishioners suffer from emotional pain and, some, from actual breakdowns. Dr. Flora's book is a much-needed asset to a community of faith that does not adequately understand, address, or support those who suffer from these issues, thus causing them to suffer in silence *or worse.*" – *Patricia Pott, MA, Ashland Theological Seminary, Author of Cans in the Dryer: Why Can't I Just Leave (From Traumatic Bonding to Freedom)*

"Papa's book has been very inspirational to me. It has an amazing storyline and I loved it! I know others will too!"
– *Kylah Smith, my 11-year-old Granddaughter*

"Dr. Flora's voice is so authentic and relatable, you will feel he is speaking these words directly to you. With palpable passion, sensitivity, and purpose, his message of sickness and healing will comfort your soul and bathe your heart and mind with hope, firmly anchored by trust in our heavenly Father." – *Blair Vick, Coordinator of Donor Relations at Vidant Health Foundation*

"We can't undo the past, but God *can heal* past wounds and bring goodness, wisdom, and forgiveness to our past, present, and future. This book *explains how* in a distinctively-fine, Flora fashion." – *Angelene Davis, Retired Registered Nurse*

"In this book you will be faced head-on with the reality of life as it impacts you daily. Then you will be inspired, encouraged and directed toward the path of HOPE which will restore you to *God's reality* as found in His word." – *Robert Skorohod, Retired Chief at Rhode Island DHS, BS in Psychology Lee University*

"Thank you, Pastor Flora, for writing *Deep, Dark, Black Hole* and transparently sharing your experience of depression. Not only persons experiencing this health crisis can benefit from reading it, but also their families, friends, and co-workers." – *Karen Bean, Executive Assistant to Vidant Health Foundation President*

"I believe God will be honored by your message of hope and many people will be inspired by your experience." – *Tim Hopkins, MDiv from Duke University, 38-Year Founding Pastor of East Wake Church of God, Wendell, North Carolina, PRN Hospice Chaplain*

"Thank you, Pastor Wayne Flora, for sharing your words of prayer, love and hope. This will be a blessing to the many who struggle each and every day with depression." – *Barbara Reaves, Retired AT&T Administrator, my former Administrative Secretary at University Church of God*

"Wow! What a journey! The author's narrative approach telling his story is very effective; I felt like I was right there with him. Dr. Flora's story amplifies the grace of God, the possibilities of satanic attacks, and then the sovereignty of God. This book illustrates how medical professionals work hand in hand with our sovereign God in treatment of serious health issues. The reader is reminded that no matter anyone's relationship with God, none of us is Superman – we are all simply humans on a journey. The outcome demonstrates that God's man, in God's will, is immortal until God has fulfilled His purpose in his life. I recommend this reading to anyone suffering this sort of crisis, and certainly to every minister and lay person, as it reveals to the reader the battles we face in life can be won by trusting in a loving and sovereign God." – *Jerry Smith, BA, MA, EdS, NC Certified Licensed Counselor, Ordained Bishop, Retired Pastor, Educator*

"Not only is this story informative – it is from the heart." – *Joyce Bratton, Retired Educator*

"What a blessing to read your work as a whole narrative! I identified with you as your honesty is evident…readers will appreciate that. Your story is well written and will make someone wish they could just sit down and chat with you about this." – *Carole Swan, Masters in Christian Education in Missions, Retired Registered Nurse*

"This book is the story of Dr. Flora's own exasperating experience in the *Deep, Dark, Black Hole!* I admire him for writing it! It will help numbers of hurting people!" – *Franklin Hunt, DD, ThD, Retired 38-year founding pastor of Cedar Creek Church of God and Licensed Counselor*

xi

Acknowledgments

As with any worthwhile effort, one rarely achieves his aspired goals working alone. Neither has the inspiration and publication of this book, *Deep, Dark, Black Hole,* happened through the efforts of a solitary individual. I am so pleased to celebrate the teamwork and diligent energies of many people who tirelessly devoted themselves to hearing this story told. All of them truly believe that, just maybe, *someone* who reads this book, may be encouraged to *find their hope in life... once again.*

I first express gratitude to my wife, Lou, who helped me survive this harrowing health crisis. I will always believe God used her to "save me" from myself when I was so terribly sick. She is my encourager and spiritual coach. She not only has great faith, but great love. She shall never need to prove it to me – she already has! I'm so glad the epitaph on my headstone will no longer read, "He said he could, but never did (write his book, that is)!" While Lou was particular about proofing and corrections, she focused primarily on chronological accuracy and exactness of event description.

I next thank my daughter, Rhapsody, whose name itself exudes with inspiration – it means "ecstasy, praise, and exuberation." She was my primary "editorial staff and proofreader." Being the Registered Nurse and nursing educator she is, she was the perfect person to critically assess my syntax and grammar, making many corrections that lent to better style, accuracy, and readability. We will always debate the use of commas...my being "old school."

I next sing the praises of my amazingly-mature granddaughter, Kylah, age 11. She was my youngest "focus group" reader (and "cheerleader")! It was important to me that she could understand my story; she was constantly begging me to finish the next chapter! She also made several corrections and suggestions that improved the readability of my story. She empathetically "heard my heart!"

I thank "Papa George" Smith, age 84, my wife's father and only remaining parent from our childhood…who now lives with us, incidentally. He and I were often up early hours together, his reading the Scriptures to start his day and me feverishly writing as "bursts of inspiration" stole my sleep. He would end his day by following my story, chapter by chapter, and offering invaluable feedback to clarify the message. It was just as important to me that Papa George could understand my story as it was my granddaughter.

I wish to thank Byron Gill, my cover design artist. The photograph of the outstretched hands is his work – in fact, so are *the hands themselves!* He is so tech-savvy! And he truly has a servant's heart; he has given of himself countless hours to make this project a reality. He is a dear friend whose devotion to Christ is a witness of God's unconditional love to so many.

Finally, I want to thank my *entire* Review Team who, chapter by chapter, graciously read, reviewed, responded, and rewrote – whew! Week after week, they read my story and openly shared how effectively it communicated the challenges of my health crisis. I received suggestions that improved the quality of the book before it ever hit the market! I listened *intently* and responded *gratefully* for each one's contribution. I would like to name them all here and appreciate each one publicly. To each, I say, "Thank you!" You will never know how much it matters that you cared to be a part of this project! Your participation added value and worth to this story that I pray will offer healing and hope to many!

So as to gracefully distribute my gratitude, I list my Review Team in alphabetical order: Karen Bean, Dr. Donald Bennett, Joyce Bratton, Ruth Craig, Dr. Robert Crick, Eddie and Nora Davenport, Angelene Davis, Dr. Al and Lori Drake, Eddie and Rita Drake, Pastor Steve Evans, Lou Flora, Byron Gill, Leslie Hawkins, Tim and Lula Hopkins, Dr. Franklin Hunt, Glenn and Sheryl Nichols, Patricia Pott, Barbara Reaves, Dr. Donald Ribeiro, Gail Roberts, Robert Skorohod, George Smith, Dr. Jerry Smith, Kylah Smith, Rhapsody Smith, Carole Swan, Blair Vick, and Joan Zachary.

When we convene for our first "book signing," I should like to cook a Barbeque for all of you and present you your own free, personalized copy of this book for your selfless devotion helping to make it happen! Let's get together and celebrate our dream that many hurting people who suffer anxiety or depression will find hope within the pages of this book *to, once again, stir their faith in Christ and restore their hope in life.*

Preface

Sunday, January 26, 2020, 5:06 am. That's when I heard God speak softly into my heart these words, "Not before now, not until now, but now." I knew what He meant. I had been working on another book for several years, and it had become rather "hit-and-miss," given all my many other duty-bound responsibilities, pastoral and otherwise. My wife, Lou, had sensed all along that I should push that project to the side and write my story of mental-emotional collapse that occurred 14 years ago in May of 2006. I should learn to listen to her – she's *almost always* right. Smile.

From the moment I heard God's voice, I began writing, promptly, passionately, feverishly. I couldn't stop. My thoughts flowed faster than my fingers could type. The rush of the experience was like nothing I had ever known before. Especially as I would awaken at 2:00 am almost daily, feeling well-rested, and ready to write…in the quiet of night…when sin slows, birds sleep, and some saints pray. Never have my thoughts been clearer at that hour than they were these past few months.

By the way, I'm writing "journalistically" with elliptical sentences as in casual conversation, double hyphens for emphases, and ellipses for trailing thought. As a college professor, my grading rubrics for literary excellence are quite rigid, and I usually will not permit the grammatical latitude I take writing this narrative. I know better, but I wanted to tell *you* my story *my way*.

I wrote this book because I love people – and now that I *better understand* mental-emotional anguish because of what I experienced, I want to encourage others who suffer similar health concerns as I did. Please note, I'm *not* a medical professional – *my* doctorate is in theology, not medicine. So, I'm cautious *not to impress* you that I understand anxiety disorder or depression. Nor should I have you believe that I ever understood what was happening medically in my body.

I have no need or desire to become rich or famous. That has no place in my motives for writing a book. In fact, I feel the Holy Spirit *purified my motives* when He whispered in my thoughts that I should write this book "as a gift to my children and grandchildren, and that *if anyone else* in the world was touched by it, *that would be a bonus.*"

While I love writing and expressing myself through the power of written words, I had never felt the need to write a book *until I truly believed* I had something meaningful and significant to say, something perhaps that could help others *if I wrote it*. That, my friend, is how I approached this challenge from day one. I wrote this book *simply because* I wish to help...*you, maybe*. Or *someone you know*.

My words are raw and visceral. They are gut-wrenching and honest. I speak plainly, sometimes bluntly. But I do so to be authentic, to share with you the *real me*. When you read the words *"it seemed"* in my story, I am saying to you *that's how reality felt to me* – though not actually as it was. I'm careful to distinguish between what *actual, current reality felt like* versus how it truly might have been.

I pray that your acquaintance with me will offer you hope and give you reason to believe that you, too, can feel better... soon. And I also pray that Jesus Christ may become a part of *your life's* most complex equations...and you find Him to be important to your quest for peace, hope, help, *and health*.

Mitchell Wayne Flora
April 10, 2020

Introduction

Deep, Dark, Black Hole

Deep, dark, black hole. I know…it sounds redundant. Like, how many shades of black can there be?! Actually, lots. But only one tone so dark that no other shades beside it could be darker. One shade *only* so dark that it can be felt, experienced even, as thick, smothering, choking, crushing, life-draining. It has been aptly described as the *dark night of the soul* by many throughout history who were searching for an explanation of the enveloping darkness enshrouding the human spirit when it seems like God has departed and does not care to present Himself.[1]

It's a horrible feeling…actually, more than a feeling – a drenching despair – an anguish of soul, the horrid sense of a loss of hope. A claustrophobic, constrictive, blinding blackness. The seemingly fatal, final snuffing of any light left to a known world. The total loss of any sense of mental,

---

[1] Evelyn Underhill, *Mysticism,* 12th ed. (New York: New American Library, 1974 [1930]), 83. This concept is derived primarily from a poem by that title written by St. John of the Cross, a 16th century Spanish mystic and poet who saw darkness as a journey toward mystical union with God (or the spiritual identity crisis experienced on that journey). However, the phraseology can be further traced back to theologians and philosophers of the 6th century.

emotional, and spiritual orientation – certainly not always *medically*, but in worst case scenarios, possibly.

And fear. No, terror! The tyranny of terror that any bad thing that might happen, likely will. The sense that Satan's let loose on you, and that maybe, just maybe, somehow, someway, you made God mad, and His wrath has been unleashed, and He's not ready to make up. The desperate, consequent dread that you won't survive, that you can't be helped, and that quality of life as you had ever known it *has ended*. And now then, alone – *all alone* in a dark, dark place, a *deep, dark, black hole*.

That's what I experienced. A Christian. A minister, *even*, of the Gospel of Jesus Christ! A pastor desiring and venturing to care for others when in this most despairing, incapacitating stretch of my life, I couldn't at all care for myself. Totally overwhelmed, outdone, vanquished, I suddenly found myself empty and demoralized, having had no *obvious* warning of this impending, ominous, now onset crisis, no explanation as to why it was happening, and no immediate hope that I would ever escape its chilling clutch.

This is my story. I hope it helps.

Chapter 1

The Broken Road[2]

Triggered? Or predisposed? I really don't know. One physician says "yes… situational stress likely." Another says, "Maybe… genetics, perhaps." Situational distress? Or genetic proclivity? The Lord knows – I don't. All *I know is* it happened…to me.

Perhaps there had been clues to which I *should have* paid attention. One of my dearest friends, a truly tried and trusted "pastor's prayer partner," retired psychiatrist, Dr. Donald Davis, had hinted early in my pastoral ministry that I might need some medical assistance, since he had noticed how over-anxious I seemed to be about everything. I always moved at breakneck speed, becoming more and more involved in the life of our "healthy," growing church as ministry became *more and more complex, and* as all the while, *it seemed,* I got "behinder and behinder."

Having been the founding pastor, I humbly acknowledge now that "letting go" of administrative responsibilities to

---

[2] Okay, so there's no asphalt or painted lines in this chapter; however, there is a "potholed," pockmarked pavement showing considerable signs of cracking and wear, ill-omened indication that my pattern and pace of life was not healthy.

broaden the base of leadership as the peak of potential was realized *was hard for me to do!* I had always involved myself in some capacity with every new and developing ministry. I remember saying to our 25-voice choir that I intended to direct it until *someone more qualified than I came along* to replace me, which eventually happened. However, I directed the choir for 10 years…STRONG SIGNAL of liable-to-come difficult days and consequences, and admittedly, *a chink in the armor of my faulty model of leadership.* But I certainly didn't see it coming. I suspect I was smitten with a trifle of demand for perfectionism – and didn't realize that perfectionism and excellence weren't exactly the same.

I also remember quite vividly saying to my leadership team one fully-flustered week that I wasn't stressed – *I was simply very busy.* Denial. And to the congregation I stated, "The church is growing faster than leadership is recruited, trained, and appointed." True, but no excuse.

MY EMERGENCY RED LIGHT STAYED ON ALL THE TIME!

Mr. Fix It! Pastor Answer All! Exemplar Everywhere-At-Once (facetious, of course – only Jesus can do that)! Ease the pain! Stop the suffering! Do all I can to make *everybody else* feel better!

Some aspects of the Type A personality *seemed* to drive me – perfectionism ("Mr. Perf," my nickname in prior youth ministries), ambition (not necessarily competition), some degree of control, and yeah – plenty of self-criticism, "tightly wound" and occasionally overreactive, usually defensive. I had clearly stated to our founding families that I was *not a maintenance pastor,* and that I would *not be content* with status quo. I expected the church to grow and I believed, as McGavran put it, *"God wants His lost sheep found!"*[3] I had no intention of playing church and becoming a typical small church statistic.

Yet aspects of the Type B personality propensity found me deeply emotive and expressive, contemplative and reflective, *very, very sentimental* – not *necessarily* a good thing when people you love pass away or become critically ill…or find themselves dreadfully bewildered by any other manner of life crisis! In fact, my clinical pastoral education experience in 1990 unveiled *my fear of intense feelings* and how *that* "unpacked baggage" was dramatically affecting the efficiency (or lack thereof) of my present ministry!

I'm not saying the church required it or even expected it, but simply that I demanded it of myself. It seemed to me I was engaging more reactive than proactive ministry most of the time – putting out fires, counseling hurt people, visiting the sick, and comforting the

> **Ministry is both proactive and reactive. Achieving balance is quite a challenge!**

bereaved.[4] *I took everything so much to heart,* it was difficult for me to differentiate between *personal and corporate* concern in the life of the church; my empathies were deep and sincere, and I chose to carry the burden of it all…not so well, I must admit.

---

[3] Donald A. McGavran, *Understanding Church Growth,* 1st ed. (Grand Rapids: Eerdmans Publishing Company, 1970), 40.

[4] The list of pastoral duties in the contemporary church is much longer than this, you understand, or at least, *I perceived it was.* But these were ones to which I gave the most attention.

Having planted the church in 1988 with four devoted and competent families, 18 persons total, University Church of God in Greenville, North Carolina had realized considerable success, according to typical "small church" standards. By the 15th year, we had strengthened to a steady 250 capacity and gone through several relocations and building phases to accommodate the growth. I had completed my doctoral program, and derivative from that, we had started quite an attractive small group ministry, incorporating at least half the congregation in close-knit discipleship studies.

By now, we had begun to staff, eventually hiring several other support persons and associate pastors, each specialized in his/her own giftings unique to the needs of the church. A rather impressive volunteer team of leaders covered all the bases of various departmental ministries, each accountable to a given staff member. These measures *should have* lightened my load, and to the extent I permitted, they did.

At long last, I remember the exact moment when, on a "take-a-deep-breath" kind of day in the office, I turned off my lights, leaned back in my faux leather executive chair, propped my feet on my nice cherry desk, and prepared to worship and offer prayer. But first, I said to myself, *"Finally, my personal finances have caught up with my arduous efforts, my pastoral staff can adequately manage ministry, the church is reasonably healthy – NOW I can ease back and enjoy coasting a bit."*

I WISH I HADN'T SAID THAT!

Chapter 2

The Warp Portal

There *is* the definitive moment when I can say for certain it began. Knowing my own personal sense of well-being, it was apparent to me that something very awry and awful was happening. True, I might have had hints that *something* was liable, but I had no idea what!

I now know that at age 49 when this crisis struck, *any counsel* I had *ever offered anybody* suffering *any form* of anxiety disorder or depression was shallow, flighty, clueless, naïve, unempathetic, and frankly – *ignorant! "Go sit under a shade tree. Pray this prayer. Think this thought. Read this Scripture. Get some rest. Take a vacation. Get a hold of yourself!"* I'm so embarrassed to recall I *really* said those things!

And I'm ashamed to admit I knew so little of the dreadful disorders of anxiety and depression that affect 40 million adults in the U.S. annually, ages 18 years and older,[5]

---

[5] "Facts and Statistics," *Anxiety and Depression Association of America,* sec. "Did You Know?" https://adaa.org/about-adaa/press-room/facts-statistics (accessed on January 22, 2020). There are overlapping symptoms as well as *distinguishing* symptoms between anxiety disorder and depression. I speak of both of these *in generality* for purposes of telling my story. I *am not a medical professional* and wish to make clear I do not speak as a medical authority on these illnesses!

and approaching 300 million worldwide,[6] not to speak of its prevalence among children and adolescents.[7] While I mean to acquaint my readers with the rather commonplace and widespread normalcy of this experience, there is *nothing I can ever say to "normalize"* the grief of it!

Enough of education just now – it was little help to me in *my hour* of crisis. *Even had I known,* it really hadn't helped!

The date was May 17, 2006. As coordinator of MIP (Ministerial Internship Program) for the Church of God in Eastern North Carolina, my wife and I were in Cleveland, Tennessee celebrating the formal commissioning of our 29 students who had just completed their nine-month intensive studies, preparing the candidate applicants for advancement to their next rank of ministry. MIP is a program of academics

---

[6] "Depression," *World Health Organization,* Dec. 4, 2019, sec. "Key Facts," https://www.who.int/en/news-room/fact-sheets/detail/depression (accessed on January 22, 2020).

[7] Karen Dineen Wagner, MD, PhD, "Anxiety Disorders in Children and Adolescents: New Findings," *Psychiatric Times,* vol. 36, Feb. 25, 2019, para. 1, https://www.psychiatrictimes.com/child-adolescent-psychiatry/anxiety-disorders-children-and-adolescents-new-findings (accessed on January 22, 2020). "Anxiety disorders are the most common psychiatric condition in youth. Lifetime prevalence rates for any anxiety disorder in adolescents is 31.9%. Anxiety disorders occur early in childhood with a median age onset of 6 years." "Adolescent Mental Health," *World Health Organization,* Oct. 23, 2019, https://www.who.int/news-room/fact-sheets/detail/adolescent-mental-health (accessed on January 22, 2020). These disorders lead to significant impairment in academic, social, and family functioning. 16% of the global burden of mental health conditions occurs in teens, ages 10-19.

and supervised ministry, awarding 16 credit hours with the Church of God School of Ministry (10 hrs. academic, 6 hrs. internship), then transferrable to Lee University[8] – a highly motivating incentive to begin and continue lifelong learning!

We had checked in early on that Wednesday afternoon as all state coordinators were scheduled for a full day of training the next day. The 500-mile trip was tiring, and we intended to have a light meal that evening, hit the sack while the night was young, get plenty of Zzzs, and start the new day soundly refreshed on Thursday morning. My wife, Lou, retired immediately upon returning to the room, and I opened my computer to check emails and to briefly peruse a CD on personal budgeting and finance management we had just purchased at the Dollar Tree.

I don't know exactly why, but one particular email from someone in the church stoked my fury – yes, *preachers get mad too!*

I work hard at developing and guarding my character and sincerely knowing the motives of my own heart in every aspect of my life and faith. I've always resented anyone questioning my integrity – ask my family! *And* I've always had the tendency to be defensive when that happens…to a fault – the issue of perfectionism? Maybe!

In any case, it happened. A decision I considered to be in the best interest of the church was being brusquely confronted – "attacked" actually…*it felt like.* The lines of

---

[8] SACS accredited (Southern Association of Colleges and Schools™).

delineation are sometimes quite unclear between one's characterization of another's behavior and his motives, or his *own person even*. In a not-so-courteous manner, this individual was affronting me, and I wasn't taking it so well!

I was physically, mentally, and emotionally tired, perhaps more than just from travel itself. This trip had been unusually exhausting (ever more so, it seemed, as I grew older). I was spent...in so many ways. I should have gone straight to bed when my wife settled in.

But now I was staring at a fight that I didn't want to engage, with a key influencer in the church, at that. In an instant, *it seemed to me that I felt a switch throw inside my being,* and *it almost seemed I heard the click when it toggled.*

The most unfamiliar and frightening symptoms began happening in my upper torso, the severest neuroreceptor burning sensations I had ever experienced, like a life's worth of inverted goose bumps raging through the dermis and epidermis of my back, shoulders, neck, and chest, but lit intensely with fire instead of chill, and painfully – no, gruelingly – agonizing! Almost as if someone has

> I felt my blood boil. My face flushed. My heart and my mind began racing. I felt heat in my head and hollow in my chest. My body started shaking!

slathered my entire upper body with Ultra Strength BenGay® penetrating, analgesic joint and muscle cream...and left me alone to die in distress. Ever tried it? Don't!

I lost my wits! I panicked. I never had before, not like this! I anguished and writhed with excruciating pain. Then I noticed to my horror that my pain was *intrinsically linked* to

my thoughts, now fearful and terrifying! Almost as if
the toggle had closed a circuit and *shorted my nerves* to my
brain. It was electrical, no – shocking! I had grounded to
a hot wire of "Adamic nature," carnal depravity, the horrid
effects of sin on the whole human race, straight-wired
directly into my soul and my fallen, sinful nature! *Or
so it seemed.*

I now noted that every thought I had, somehow,
someway, *directly and immediately* communicated to my
physical being, almost as if when one thinks a pleasant
thought, he feels *pleasant shivers* down his spine, except
exactly the opposite was occurring. Quakes and tremors
of insufferable throbbing, stinging, smarting in wakes
and swells, surges and billows. And it was becoming
worse by the minute and not easing in the least, but rather
more and more intense, rhythmically attuned to my
frantic thought processes. My patterns of thought themselves
compounded the problem, strengthening the symptoms, accentuating the grief, in a sort of cyclical, reciprocating, hellish manner. In fact, I *thought* of hell.

And I imagined for just a moment *how like this horrible experience* eternal torment in hell might be.

I later came to understand what high, *very high,* blood
pressure feels like, and heart palpitations bent on breaching
the chest wall and heaving this misbehaving organ out of the
cavity where it belongs to simply *slow it down* and *prevent its
exploding* self-destructively! Mine felt like that. I was sweating
profusely, soaking my clothes, beginning now to cry, to weep
uncontrollably…as I hadn't in a long while.

Not because my "heart" was deeply touched in a moving manner by some stirring sentiment, but because my body was wrecking, and my sympathetic nervous system was reporting in bold, blatant bursts: **"Warning! Warning! Shutdown! Shutdown!"**

I was facing the severest test of my entire life, to that point…a frightening season of *non-functional humanity*.

I never answered the email. I never addressed the issue. I never acknowledged to that person my egregious response. I soon realized I had greater concerns to deal with, and that wasn't one of them.

Chapter 3

Anguish Amplified

I wanted to wake my wife, but I had presence of mind enough (or *was that* presence of mind?) to feel it would unduly alarm her. After all, I wasn't sure how long this would last. A few hours? The night? A couple of days? I just knew that interrupting her rest would *likely ensure* a trip to the Emergency Department in a hospital far away from home, out of our insurance network, and for certain, would spoil our plans for the next few days.

I could not have told you *then* what was happening to me. Not having *ever experienced* anything like this, I didn't know the difference between a heart attack or a stroke event, high or low blood pressure or a sugar spike or drop, an onset seizure or salmonella symptoms. For all I knew, my tea had been poisoned, or someone had slipped a crazy pill into a side dish of my evening meal, maybe something toxic, lethal. I didn't know if by break of day I would be dead or alive. It disturbs me now to confess I plead such flagrant ignorance.

As the symptoms worsened, I tried to get a handle on the situation – calm my nerves, lower my anxieties, arrest my emotions, focus my attention – but I couldn't. I had crossed over into a region of foreign and strange complexities, an alien zone of mounting fear and unconstrained despair, and I couldn't stop it. I prayed in frenzied, "out loud" whispers; I sniveled and sobbed in low, lamenting moans; I begged God to help me, but *it seemed* He wasn't listening. *It seemed* He wasn't there.

> The poorly lit shadows in the room began to resemble demon spirits taunting my testimony, jeering my Jesus, mocking my faith.

Somehow, I knew the night would be long. After exhausting myself weeping, writhing, and wrestling with God, I decided to preview the finance management CD[9] previously mentioned and "get my mind off" myself, if I could, and force myself to *think* of something else. I placed the CD in the tray of my laptop and opened the app. It was a well-organized study on the benefits of a full-life finance plan for clearing indebtedness at an early age and securing one's family for a comfortable retirement. Family budgeting, disposable vs. discretionary income, emergency funding, savings (and investing), debt control (and relief), financial goals by when (?), retirement, etc.

I was *temporarily* intrigued by the genius of the sage wisdom presented…until I saw sample charts proposing where persons my age should be by this time in their life, and *I wasn't there!* A chilling surge of utter shame and degradation ruptured the momentary façade of calm in my soul. And suddenly another gushing rush of tortuous,

---

[9] Deaver Brown, "Personal Finance & Investing Survival Kit," *Simply Media, Inc.* (Lincoln, MA: Simply Media, Inc., 1999), 8-10, compact disc.

tantalizing, neuroreceptor pangs, worse than the first, coursed like demonic energy through the nerves in my body, burning like liquid fire poured over my being.

I thought, "Oh my God! What have I done?" The best I knew how, *I thought,* I had answered God's calling in my life, *but must have supposedly imagined* I should be further along than this by now. We had just bought a brand-new house, six months before in December of 2005, 2500 square feet, in a nice, new neighborhood, for "equity upgrade" purposes. Our intentions had been to stay there five years, then sell, and move the equity to a downsized retirement home and be debt free. But the housing industry *had just upturned* at the top of 2006 and home values were dropping like lead balloons. It dawned on me we were probably so upside down we could never recover! What a fool! Had I become so self-reliant that I had not prayed earnestly enough to discern God's will in the matter? Had I presumed upon His grace and "stepped out" in careless foolishness instead of confident faith?

Had I tested the Lord and angered Him with my dismissive and contemptuous display of fakery and hypocrisy?

My wife and I have only purchased two new cars in our entire marriage, well, three. A 1980 Volkswagen® Rabbit Diesel, popular in the day, *especially* touting 50 miles per gallon. But whew! That $8000 purchase was a chunk of change – too much for our budget at that time! We decided *we'd likely* never purchase another new car – we'd let someone else bite that bullet, and we'd buy *the used vehicles* after someone else drove them off the lot.

But in 2004 when a peer minister friend asked if we "intended to drive our 1990 Buick LeSabre [which my parents gave us] right into the museum," I began to think my wife was more deserving than this. I suggested we purchase a new car as we felt financially stable enough to afford the payment. After shopping around, we landed the Toyota Highlander... nice ride, indeed, but I soon realized it was not big enough. My knees felt trapped by the obtrusive door design, and besides that, we anticipated more grandchildren now, and we'd be needing more room. I suggested 18 months later that we "upgrade." We went back to the same dealer and traded for the Toyota Sienna, "the grandparents' auto," our kids called it. And of course, we'd just hiked our payment, and yes – *we really were upside down now!*

All this flooded into my head in a matter of moments. And there I sat – stupefied and dumbfounded at my own idiocy. Taking on excessive debt at that point in our lives when my high school buddies were retiring with pensions and 401(k)s, easing up and reining back, approaching a stretch of genuine ease while I was encumbering – no, burdening – my family *and my future* with needless grief! A revolting shame, a repulsive, disgusting, nauseating sense of self-worth enshrouded me – no, no, *not worth* – "worth" isn't the right word!

> How could I even ascribe the use of that word to someone so reckless and foolhardy? *"Worthlessness"* is a better word!

By now, the ruddiness of my cheeks, the flush of my face, and the pace of my heart were peaking evidence of an onset health crisis – or spiritual problem...maybe both. The profusion of sweat, my over-exaggerated but thoroughly panicked emotions, and the rhythmic coursing of incessant, yet escalating spasms of my tender, torched nerves was driving me insane. And fear. Fear of losing my church – my job! Fear of losing our home, our possessions. Fear of failing my wife and children. Fear of humiliation and embarrassment before all my family and friends. Fear of reproaching the Church, the body of Christ. Fear of death, fear of life, fear of judgment, fear of God – *terror really*, that I was about to meet my Maker, and I really wasn't prepared as I always thought I was. Surely, I had played the fool and gotten caught.

I felt I was awakening from a Rip Van Winkle sleep of ease to a nightmare of disappointment and despair, and I was standing before God naked and ashamed and empty-handed. I was feeling as if I had made costly mistakes for which I was about to pay, and it was time.

I never went to sleep that night, nor *for 16 nights more* to come.

Chapter 4

Zombied-Out

By daybreak I was drained, depleted, diminished. Consumed, expended, exhausted. *Absent, really.* No longer present. Checked-out. MIA…at least, from life, the world, humanity. To myself, I seemed another person, actually. Someone I had never met or known. Someone who frightened me, whose thoughts, now totally illogical and incoherent, were rampant, intemperate, uncontrolled – dangerous, maybe. I was scaring myself, imagining the worst, envisioning the worst – conjuring any and all conceivably horrifying outcomes and liabilities.

Ultimately dropping, tumbling, spiraling, downward, …fast. Off the platform, off the planet, offline. Reality "no longer was." Or at least, it was different. My understanding of it changed that night; it wasn't what I thought it was. Distinctions and differentiations "weren't" any longer. I couldn't think, I couldn't reason, I couldn't feel, at least, sensibly, logically, humanly.

I had spent the night "spinning the cube," frantically but vainly daring to imagine every disastrous end result possible, for *it seemed* at this point, "disastrous end result" was all I could see. Perhaps not even Rubik himself had known with certainty the implications of a puzzle so mesmerizing that any of its 43 quintillion combinations and outcomes had all been possible (43,252,003,274,489,856,000).[10] Through the night, *it seemed* I had examined *every one of them* (absurdly-intended)!

By now, I regret to admit, my faith had faded to fate. I felt stricken, beaten down, badly bruised, abandoned by God, and left *alone* to my own devices. Totally exasperated and bewildered. A sickened puppy, a shivering lamb, lost on a crag at the edge of existence, or space, or time – I couldn't tell which. Just lost.

Zombied-out. Dead, but living. A being, but barely. A smitten spirit within a "living" corpse, looking out at an unknown world through beady, glass eyes.

And hollow, oh so hollow in my chest, like something of value, something that belonged, had vacated. That's how I felt by the time my wife awakened.

I was quiet, very quiet when she got up. I said little. She didn't know just yet I had been up all night. She began making ready for the new day, intending to visit old friends she had known as an employee in the World Missions Department of the Church of God Headquarters years ago when I was in college and seminary. I was scheduled to be

---

[10] "Welcome to the Rubik Zone," *The Rubik Zone,* para. 10, https://www.therubikzone.com/ (accessed on January 26, 2020). 43 billion billion is the equivalent of Rubik's Cubes stacked almost 10 miles high on Planet Earth (9.32 mi.). "Number of Combinations," *The Rubik Zone,* para. 3, https://www.therubikzone.com/number-of-combinations/ (accessed on January 26, 2020). This number is a "little less than the square of earth's population," yet, "a manageably imaginable number."

in meetings all day. She would drop me off at the appointed time, then pick me up when I would call her sometime mid-late afternoon.

I was covering as best I could, but she shortly sensed something was wrong. I wasn't my usual self. First of all, I never get up first. I love sleeping, and almost always, I'm last up and out. Sorry, folks…I'm not a morning person. I know my prime time, and it isn't sunrise – I miss a lot of them. When she inquired, I limited my response so as not to raise suspicion. "You look tired," she said. "I am," I replied. "I didn't rest well last night." That's as far as I went. I wasn't ready to explain; besides, I didn't know what to say. And I certainly didn't want to concern her.

I don't know how now, but I managed the meetings, and made the worship services and formal commissioning of my students. Those who knew me best – and there were several – my board members, a few of my students, my peer leaders, knew something was wrong, and several asked. But I put them off, not being dishonest, just being sketchy. I simply said, "I don't know, I just don't feel well."

My feeling unenthusiastically compelled to oblige, we shared meals together, chatted small talk around service times, and simply did what *I felt we had to do* to clear our duties by the students, and not dampen the

I tried to put on a face and pretend to be "me." I was present in body but *absent in spirit*.

excitement of their achievements. But all my ministerial development team left Cleveland that weekend knowing something wasn't right with Dr. Flora, but unable to put their finger on it. His usual personality had been quite subdued, and they easily perceived it. And my wife *certainly knew* something wasn't right, and moment by moment, began to feel more and more concerned that, for sure, something terrible and foreboding was happening *to and inside* her husband.

She knew me, and she knew me well. I had *never been able* to hide my feelings from her, and she could usually read me like a book. She began to realize I wasn't *telling everything*, nor sharing enough information for her to be at ease about my well-being. She began to probe and inquire investigatively until, little by little, I had detailed what had happened and what *was happening*.

But I had no explanation to offer...nor did she in response.

The symptoms continued the remainder of the trip, rising, cresting, then falling like swells in mechanical waves...timed by nature, *it seemed*, now establishing a noticeable pattern of ominous predictability. It was becoming more and more obvious to me the intrinsic link between these symptoms and my mental-emotional state, the thought processes that were both *cause AND consequence* of these symptoms. So, I came to realize that *to the extent possible*, nominal as it was, when I was forced to focus on the event at hand, the symptoms *slightly subsided,* though ever-brewing beneath the surface like the boiling lava of an imperiling volcano threatening imminent eruption.

I was scared. And so was Lou. She insisted we should leave and go home early, but I refused, and suggested we just needed to make it through this weekend. Once we *did get home*, I thought, I'd feel safe, and could get some rest, and would hope to feel better. It didn't happen that way. I found myself feeling frantic, desperate, panicky every waking hour, virtually *most of them* for these first 17 days in a row, becoming less and less capable of controlling my emotions, and *lesser still*, my thoughts.

Since before completing my doctorate in 2002, when I was always reading books, usually 15 average per semester, and using the AC power outlet in our car to work on my computer, I had long ago taken the passenger seat, and Lou always drove. She preferred to – she knew I got sleepy behind the wheel, and she never did. I liked being chauffeured and we were used to it.

I remember the drive home. It was quiet, somber quiet. Lou was afraid to speak, and I didn't want her to. I was hurting inside, grieving, whimpering, worrying, panicking...and *staring out the window* all the way home. I watched how quickly the fields, and woods, and homes sped by, and thought how *so like life* that was – the weaver's shuttle (Job 7:6),[11] the lightning flash (Mt. 24:27), the twinkling eye (I Cor. 15:52), the blade of grass (Ps. 103:15, 16), the vapor trail (Jms. 4:14).[12] *In that moment, I felt like* I was nearing the end of mine. I couldn't know, I didn't know. I just felt like it.

---

[11] *The Holy Bible, New International Version,* (Grand Rapids: Zondervan Publishing House, 1984). Unless otherwise noted, all biblical passages referenced are from the *New International Version.*
[12] "[6]My days are swifter than a weaver's shuttle, and they come to an end without hope" (Job 7:6). "[27]For as lightning that comes from the east is visible even in the west, so will be the coming of the Son of Man" (Mt. 24:27).

The end of that *road journey was not* the end of this *life journey*. In fact, this despicable, depressing adjustment in the course and quality of my life was just beginning. I had no idea what lay ahead, and I was *not at all eager to know.*

"Why, you do not even know what will happen tomorrow. What is your life? You are a mist that appears for a little while and then vanishes."

(James 4:14)

"52...in a flash, in the twinkling of an eye, at the last trumpet. For the trumpet will sound, the dead will be raised imperishable, and we will be changed" (I Cor. 15:52). "15The life of mortals is like grass, they flourish like a flower of the field; 16the wind blows over it and it is gone, and its place remembers it no more" (Ps. 103:15, 16).

Chapter 5

Fragmented, Frail, and Falling to Pieces

Sometimes it's better to have something constructive on your mind. The old adage, *English Proverb, actually,* that "an idle mind is the devil's workshop," though not a Scriptural quote, isn't far from the truth. In fact, a couple of famous persons have offered similar quotes concerning the ills of idleness: *"There is no greater cause of melancholy than idleness"* (Robert Burton). And *"It is in our idleness, in our dreams, that the submerged truth sometimes comes to the top"* (Virginia Woolf).[13]

It is certainly true that melancholy had taken hold and was clenching tightly, actually seizing, strangling like a wet ligature about my neck, slowly drying, tautening, choking the spirit life force from my being. I could *only hope* no hideous truth or ignominy was surfacing.

We were home now, but I *didn't* feel safe. I wasn't resting, and I wasn't better. And I certainly wasn't constructive. Any semblance of structure had ended with the scheduled meetings in Tennessee. And while we had begun office hours

---

[13] "Thoughts on The Business of Life," *Forbes Quotes,* Forbes Quotes.com LLC™, 2015, https://www.forbes.com/quotes/2656/ (accessed on January 27, 2020). Both Burton's and Woolf's quotes are from the same source.

at the church in 2003, I was in no condition to show up *any* the next week. Nor did I have any intentions of doing so.

Having returned home late Sunday evening, I dreaded my wife leaving me to go back to work on Monday morning. I needed her close, *really close.* She loved me dearly, and I her, and more now *than ever*, it mattered.[14] Although Lou has always been an incredibly strong person – and *strong-willed*, quite capable of defending herself in any face-off or showdown, typically terse and forthwith expressing herself – in *this* situation, she was tender and sensitive, *incredibly* sensitive.

> She spoke softly, gingerly, with deepest empathy, in gentlest tone.

She knew I was frail and never once *EVER* raised her voice to me throughout this entire crisis. I am absolutely sure she was God's primary agent of repair, restoration, and recovery to me, and I will always credit her with saving my life...certainly, and of course, by God's grace! The Holy Spirit *through her* painted a perfect picture of the image of Christ on the opaque and murky fog of my overcast future.

Lou *did* go to work; we felt she had to. And when she did, I felt very alone in this strange, new, unfamiliar *"palace of pain"* that I *had already begun to despise* – a taunting reminder of my foolish financial decisions that now tormented my mind...scoffing my judgment and disparaging my faith. This "transition" *mansion of mockery* became my hellhole for almost the whole of a year.

---

[14] At that time, Lou and I had been married 31 years. At the time of this writing we shall have been married 45 years on July 31, 2020.

I shut myself away…and out…and down. I closed the blinds and covered any windows that had none. Houses were in close proximity in this community, and I thought my neighbors were watching me. I felt paranoid. I closed all interior doors, especially the ones I was behind. Noises and lights began to bother me, even the slightest. I begged my wife to *please* not run the washer or dryer or dishwasher or vacuum. To *please* not turn on the TV or answer the phone or even the doorbell. To *please* not talk to anyone about my situation, at least in my presence.

> I began to *feel dysfunctional.* I couldn't think clearly at all. I couldn't stop crying and I didn't know why.

One morning it took me two hours to make our bed after Lou had left for work. Two pillows, the sheet, a comforter, and decorative throws. My mind was racing irrationally trying to figure out how this had happened, and every few seconds my emotions would break, and my soul would heave, *convulse, it seemed.* I would shake uncontrollably and cry hysterically, and my tears would cloud my vision so badly, I couldn't see. I would walk away from the bed and pace the house, crying out to God to help me, to save me, to deliver me. Then I would remember I hadn't finished the bed and would go back and try again. The same episodes of eruptions and outbursts would happen over and over before I ever finished making the bed.

I began to loathe myself, wishing I could "part" my own company – I didn't enjoy being around me and couldn't imagine why anyone else would (or ever did). I felt I was *ruining my wife's life* and wondered why God was punishing her after she had loved me so graciously all these years.

My thoughts were no longer rational. My behavior was bizarre. I was hearing things, truthfully, and couldn't believe it was so until Lou and I together "confirmed it." Several nights in a row, when in futile effort to try and rest (which I didn't) in the bed next to Lou, I kept hearing the low, steady droning of a bass guitar and drumbeat just down the road from where we lived. It was in the wee hours of the morning, and I couldn't imagine who in this nice neighborhood had the gall to be up at such an irreverent hour, daring to keep everyone else awake with his distasteful and "unmusical" drum-banging and bass-strumming.

> I could feel the vibrations in my chest, though several houses removed, and it was driving me insane!

Aside from the harassing pangs of the usual symptoms that had become so bedeviling and tortuous that I could no longer control my terrorizing thoughts *at all* nor the consequent neuroreceptor burning sensations that accompanied them – *I now had this to contend with*! Here I lay with heart racing at 150-160 beats per minute like a jogger running track. Adrenal gland wide open, I'm confident. Blood pressure high, I'm sure. Pooling sweat in my 18 inches of king-size bed space, and having to move left or right every few minutes to get out of a puddle of wet bedding to a dry spot – *and this bozo down the road is practicing monotones and rhythms at this ungodly time of night!*

I expressed aloud to Lou, (who herself had now become quite restless worrying for me) my annoyance with this kid's menacing, monotonous droning in his outlandish hour of practice and complete disregard for others. "What?" She asked. "The bass, the drum!" I said. "It's driving me crazy!" She listened for a few seconds, then replied, "What bass, what drums, Honey? I don't hear anything." "Shhh!" I said. "Be quiet! Listen! It's in the distance, down the street. Don't you hear it? That low, droning, 'Bong, bong, bang! Bong, bong, bang?!'"

We both listened together – it was very distinct and clear to me. Just low, moaning, and tormenting, *almost as if this kid knew I didn't feel well* and meant to finish me off! "I'm sorry, Wayne – I don't hear anything at all…nothing," she answered. All at once, *it seemed to me,* the torrid horror of hell's hottest flames coursed through my delicate nervous system. Fire shot through my body like surging currents of a lightning bolt! *It dawned on me I was hearing things! It was in my head!* "Are you sure?" I asked. "Yes," she said. "I hear nothing, Honey."

I put my head under my pillow and pulled it tight to my ears, and it was still there! Just as clear as before –

> **Totally in my head, but still there!**

no difference. Yet no ambient sound at all! I burst into tears and wondered what was becoming of me. I was falling apart, piece by piece, losing my mind – going crazy, dying slowly, and couldn't stop it! Night after night this happened. I began to feel the devil was playing my funeral dirge and wanted to be conclusively sure *I heard it before I drew my last breath! It seemed* he was bent with vengeance on punishing me for my many years of love for Christ and service to Him and was determined to *end my life to stop my ministry!* And in that moment, *it seemed* he was hurting God by striking His child!

"Disorientation" is a medical term, usually reserved only for use in its strictest sense – "an altered mental state" characterized by a loss of orientation as to "location and identity…time and date."[15] Accompanying symptoms often include confusion, delirium, delusion, agitation, and hallucinations. But its causes are many, commonly delirium and dementia, but not solely. A short list might include amnesia, liver failure, encephalitis/meningitis, dehydration, hypoxia, sepsis, to name but a few, but the many causes are too numerous to mention here in the body of this text.[16]

That said, I am *very careful* mentioning this word, wanting conscientiously to guard its proper diagnosis. But in the sense of *very restrictive analogy,* hyperbole perhaps, what I experienced over the next few days and weeks *seemed like disorientation* to me. My mental state *was altered!* I was beginning, *I thought,* to experience many of these symptoms, in fact, *all of them, it seemed* – confusion, delirium, delusion, agitation, and hallucinations. If I *wasn't* disoriented, I was dreadfully close.

---

[15] Emma Nicholls, reviewed by Seunggu Han, MD, "What Causes Disorientation?" *Healthline,* Aug. 22, 2019, sec. "Overview," https://www.healthline.com/ health/disorientation (accessed on January 28, 2020).

[16] Ibid. Other causes can be the side effects of some drugs, withdrawal from certain drugs, amnesia, carbon monoxide poisoning, cerebral arteritis, cirrhosis, liver failure, central nervous system infections, complex partial seizures, concussion, dehydration, drug overdoses, electrolyte abnormalities, epilepsy, fever, heat-related illnesses, hypoglycemia or hyperglycemia, hypothermia, hypothyroidism or hyperthyroidism, hypoxia, brain tumor or hematoma, mitochondrial disease, orthostatic hypotension, renal failure, Reye's syndrome, sepsis, stroke, vitamin deficiency, vestibular disorders; even an emergency can trigger distress that causes disorientation.

I couldn't sleep. I couldn't lay. I couldn't sit. I couldn't kneel. I crawled. I wriggled. I slithered on the floor. I groveled in prayer. In myriad patterns of fetal forms, I wailed and whined before God. I walked the floors *and* the stairs. Back and forth, back and forth, back and forth – to the overhead bonus room, to the master bedroom, to the restrooms, to the walk-in closets. Sprawling on my face before God, crying out to Him, bellowing, bawling, but hearing no reply, sensing no "Presence." *It seemed* as though I was trapped in a vacuum that not even God could penetrate...or cared to. Or maybe a deep, dark, cavernous hollow in the heart of the earth, and God couldn't find me...or didn't wish to. I *felt very disoriented, at least spiritually!* And very lost as to any sense of meaningful direction!

As to time? It stood still. But not because I was having fun; rather because I was hurting, grieving, and frightened, and *it seemed* this mounting misery of deteriorating health would never end. I wished it would. I began to ponder *very, very,* private thoughts of how to help it along...to finally stop the pain.

Chapter 6

Honest Confessions, Good for the Soul

But for the grace of God, I'll never understand how we made it through that first week. It was so upheaving and cataclysmic to the small sphere of our normal, everyday lives. Nothing before nor since has ever been so distressful and disruptive, *not even* my mother's death a year later and my dad's in 2011 – and I preached both their funerals!

Not at all dare I say it could not happen again nor be worse still if it did. Nor should I say the phone might not ring today and bring news to my ears that could make my crisis *then* seem so modest and elementary *now*. Please *do not hear me* presuming upon God's grace to say that in His awesome sovereignty and perfect pleasure for every man, woman, boy, and girl that *I am the only one* who has ever experienced anything this vexing. Or that I have *already experienced* my share of life's pain and am not liable to experience more. I shall not be so foolish!

I am simply saying that life in that dizzying, surreal, bewildering world is the worst I have ever known, even to this day. And I am trying to communicate to my readers the desperation and despair of that crisis as honestly and accurately as I possibly can – *yet words still fail me* to convey it as tangibly and realistically as it actually was!

Sunday was coming, May 28, and I wasn't thrilled about it. The usual, ecstatic anticipation most pastors feel looking forward to fellowshipping their beloved church family and sharing God's Word with them *was gone.* *Absent my spirit. Departed.* It had drained from my being when the love of life itself had left.

> I was wretched, base, and squalid, morally and spiritually. The mere shell of a man.

I had stopped eating. I wasn't hungry. I didn't know why *then*, but I suspected it was physiological. I had always loved food – don't all preachers?! It has been said that most of us pastors who carry the Gospel and preach against the sins of others *are ourselves guilty* of "overdosing" on fried chicken. I confess – I was one of them! But now I was dropping weight…fast. And could do little about it. Food was repulsive to me, and I had to make myself eat to simply maintain any modicum of energy and survivability. By the time my health calamity was averted, I had lost 45 pounds in six weeks and was back to my wedding weight 31 years before. This was not the weight loss plan I would have chosen.

Yes, Sunday *was* upon us, and I was pastor…of a wonderful, loving, healthy church. They deserved *to know something*, didn't they? But how to communicate it, or by whom, I didn't know. So, as the toilsome week edged into the weekend, I began to feel obligated, even duty-bound, to be there, no matter my condition.

I really had so little composure approaching the weekend that study was impossible. All I could do was agonize in prayer amid the misery of my symptoms and ask God to

please point me in the right direction. As best I could, I
rehearsed favorite Scriptures and decided upon a subject,
and *only hoped* the gift of discernment was still operative in
my spirit.

We didn't go to Sunday School – we always had. I felt
it was important for the pastor *to be ministered to* and had
always been supportive of our educational program. I
believed the church seeing the pastor *as a student-learner*
was as integral to *their experience* of discipleship (and *mine)*
as seeing me in the pulpit. However, in weeks to come, I
wouldn't go to Sunday School at all, but would hide away
in my office until church time to avoid socializing. That was
so unlike me – I have *always been* a sociable person, quite
affable and outgoing. And it had *always been* important to
me that I should greet every person in the church, especially
our guests. But that day, I couldn't…I just couldn't.

As we entered the sanctuary, I was anxiously reticent,
timidly guarded, cowed like a caged animal shivering
franticly in fear that its master was displeased with him and
about to exact overdue punishment. I
was overwhelmed that this place of
safety and solace just two weeks ago
now seemed so foreign and so frightful
to me.

> "I shouldn't
> have come," I
> thought. "I
> can't do this."

There's no way these people I loved
so much – and I knew loved me – did
not notice. I hadn't slept nor eaten in days – it was easy to
tell. My gait was feeble, my body was frail, and my face was
ashen. Past pale to pallid, colorless, like "death warmed
over." My wife clung to me, protective and wary, shielding

x

me from the usual hugs, handshakes, and back pats they were so accustomed to extending. I know it had to be awkward and unsettling *for them*, yes; but it was *evermore* panicky and terrifying for me. I really wanted to turn around and walk out, just leave – spare them the discomfort, and me the pain…but I couldn't.

Some things I remember crisply that morning, some vaguely. I really can't recall the order of the service nor the songs that were sung. That's all a blur. We sat on the front row where, as pastor, I had always "led" worship simply by participating, one of the crowd, the "laos,"[17] the people, the laity. But to me, the air was thick, and the music was muffled; I felt like I was in a drum, a hollow, a void maybe.

I was dizzy and dazed, stunned really, that I had even come. I should have known better.

When it was time to preach, I walked from my seat slowly. Lou hated to let me go – she was afraid I would collapse and later admitted she was amazed I didn't. I climbed the steps cautiously and greeted the congregation clumsily. I don't know all I said, nor how I preached. My journal[18] states my message topic that morning was, "The

---

[17] Joseph Henry Thayer, DD, "Laos," *A Greek-English Lexicon of the New Testament* (New York: Harper and Brothers, 1889), 372. Defined as: 1) "a people, people group, tribe, nation, all those who are of the same stock and language," and 2) "of a great part of the population gathered together anywhere."
[18] Wayne Flora, *Personal Spiritual Journal,* May 31, 2006, 1.

Bottom Line for Highest Hope," and I took my text from II
Corinthians 12:6-11. Permit me to share it with you below:

> *6For though I would desire to glory, I shall not be a fool; for
> I will say the truth: but now I forbear, lest any man should
> think of me above that which he seeth me to be, or that he
> heareth of me. 7And lest I should be exalted above measure
> through the abundance of the revelations, there was given to
> me a thorn in the flesh, the messenger of Satan to buffet me,
> lest I should be exalted above measure. 8For this thing I
> besought the Lord thrice, that it might depart from me. 9And
> he said unto me, My grace is sufficient for thee: for my
> strength is made perfect in weakness. Most gladly therefore
> will I rather glory in my infirmities, that the power of
> Christ may rest upon me. 10Therefore I take pleasure in
> infirmities, in reproaches, in necessities, in persecutions, in
> distresses for Christ's sake: for when I am weak, then am I
> strong. 11I am become a fool in glorying; ye have compelled
> me: for I ought to have been commended of you: for in
> nothing am I behind the very chiefest apostles, though I
> be nothing (KJV).*

I don't really remember the specifics of the message,
but from the text selected, I can only imagine. I can't find
my handwritten hardcopy of this sermon; perhaps I threw
it away, supposing it was the worst one I had ever preached.
I don't know. I'm sure I'd be permitted to go back to the
church, from which I have since retired, to comb through the
cassette masters and find the actual audio recording of the
sermon for that day. But I don't want to. I don't care to know

what I said nor how ineptly I might have preached; I don't want to hear myself *in that condition*…ever again. Hopefully.

But I DO clearly remember detailing the concerns of the past week – loss of sleep, loss of appetite, runaway anxiety, incessant crying, and tattered emotions. And I remember offering, in essence, this *raw, visceral confession:* "You are my family, and I love you. And I need for you to know that I'm not as strong as I thought I was. I'm not as good as I thought I was. And I'm certainly not as spiritual as I thought I was. My wife and I desperately desire your prayers this morning, and I would welcome your ministry to me here in these altars before we leave church today."

I slowly stepped from behind the pulpit, down to the ground floor, reached out my hand for my dear wife, who by now, along with me, was openly crying, soulfully and sorrowfully. We centered before the communion table facing the congregation, hands lifted, tears flowing, crying aloud to God for His help, His mercy, His healing. Immediately, our Elders and wives stepped out and hurriedly rushed to the front of the church, surrounding us as would parents in defense of their children when danger lurked.

Instinctively, the congregation at large streamed from their seats and swarmed us, reaching forth, hands upon us, and hands upon those *touching us,* until everyone in the house, *it seemed*, was intensely and empathetically connective in prayer. In corporate unity and earnest appeal, the entire congregation was deeply, emotionally, and passionately engaged in supplication to God. Crying out fervently and boldly *in our behalf,* interceding with us for a miracle from God, for His help in this hour, for His mercy to this need.

> It was like revival, though pensive; like a long-desired homecoming (or a *going away*, perhaps), but seriously sobering.

It reminded me of Paul's Ephesian elders weeping unconsolably for him as he left for Rome, certain they might never see him again...in this life (Acts 20:36, 37).[19] It was ardent and heartfelt, and it lasted and lasted until all sensed relief that God had heard our prayers, and answers were on the way! We all wept, and hugged, and consoled each other, reassuring one another that God was in control, that He loved us, and that everything was going to be okay.

Prophetic words were spoken to the church at large and to Lou and me, *in particular*. Tommy sensed the Lord saying that God had heard our prayers and honored our brokenness and would bless the church for our faithfulness. Barbara offered encouragement with these words: "Courage, help, and hope." Edna whispered softly in our ears for only Lou and me to hear, "Let not your hearts be troubled, neither be afraid – listen to your Father's voice." Amy consoled, "Peace, wisdom, strength, and rest." Many came to us, deeply moved by the Holy Spirit, with expressions of spiritual counsel and authentic concern. Each expressed his or her resolute support for us and declared intentions to continue in prayer for us in the coming days.

---

[19] "36When Paul had finished speaking, he knelt down with all of them and prayed. 37They all wept as they embraced him and kissed him" (Acts 20:36, 37). The whole of Acts 20 is now personally touching to me. It is the text I took for my farewell message to University Church of God when I announced my retirement in April of 2014.

Some hugged and held on tightly, for some duration. And one in particular, Abbey, a beautiful young woman now, whom as an infant, I had dedicated to the Lord and felt

> Some said nothing – they didn't have to. Their tearful embrace said it all.

much like a spiritual father to her, was so broken for us, and so moved by the service and the prayers. She was among the last to leave. I recorded these words in my journal about her inspiration to me that morning: "Abbey so ministered love and grace to me today, with barely a word spoken. She just hugged me and held me, weeping with me – so precious, so sweet! I love her so much."[20]

Lou and I had not known what to expect when we went to church that day. The outcome was more favorable than we could possibly have imagined. Our hearts were truly touched by the genuine love of our caring congregation, and we were immensely grateful that *they now knew…*

We knew God heard our prayers, and once again, we were reminded He was on His throne. We believed things would get better.

And we hoped they would…*soon!*

---

[20] Ibid., Flora, *Journal,* 1. I am only calling first names of these persons to protect their interests in the general public.

Chapter 7

The Doctor Is In

In the United States alone, upwards of 25% of adults suffering any form of anxiety disorder are not seeking treatment, and just over 70% of youth suffering "major depression are still in need of treatment."[21] Some data suggests the percentages are higher for adults than 25% (40%-60%), taking into consideration the *nature and extent* of the illness. Perhaps of greater concern still is the average duration of time *between onset and treatment* – 11 years![22] I could easily have been one of these statistics.

There is a plethora of reasons as to why treatment doesn't occur, most prominently among which are costs, scheduling, insurance, embarrassment, shame, stigma, denial, trust, fear, and *amazingly enough, just not knowing where to go, or who to*

---

[21] "The State of Mental Health in America," *Mental Health America,* 2020, sec. "Adults with AMI Who Did Not Receive Treatment 2020," https://www.mhanational.org/issues/mental-health-america-adult-data and sec. "Key Findings," https://www.mhanational.org/issues/state-mental-health-america (accessed on January 31, 2020).

[22] "Mental Health Care by the Numbers," *National Alliance on Mental Health,* 2019, sec. "Mental Health Care Matters," https://www.nami.org/learn-more/mental-health-by-the-numbers (accessed on January 31, 2020).

turn to.[23] I will confess that I am "guilty" (smile welcomed) of some of these, but not all of them.

My family was pleading with me to seek medical attention. I had vehemently reneged all throughout the previous week; and now into the next, they continued to implore me to *please see a doctor.* Yes, even after that most moving church service we had experienced on Sunday morning! Don't mistake me, it mattered. But it didn't "fix me." I was much comforted by it, and greatly encouraged, indeed, that God had heard our prayers, and certainly that the loving people I had served as pastor sixteen years to date when this crisis occurred, truly and sincerely cared! But the miserable afternoon that Sunday gave way to a dusk of despicable grief and anguish as yet *another night* of unbearable pain and suffering came upon us.

It wasn't that I didn't trust God – it was simply that I couldn't stop the agony and end the grief with the snap of my fingers! After Sunday's service, did I *at least believe God loved me?*

Yes, but I could not understand why He was allowing this to happen to me.

Okay, stigma…and denial, maybe. *These were* issues *for me* as is likely *for most persons* suffering this disorder. But keep in mind that not only was I a Christian of 35 years, but

[23] Neighborhood Psychiatry, "Why 75% of Anxiety Sufferers Fail to Get Proper Care," *Psychology Today,* Aug. 13, 2018, para. 10, https://www.psychologytoday.com/us/blog/psychiatry-the-people/201808/why-75-percent-anxiety-sufferers-fail-get-proper-care (accessed on January 31, 2020). Note that in this article, the authors suggest as high as 75% of persons needing help do not seek treatment. Other reasons as to why are also listed in this article.

a minister of the Gospel of Jesus Christ for 30. I had been credentialed in our organization for that long and had developed quite a standing of prominence and distinction among my peers in our state.

I was a graduate of Lee University (Lee College) in Cleveland, Tennessee as well as the Pentecostal Theological Seminary (Church of God School of Theology). I had earned an Associate degree in Business Communications at Pitt Community College to enhance business administration and marketing in my pastoral ministry. I had engaged a very intense unit of clinical pastoral education at our prestigious tertiary teaching hospital in the region. I had completed my doctoral studies at Columbia Theological Seminary in Decatur, Georgia with emphasis in missional intentionality and leadership development.

Besides that, I had been involved with ministerial development in Eastern North Carolina since 1993 and had been coordinator of the program for eight years at that time. I was respected and beloved by my peers and leadership. *And* had also been selected by them to serve on our esteemed State Council several times. I was endeared to the church we had planted and the loving people who graced me to serve them these many years!

**Can't you see?! This couldn't
happen to me!
Could it?**

It wasn't possible that someone *so important and so valuable to the kingdom of God as I* could experience anything like this, was it (facetiously intended)?[24] And further, what about my future? We can't forget that, can we? All the things that God had planned for me that I'd aspired and worked hard for, and was looking forward to, but hadn't happened yet? We couldn't waste a perfectly picturesque, fine-tuned future, could we? COULD WE?!

And yet, *it was happening!* Occurring in *my life – not just* someone else's! And like a runaway train on a downhill grade or an avalanche rushing the slopes of the steepest mountain, it was shoving its way along – *gaining speed even –* and I could do *absolutely nothing* about it! Except cry. And cry some more. And more still.

I had witnessed God heal many people throughout our ministry, some in our very own family. A most notable article in our Declaration of Faith states that, "We believe divine healing is provided for all in the atonement."[25] I could not possibly forget the time my wife was miraculously healed of a pneumothorax – I was a witness! After

> Hey, we believed in divine healing! What about that?

---

[24] I wish for my readers to understand that I am being *deliberately hyperbolic* (a bit exaggerated) in this long list of personal accomplishments *as was Paul* in Philippians chapter 3:3-6 *only to say in verse 7 that, "...what things were gain to me, those I counted loss for Christ"* (KJV*). His point, as well as mine, is to demonstrate *by example* that no matter how important any of us thinks he/she is, or how much any of us thinks he/she has achieved in this life, *none of us* is anything without Jesus Christ as Savior and Lord! *And w*hat happened to me *can happen to anyone!* We *must* be sober concerning this evident reality!

[25] Article 11, Declaration of Faith, "Beliefs," *Church of God,* http://www.churchofgod.org/beliefs/declaration-of-faith (accessed on January 31, 2020).

having prayed for her wart-infected fingers, I saw *with my own eyes* her peel them off and toss them out the window on a road trip to visit family – *less than a week after the prayer!* We were young in marriage at that time, and her hands have been completely blemish-free ever since! Those are the talented hands that play so gracefully on the grand piano, and *everyone has seen* how beautiful they are! I had personally seen God heal people I pastored when medical science had rendered its final verdict and there was no more hope! I knew beyond the shadow of a doubt what God could do!

But *now, this* wasn't someone else's well-being at stake, *someone else's* health in crisis for whom I *might have had* greatest faith to believe that God could *and would heal them.*

> **This *was me and my life!*** Baffled me. Broken me. Beaten me. Tortured me. At the end of my rope. The end of my wits.

And *completely confounded and confused, totally exasperated* trying to figure it out and make sense of it!

My wife and my children had had enough of my relentless non-persuasion! They were as concerned as I…and *just as weary!* So, on Monday, *they took control!* They saw I wasn't helping myself and had no intentions to. Taking the reins, my wife and daughter made an immediate appointment for the next day with my primary care physician. I could kick and scream and yell (which I didn't) all I wanted to – they weren't taking "no" for an answer! I was going to see the doctor whether I was pleased or not! Even if it meant my son had to straitjacket me, which he could easily have done if I had not behaved!

I dreaded it. I despised the thought. I knew where this was headed and was terrified what this might mean for my future in ministry! The general populace is uninformed (or *ill-informed*) about anxiety disorders – even the Christian community (as *was I*)! And good-bad-or-indifferent, *I knew how unforgiving, or at least, unsympathetic,* the world could be toward persons deemed mentally sick or distressed! I knew my career was coming to an end…*and possibly my life!*

> Like an elementary school kid throwing a tantrum when he's forced to take his school vaccinations, or like me as a child *every time I went to the doctor* for bad colds or infections, *I always got a shot – in my rear!*

And consequently, I had grown to *hate going* to the doctor! Okay, okay, *it wasn't quite that bad this time,* but my feelings hadn't changed! I was going to the doctor (like it or not)… *in my body,* yes…but *in my mind,* I was staying home.

On Tuesday, May 30, my wife, my daughter, and I went to the doctor…and yes, "the doctor was in!" Actually, I loved this man. Dr. Donald Ribeiro[26] was the community favorite in

---

[26] "Greenville Express Care," *Donald A. Ribeiro,* 2020, https://www.ribeiromd.com/?site=Expresscare (accessed on February 25, 2020). "Dr. Ribeiro received his Bachelor of Science in Biochemistry in 1982 at East Carolina University (ECU). He received his MD Degree at ECU School of Medicine in 1986. His Family Practice Residency was at Pitt County Memorial Hospital 1986-1989. He was Chief Resident for the Family Practice Residency Program in 1989. He was Board Certified in Family Practice in 1989. He has been practicing in Primary Care Medicine since 1989 in Pitt County and Greene County. In 1983, Dr. Ribeiro became an Ordained Minister by the NC Convention of the Original Free Will Baptist Church. He has served as the pastor of the Ormondsville Original Free Will Baptist Church since 1998. Dr. Ribeiro was certified by the American Academy of Medical Review Officers in 2004. Dr. Ribeiro was named Physician of the Year by the NC Academy of Family Practice in 2011."

several towns. At that time, he was a primary care physician at several clinics and was practicing family medicine at each one certain days of the week. It was not uncommon for him to always have a young intern by his side, training him or her in the art of medicine to serve their patients with excellence as he himself did. Several years younger than I, he himself was a minister of the Gospel of Jesus Christ and pastored a community church in a nearby town. He was dearly beloved by all, both as pastor and clinician. I had *never heard one unfavorable remark about him* from anybody. The truth is, I respected him highly and had already "trusted him" with my health in numerous prior visits.

That day was different. I didn't trust anybody.

My guard was up, and I had brought my emotion-protective "animal cage" right along with me; in fact, I was rather audacious and defensive, intending not to "give in" and accept *any form* of recommended treatment! I dug in my heels and stood my ground. But a good doctor will not permit his patient to instruct him *how to practice* medicine. Neither did Dr. Ribeiro.

It was obvious to me that he was *seriously* concerned for me when I entered...well – *actually, "we entered"* – the examining room. He asked for a full description of my story, questioning me, but *primarily* questioning my wife and daughter. They detailed the particulars and *left nothing out*.

He knew I was frightened. He had never seen me like this before, and he knew me well. And he loved me as genuinely as I loved him. After "assessing" the situation, he began offering his recommendation for treatment, *and* began writing out the Paxil prescription. I-HIT-THE-CEILING! I came unglued and had a tantrum right there in his clinic! I began bawling like a toddler on his daddy's shoulder, headed out of the church sanctuary for a decent smack on the behind (I had seen this plenty of times!)! And I couldn't get it under control!

You should have heard me! I was pitiful! I shouted hysterically, hardly able to speak clearly through my sobs and sniffles, "I'm not taking that!" I yelled. "You might as well tear that up right now! I'm not becoming a druggie and ruining my ministry for an antidepressant!" I was vehement and passionate, almost volatile and explosive, like water droplets bursting angrily on a sizzling hot griddle – no, actually, *more like verbal shrapnel flying* when a bomb detonates from a hairpin-triggered, *dead wrong, misspoken word!*

He saw that I was desperate *and* unrelenting, and he knew *this was not going to be an easy street* for either of us. "Pastor Flora," he pled earnestly, "I can't help you if you don't let me. You need treatment *now* and the longer you delay, the worse it can become." He was gravely serious. "I'll be okay, Dr. Ribeiro," I cried, literally. "I just need help sleeping. Please, just give me *something to help me sleep.*" "I can't," he responded. "I can put your body to rest, but I can't put your mind to rest. Sleep medication is not the proper treatment for your situation. You need to start an

 antidepressant right away." "NO!" I retorted. "I'm not doing it. I'm NOT taking antidepressants. We can leave *right now* if you can't help me!"

I saw Dr. Ribeiro studying the faces of my wife and daughter who themselves were experiencing rightfully heightened concern. Neither of them believed we should leave before *some plan* of treatment had been decided, and some resolution to this rapidly developing heath crisis had been determined.

> It was urgently tense in that room, and for a few moments, eerily quiet.

Dr. Ribeiro reluctantly suggested that we *might try* using Xanax®,[27] to help me sleep, but *only for a few days*, perhaps weeks at most. He knew full well the limited capacity of this medicine to treat any formal diagnosis of anxiety disorder *long term*. He also knew it had a short half-life, meaning that while it was perfectly acceptable to prescribe for sleep aid *temporarily*, it was *less likely to be helpful as a sleep aid* from the point it had eventually reached its half-life.[28] He also strongly cautioned that this medication should be used judiciously as it could easily become dependently addictive.

For now, he would diagnose me with "sleep disorder" – not clinical depression. *I'm conjecturing,* looking back, that he *likely felt it was too soon* to diagnose me formally with clinical

---

[27] Kaci Durbin, MD, reviewer, "Xanax," *Drugs.com,* Mar. 4, 2019, https://www.drugs.com/xanax.html (accessed on February 1, 2020).
[28] Yolanda Smith, B. Pharm., reviewed by Liji Thomas, MD, "What is the Half-Life of a Drug?" *News-Medical, Life Sciences,* Aug. 23, 2018, https://www.news-medical.net/health/What-is-the-Half-Life-of-a-Drug.aspx (accessed on February 1, 2020). "The elimination half-life of a drug is a pharmacokinetic parameter that is defined as the time it takes for the concentration of the drug in the plasma or the total amount in the body to be reduced by 50%. In other words, after one half-life, the concentration of the drug in the body will be half of the starting dose." *Remember this thought – it will resurface in the next chapter as an explanation for adjustments in my medications.*

PRESCRIPTION

Rx

Remember, I said he was a good doctor!

depression *without other data and a more complete study of my medical history.* Further, he knew my status would require a *very close monitoring* for weeks to come before he could rule definitively…*or refer.*

I must issue complete disclaimer on behalf of my dearest doctor/pastor friend and say that I really gave Dr. Ribeiro *little or no choice* that first visit! Had he insisted on prescribing antidepressants *that day,* I WOULD HAVE WALKED OUT and not gone back. If he had dared to refer me to any medical professionals in the field of psychiatry, I had gone ONLY by force as men in white suits hauled me out. Even though there was as an "elephant in the room," he knew how strongly I felt, as did my wife and daughter, *and I certainly meant it!*

In any event, we filled the prescription and promised to come back *as a family* EVERY WEEK until my symptoms subsided and my health improved.

I suspect I *really*

am a statistic…

refusing help.

Chapter 8

Rebound Anxiety

Some things are too incredible to imagine. This is. I had been duly advised.

But stubbornness has no restraints, even when someone was as pitiably sick *as I was*...or certainly as *I thought I was. I was once* a good listener, but now I wasn't. Not anymore. It seems I couldn't hear – not literally – but figuratively. Not with my ears anyway, but with my mind.

I had been properly instructed how to administer the Xanax®. I will tell you this – I *never once played with* my meds. *Never!* I sensed the seriousness of my health crisis and realized my life was potentially endangered. I didn't play "doctor." To that extent, and perhaps to that extent *only*, I was a good patient.

At first, I was impressed with the effects of this new regimen of treatment. I liked how it made me feel *within minutes* after taking it. Relaxed. Carefree, kind of. At least for a little while. *Able to breathe, easily.* To be truthful, I really hadn't noticed through the progression of my illness how labored and strenuous my breathing had become, that simple, involuntary function of the autonomic nervous system. Amazing, really…breathing – something I had done all my life *without thinking* up until age 49.

It now dawned on me while adjusting to this medication that part of my panic was the need for air, the yearning to breathe…just breathe. Live. Survive. Nothing else. That natural, instinctive, "taken-for-granted," biological process required for living, even merely to sustain existence.

It really hadn't occurred to me that throughout *all of my frantic pace of life*, I had *done that* since the day of my birth.

Dr. J. E. Wright, the doctor delivering me in that white plank house on Crisp Sandpit Road in Crisp, North Carolina that Saturday afternoon, 3:16 pm, November 17, 1956,[29] had suspended me by my ankles in his strong left hand and slapped me *quite forcefully* across my tiny little butt cheeks…*several times*, to get it started…breathing, that is. I remember because that had been *quite a story* for Mom to tell and retell throughout the whole of her life, *my being her favorite of three children*, an older brother now deceased and my baby sister, Rita Kay, whom I've not introduced just yet. [I'm having so much fun teasing you, Rita! We've *always declared* each of us was the favorite, haven't we?!]

Why is this so memorable? Because Mom said the doctor was terribly distracted that day; he and Dad were engrossed in an NBA Eastern Division Basketball Game, watching it on our black and white TV. And she was pretty much on her

---

[29] Wayne Flora, *Authentic Copy of Handwritten Birth Certificate* completed by Dr. J. E. Wright two days after my birth (Nov. 17) on November 19, 1956.

own. As best we can determine (Help me, Sports Buffs!),
the Boston Celtics beat the Rochester Royals in Boston that
Saturday afternoon, 108-86.[30] Furthermore, Mom admitted
that having already had one son, Ronnie, her firstborn, she
really wanted a girl, and when I born – she cussed![31] Of course,
she got over it, and pretty much came to like me quite well as
I won her heart throughout the whole of my life until she
passed in 2007 when I was just turning 50. I'm smiling – I
hope you are!

But since then, I've been breathing. Regularly,
rhythmically, and easily. Until I got sick. And then *it wasn't*
so easy! The Xanax® brought it to my attention. And now, *it
seemed,* breathing normally was about *all I could focus on* in
this delicate and scant stretch of my
life. The medicine helped…some…
for a while. I took it regularly at first
(later *as needed*), and as prescribed,
four times a day.

> My evening dosage
> was most important
> of all – that was
> my sleep aid.

Since there was little to do in life anymore, *except*
breathe…and survive, my wife and I started going to
bed early, 8 pm, for the next several days. She was *totally*

---

[30] "1956-57 Boston Celtics Schedule and Results," *Basketball Reference,*
https://www.basketball-reference.com/teams/BOS/1957_games.html
(accessed on February 2, 2020).
[31] Keep in mind this was *long before* ultrasound and other forms of pre-disclosure as to what gender the newborn would be. By the way, there *is a difference* between "cussing" and "cursing," at least in my southern impression of it. Mom didn't *curse me* (as if to cast a spell or wish evil upon me) – she simply "cussed the situation" (said some bad words) that brought her a degree of disappointment with this particular outcome. I just thought you ought to know that I humor the incident and really didn't "take it personally." After all, I became her favorite, *didn't I?!* Smile.

exhausted and certainly needed her rest; the idea of retiring early was quite appealing to her, and she was desperately hoping this medication would help me rest as well. And indeed, it did. For a few hours.

But then, given its "half-life" – (remember that?) – I began awakening at 1 – 2 am in the wee hours of the night, way before cockcrow or crack of dawn, *with horrific REBOUND ANXIETY!* Frankly, I had never heard this term. But I learned in short notice what it was. I *thought I had already suffered,* but not until now. The usual symptoms were no longer "usual." Every pain was intensified! Every grief was accentuated! Every anguish was compounded! The burning sensations, the liquid fire, the racing heart, the drenching sweat, and the terror – oh, yes, the terror! *The runaway thoughts and out-of-control emotions terrified me!* And I thought I couldn't handle them before? I *certainly* couldn't handle them now!

Oh – and remember the bass guitar and drums?!

NOW, they were *amplified!* They weren't just "down the street" anymore! They were right there in my own home...*in my bedroom! That menacing kid* – or *devil* – who wanted to kill me with his nerve-wracking practice at ungodly hours was at it again, and NOW with *ruthless and merciless ferocity!* I couldn't stand it! There was no way to stop it! The pillows over my head made it worse – they seemed to be the baffling that "confined" the music in my mind, making absolutely sure I didn't miss a single stanza of, "Bong, bong, bang! Bong, bong, bang?!"

To my dismay, I began to notice a breathing distress unique from my prior challenge to simply draw air – my breathing cycle *inverted!* I don't know how else to explain it, except to say that one's usual breathing pattern is "inhale – exhale, inhale – exhale." But mine was now reversed: *"exhale – inhale, exhale – inhale."* And the breaths were not long, deep, and full, but were short, rapid, and shallow.

> It was frightening because *it seemed* I was "drowning" in a watery grave of carbon dioxide and couldn't come up for air.

Sounding somewhat like the whimpering of a small child who just got a spanking, and his parents have issued the ultimatum – "You'd better stop crying right now, or I'll give you something to cry about!" Snuffling, sniveling, *snorting even*, trying "his little heart's best" to stop this involuntary, uncontrollable, puffing and blowing to prevent yet another trip out "behind the barn!"

I kept going under, trying frantically to grab a good breath, a deep drawl. *A long-lasting yawn would have been nice*, the kind you have *right before* you trail off to sleep. But nothing doing. I was dying, I thought. Right there in my bed. *There beside* my sleep-deprived wife who *already* hadn't rested well for days and days on end by now.

I ached for daybreak, but when it came, it didn't end. All alone in this horrible house I now hated with a passion, I cried and cried, and paced and paced, and prayed and prayed. Waiting anxiously, *oh so anxiously,* for Lou to come home and be with me. And hold me. And speak tenderly to me…*as she always did.* And comfort me *as no one else knew how.* And give me hope that somehow, someway, *it would be okay, it would get better. And that it would not always be this way.*

But then, I would despise the sun setting, the night falling, and dark coming. I knew what the night would be like and I was weary of it. I was *never ready* for the next one. But as sure as the day is long, the next night would come.

Church was becoming quite "hit-and-miss," in rhythm with my panic cycles. The first several Sundays of June, we went to church, although we probably shouldn't have. I eked out desperate messages, no sleep at all the night before. In fact, I preached nine of eleven double-AM services with no rest going into the pulpit. I couldn't go on June 25. Had I gone, I would have been on a stretcher, likely strapped in. The next Sunday, July 2, I besought my Associate Pastor, Glenn Nichols, to preach in my place – I just didn't think I could handle it. It was becoming harder and harder to focus, to control my thoughts and dampen my fears.

> I was present that day, *but absent.*

"There," but "signed out." Coming into church, I felt like a newborn calf staring at a new gate, and once in, *felt as timid as* a mouse in a minefield of mouse traps. Almost paralyzed. So scared of all these people I loved so much, and so afraid I might "let on" I was falling apart and *not be able* to continue being their pastor.

I was frailer than the week before, and it was obvious how quickly I was losing weight and strength...*and confidence.* I didn't want to be there. I didn't want anyone to see me like this. I was suffering severe panic attacks recurrently now, and I was afraid I would *come completely apart* if it happened right there in church.

Caring medical professionals in our congregation were telling me, in private of course, that I needed to relent and listen to my doctor, that I was a likely stroke candidate with this high heart rate and dangerously elevated blood pressure. Their compassion was unpretentious and compelling. In days to come, I would carefully consider the sincerity of their counsel, and it would be integral to the saving grace that got me through this crisis.

Pastor Glenn preached that morning, graciously willing to cover for me. Promptly and assertively, he stepped into the role of an "armor-bearer," and began to *proactively and protectively relieve me* of overburdensome duties and responsibilities. Without missing a beat, he swiftly shifted "into the main lane" and began covering my bases...and taking my "hits." He empathetically and conscientiously started attending to the needs and health of the church... *and mine.*

Having been a highly regarded and much-beloved leader in the church since the day we conducted our first service, October 9, 1988, Glenn *had been there* -- training, leading, serving, and caring. And now, he was demonstrating the moxie required to take the brunt and burden of pastoral ministry as I found my way through this maze of misery, this mysterious and muddled misfortune that I feared would be *my last and only reminder* to anyone I had ever existed.

Glenn was my dearest friend. He knew me and understood me. I will tell you later how I learned it to be so. But for now, suffice it to say how much it mattered that a brother in Christ sincerely cared for me as deeply as he. I survived that day. But there were *many more* to come.

Chapter 9

The Switch

Flip it up – lights on. Flip it down – lights off. That's how it works. It's that simple. On, off, on, off. And that's what switches do – turn things "on" or "off." They open and close circuits, either permitting, breaking, or directing flow…of electrical current, data packets, information…even optical light. And it's quite interesting that they are often referred to as "traffic cops."[32] Directing "flow of traffic." Sending energy, information, or light in different directions.

Our bodies have switches, designed by God to do this very same thing. Okay, with *more technical design*, perhaps, than a single pole light switch. But nevertheless, functioning in quite the same manner, accomplishing similar purposes, yet on a grander scale…well actually, a grander *microscopic scale*. The human body is an amazing "machine!" Over eons of time, *as many* remarkable inventions as intelligent human beings have designed, built, or replicated, the human body isn't one of them. Humans can't create a human body – they aren't "Creator" – only God is!

---

[32] Dan Hogan, ed., University of California – Berkeley, "Largest, Fastest Array Of Microscopic 'Traffic Cops' For Optical Communications," *ScienceDaily*, 12 April 2019, www.sciencedaily.com/releases/2019/04/190412094745.htm (accessed on February 3, 2020).

The psalmist so eloquently exclaimed, "I praise you because I am fearfully and wonderfully made; your works are wonderful, I know that full well" (Ps. 139:14). One particular rendering of this verse reads like this, "I will give you praise, for I am strangely and delicately formed; your works are great wonders, and of this my soul is fully conscious" (BBE).[33]

Throughout the ages, scientists and medical professionals have studied the human body, and in our modern era, we've become quite knowledgeable of it. How and why it functions the way it does, all its many organs and systems that just *simply must* work well together for a person to be healthy. And the diseases and disorders that can happen in the human body to deteriorate its well-being.

We are way ahead of the curve understanding the complex machine that it is, but *way behind the curve of God's infinite knowledge of it,* our Creator who made it. And I've learned, as have you, that no matter how wealthy a person is, or how vast the unlimited resources he has to allocate for saving his own life, it may not make a difference at all in the end. There's only so much mankind can do to sustain one's life. And when it's time to meet the Maker, life ends.

> "Just as people are destined to die once, and after that to face judgment..."
>
> Heb. 9:27

---

[33] *The Bible in Basic English,* S. H. Hooke, trans. (New York: E. P. Dutton & Co., 1949).

I know that quite well, having been a minister and student of the Bible most of my life (and now a Licensed Funeral Director). I've served families whose loved one was passing and been there holding their hand when the last breath was drawn. I've preached hundreds of funerals and comforted hundreds of families in ministry *and* the funeral industry.

I *get the reality* of my mortality…
I live with it *every single day* of my life.
In my calling, I'm not permitted to forget it, at all.

So, I know as amazing as the human body is, as complex a "machine" as we know it to be, and as brilliant as all professionals in any field of science and medicine may be, the body ultimately fails. Systems fail, organs fail… *switches* fail.

Perhaps I am overstating a bit my analogy of switches in the human body, but I don't know how else to convey what I wish to share. These "traffic cops" posted at millions of tiny intersections in the body are designed by God to open and close lanes, "circuits," if you will, and to "direct traffic," instructing chemicals and currents and fluids *when and which way* to go. When they work well, the body *functions well.* And when they don't, the body doesn't.

There was once a time when after a *really busy* day in pastoral ministry, I could lay down at night, *flip that switch,* and go to sleep. And sleep really well – remember, I love sleep! But then, *it seems,* that switch broke. Or at least, it began malfunctioning. It didn't work well anymore.

I don't know *which switch it was.* Or *where it was.* My brain? My chest? My heart, maybe? I didn't study medicine – I studied theology, and the heart in theology isn't an organ like the blood pump in the human body. Instead, it is the seat of human emotions, that place in the soul (or the spirit...I don't know which) that God touches with tenderness when the "patient" is ready. The brain in theology, *I think,* is *really* the conscience, *the mind of the human spirit* that lives on forever even when the body and its organs have died. Of course, that's debatable. That said, I *certainly don't know* what all the switches are and what they're for *nor* how they work. I just know this – *mine quit!*

> It made me into another person, one I didn't know, and didn't like.

I couldn't control it anymore. Maybe the handle broke off and got lost, and I couldn't find it. Maybe it rusted out. Or jammed or locked up. In any event, it affected my health dramatically and it changed my life radically.

I told my wife more than a few times that I "felt" that switch throw inside my body. It was quite noticeable. *It seemed like* it was in my chest, and when it clicked, circuits opened or closed. I would instantly feel some better, or *much worse!* Ask her how many times I said to her, "Oh, honey – it's over!" I felt that switch click inside, and *when it did,* I began to feel better right away. My hopes would build, and I would feel encouraged that I *really was* getting better, that my health was improving, and I was going to be well again.

And then, just like that – it would flip the other way, and it would start again...all with the "click of a switch." I would feel it...and be despaired. And the horrible health issues I wished **Surreal, otherworldly, trancelike, illusory... but real,** *very, very, very real.* were behind me and the symptoms I had been experiencing would resume all over again, most often, *worse than before.* The nightmare just wouldn't end, and I felt I truly was in a warp zone, the *Twilight Zone,* maybe.

Curious, isn't it? That I would describe my experience of this mysterious manifestation of bizarre and inexplicable symptoms in such elementary manner. But to the extent one *can* describe it, that's the *easiest way* for me to say it for my readers to *understand.*

Okay, for the tech buffs in my audience, I offer you this highly technical explanation of how the brain and body work and *why* anxiety disorders *can happen* – skip if you wish not to be that technical (Smile).

> An important aspect of neuroplasticity [our brain's flexible ability to grow and assume new shapes, and thereby enable memory and learning] involves the monitoring of neurotransmitter activities. Specific receptors help neurons sense the environment and turn the genes which cause production of neurotransmitters and their receptors on or off [*I like this terminology!*]. For example, if an individual has just

experienced a stressful situation, the brain senses the rise in stress level and may turn off or turn down the genes that make neurotransmitter receptors. When fewer receptors are available, messages sent across synapses are received more slowly or with less sensitivity. If the receptors that have been downgraded or upgraded are also involved in regulating mood, then receptor up and downgrading will have an effect on mood…research suggests that antidepressant medications and electroconvulsive therapy (ECT) seem to increase the growth of new neurons in these key brain areas. In contrast, chronic stress seems to decrease cell growth in these areas. Based on this evidence, we can conclude that a decreased number of neurons in the emotional centers of the brain can lead to slower reactivity and depressive symptoms.[34]

That said, chemistry in the brain *may not be* the *only cause* of anxiety or depression. The endocrine system plays a big part as well! Comprised primarily of glandular organs (pituitary, pineal, hypothalamus, thyroid,

> **When any aspect of the endocrine system fouls up, *depression can occur!***

---

[34] "Biology of Depression – Neuroplasticity and Endocrinology," *MentalHelp.net*, a subsidiary of *American Addiction Centers, Inc.*, para. 2, https://www.mentalhelp.net/depression/neuroplasticity-and-endocrinology/ (accessed on February 4, 2020).

parathyroid, thymus, adrenal, pancreas, ovaries, testes) in the body that make and secrete hormones, the endocrine system carries these *hormones* through the bloodstream to do specific tasks in the body.[35]

So, while the brain controls neurotransmitter *chemical traffic* in the body (via brain and nervous system), the endocrine system controls *hormonal traffic* in the body (via the bloodstream and between organs). The *"central switching station"* between the nervous system and the endocrine system is the *hypothalamus* and "is an exceptionally complex brain region, which controls many different body functions such as blood pressure, appetite, immune responses, body temperature, maternal behavior, and body rhythms pertaining to circadian and seasonal rhythms."[36]

Keep in mind, genetic proclivities, environmental stimuli, and *certainly, stress*, are ALL likely culprits!

Feeling depressed? My goodness – just studying it can "throw the switch," can't it?! Okay, I'm not well-versed in this stuff, so I've only included this bit of research to satisfy the "inquiring minds" of those who need to know how

---

[35] "The Endocrine System and Glands of the Human Body," *WebMD*, sec. "What Is a Gland?" https://www.webmd.com/diabetes/endocrine-system-facts#1 (accessed on February 4, 2020). "Many glands make up the endocrine system. The hypothalamus, pituitary gland, and pineal gland are in your brain. The thyroid and parathyroid glands are in your neck. The thymus is between your lungs, the adrenals are on top of your kidneys, and the pancreas is behind your stomach. Your ovaries (if you're a woman) or testes (if you're a man) are in your pelvic region."
[36] "Biology of Depression…," *MentalHelp.net*, sec. "Endocrinology," para. 2.

incredibly complicated and delicate the human body is! And consequently, how *easy it can be* to trigger an eruption, quake, or avalanche of nightmarish anxiety…however *you* might describe it!

I'm intending to be a bit blunt closing this chapter. It bothers me badly when *anyone* makes light of depression, anxiety disorders, or chemical imbalance. I've heard so many say of others *before I got* sick, "It's all in his head." Or, "it isn't real – she *just thinks* it is." Or, "It's imaginary. If they would just get up and be productive, they wouldn't feel that way."

I'm *really* a nice person, so please take what I'm about to say with a grain of salt…and then get over it.[37] [Free Speech – First Amendment! Smile!] If you are one of those individuals who trivializes the illnesses of people who suffer physiological impairments caused by chemical imbalances in the human body, then I wish for you that all your favorite parking spaces will be taken, the fleas of a thousand camels would infest your armpits, and that someone who doesn't like you very well would bloody your nose…but not break it.

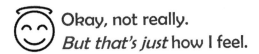 **Okay, not really.**
But that's just **how I feel.**

---

[37] Please grace me to be facetious and overbearing *just* this one time! I certainly *do not want* this to happen *to anyone!* I'm truly a caring person, *but it does make my point,* don't you think?!

Chapter 10

Caleb Courage

My firstborn grandson of six grandchildren total (the circle is complete) was born June 5, 2002. That's also the same year my wife's mother passed away. She was the first among either of our parents to go and be with the Lord. Lou and I both had felt so sad that her mother, Ruth Ellen Smith, had not lived to see her first great-grandchild. Her mother loved children and had operated a daycare for 35 years, loving on all the children in the community...*everyone else's*, that is.

Ruth was boasted to be the best childcare giver in the entire region, not of herself, of course, but by all the parents who trusted her with their children's care. She loved those kids so much and showed them such affection that my wife, being an *only* child, *never really felt like one*. For all she knew, every kid in town was her sibling! It was said of Ruth that she could cure ADD and ADHD.[38] Folks were saying, "Give her a week, and she can fix your youngin!"

To this day, people who knew her *still brag about her*. In fact, my father-in-law, George, our only remaining parent, age 84, still works at the same furniture company that he

---

[38] Attention Deficit Disorder and Attention-Deficit/Hyperactivity Disorder.

always has since age 17 (67 years – beat that, will ya'!)! He is still invaluable to the company vision! And guess who *his boss* is?! A brilliant and handsome Christian gentleman, grandson of the family company owners, that "Ms. Ruth" kept when he was a child, *one of her favorites,* I might add! I guess it would be okay to acknowledge that he has probably put that company on the map in a really big way, being market- and tech-savvy and all. *We'd like to think Lou's mom had something to do with that!*

But now *her first great-grandchild was coming,* and we were so happy for her, and *she was so excited!* But she took ill in late 2001 with complications from congestive heart failure...you know, that delicate balance between functions of the heart, lungs, and kidneys. And when my son, Mitchell, and his wife, Amy, visited Ruth in the hospital, they *let her feel her great-grandchild* moving in Mommy's tummy. But she said to them with an uncanny certainty that she wouldn't live to see this child in person. "Don't say that, Ms. Ruth," Amy implored. "Yes, you will!"

> But Ruth was right. She died February 18, 2002...
> four months before the baby arrived.

I guess it's true that *most firstborn* grandchildren get all the doting from both sides of the family – Caleb sure did! And it was so much fun learning to be a grandparent! I now wish my grandchildren had come first, *then I would have known* how to be a better daddy. But I'm afraid I "practiced" *on my kids* and only *then got it right* with my grandkids! Perhaps most grandparents feel this way.

I'm so proud of Mitchell and Amy that they gave all three of their children Christian names. Caleb's two sisters, five and seven years younger than he, are named Hannah which means "Grace" and Bethany which means "House of Figs or Dates." Grace more specifically means "gift or virtue coming from God," and most commonly means "favor undeserved and love unconditional." The name, Bethany, represents a state of spiritual goodness, "springing from an understanding of spiritual ideas and the love of serving others."[39]

Caleb means "courageous," and his middle name, "Nathaniel" means "gift of God." Together they mean "courageous gift of God." He and I had become "buddies" from the day he was born.

> ### Caleb Nathaniel
> This is who Caleb was to me – a *conveyor of courage* and *a gracious gift from God!*

My son was a drafting and design artist at the time, and my daughter-in-law was a talented teacher, employed in a local private school. Not having church office hours in 2002, I had more latitude *then* than in later years. Mitchell and Amy graced me to keep Caleb while they worked. I purchased a Sony camcorder to make memories of my firstborn grandson and *filled 38 four-hour cassettes* with precious memories of those first years with him.

I taught Caleb how to fry an egg (at two years old…*not by himself,* of course), how to dance (well, kind of – if you can

---

[39] "Bethany, Bible Word Meanings," *New Christian Study Bible,* para. 3, https://newchristianbiblestudy.org/concept/bethany (accessed on February 5, 2020).

call *how I boogied* "dancing"), and how to play "hide and seek." His favorite song was Sara Evans', *Born to Fly.*[40] I would crank up my sweet-sounding Onkyo entertainment system, and swing that boy all over the dance floor, playing that song over and over at his beckoned behest, "Agin! Agin!" We loved playing "hide and seek." And you should have seen *how cleverly inconspicuous* he was when it was *his* turn to hide! It's still so funny seeing that memory in my

 mind's eye, his tiny little body stretched out from under the bed with only his head hidden, *thinking he was hiding from Grandpa* and I couldn't see him.

And, *of course, I couldn't* – not until I looked really hard for him and finally found him!

On one particular occasion later in August when Caleb was overnighting with us, he and I planned to sleep on the floor in our little pop-up tent at the end of our kingsize bed. I felt so sad for Caleb that night because we had not finished unpacking all of our boxes in this new house, and many, maybe most, of Caleb's plush animals we had purchased for him to play and sleep with were nowhere to be found. I was so concerned he would not be happy to sleep without them.

I said to Caleb as we lay down in the tent and readied to say our prayers, "Caleb, Grandpa's so sorry we haven't found your plush animals yet, and you won't be able to sleep with

[40] Sara Evans, Marcus Hummin, and Darrell Scott, *Born to Fly,* CD Single and Album, Sara Evans and Paul Worley, prod., Updated June 26, 2000, RCA Nashville, *Wikipedia, The Free Encyclopedia,* https://en.wikipedia.org/wiki/Born to Fly (accessed on February 5, 2020).

them tonight. Give me some time, and I'll find *all the things* that make our lives special." Caleb's response (for a four-year-old, especially) was both profound and prophetic!

He sat up promptly and declared gallantly,
"We already have all the things we need to make our lives special, Grandpa! Now think about that!"

And Grandma, eavesdropping from her pillow on the bed echoed back, "Amen! Preach it, Caleb!" I was so amazed how the Lord could speak through the heart of a child! I take great comfort in those words, *even to this day!* They helped to bring balance and inspiration to my life!

I needed inspiration! *It seemed* my life was worsening by the hour...no, by the moment. My health was failing. My symptoms were intensifying. My medication wasn't working. And my will to live was fading fast. My son and his wife knew this, and they understood how important it was for me to "focus." So, they brought Caleb to visit as often as they could to help me get my mind off myself and my pervasive melancholy and misery.

It wasn't easy. When Caleb was with me, I still hurt, I still mourned, and I still panicked. *But I tried not to cry!* I didn't want Caleb to be concerned for me at his age, and I didn't want anything to encumber the relationship I had with him at that time. So, we managed, and it helped.

The most durable and longest-lasting patio set we ever bought, *Caleb helped me put together!* I had purchased it from Kmart weeks before but had been too sick to pick it up. My son did that for me. To my dismay, it was boxed and required assembly – I should have known that. But how fitting, Caleb, having just turned four years old, loved working with tools, and his little hands *touched every screw!* And he knew how to use my tools as well! That was a good day for me. I felt like I had accomplished something, and I had done it with the assistance of someone I loved dearly!

This entire chapter is dedicated to Caleb in celebration of the spiritual inspiration he imparted to me in the darkest days of my life! He will be 18 years old this June, and I am so very proud of my firstborn grandson!

I am *absolutely convinced* my family's support was crucial to my recovery, and Caleb's love was integral to my healing and restoration back to good health. I will always love him for that and will never forget how he helped to "save" me from myself. Proverbs 23:24 says that a righteous person's parents ['*and grandparents,*' may I add] have "good reason to be happy" (GNB).[41]

Thank you, Caleb, "Buddy!"[42] And here's that song I made up for you that you *always loved to hear* "Agin!" and "Agin!" [...to the tune of, "The Devil Is a Sly Ole Fox"]:

Caleb is a sweet little boy, and he brings me lots of joy!
I will love him all the day, 'cause he makes me feel that way!
Caleb is my grandson, and he is so much fun!
Caleb is my grandson, I love him, O' so much!

---

[41] *The Good News Bible* (Philadelphia, Pennsylvania: American Bible Society, 1966).
[42] I've always called Caleb "Buddy" from the day he was born. It's kind of a grandfather-grandson tenderness that sparked the moment I saw his face and realized I was a Grandpa!

Chapter 11

My Baby Sister

You haven't met my baby sister yet. *You oughta!* She's a
hoot! She's the "class clown" in our family who always keeps
everyone laughing! I still have mental images of her doing
"The Washing Machine."[43] She could move *every part of her
body* at the same time – she's so talented! She could bust a
move to the tune, "She's a Brick House."[44] In fact, she actually
hurt her knee quite seriously one time cutting up, strutting
her stuff, dancing to that song! Incidentally, *that knee* has
since been surgically replaced!

Five years younger than I, Rita Kay Drake and I have
always loved each other *dearly!* But when I got sick, that
loved deepened immensely as she became my wife's "second
line of defense." Between the two of them, they weren't about
to let their husband-brother go down! Not if their lives
depended on it! And while she and I talked lots – I mean *lots*
– she and Lou talked a lot as well. She has become my wife's

---

[43] NOT the seductive "Jennifer Lopez version!" *Rather, my sister's
generation's own* version, more like the "Twist."
[44] The Commodores, "She's a Brick House," *Commodores, Brick House,*
Motown Records, August 26, 1977, Album, *Genius,* https://genius.com/
Commodores-brick-house-lyrics (accessed on February 7, 2020).

sister that she never had, being an only child. She and Lou are very close, and she knew when *I wasn't capable* of being objective, Lou was.

> She got the *impressions* from me, but she got the *facts* from Lou. She kept up *with both!*

Rita is "my mama" now that our mother has passed away. It's quite amazing how prominent the genes are in our family. I look and behave just like our daddy, Rudolph Casper. You should see my profile – if you didn't know better, you would think he had come back…from heaven! And Rita looks *and behaves* just like our mother, Mahala Jane, "Janie." She *walks like her, literally* – with a back-bent gait, because her back *and* knees are giving way. She *cooks like* her! In fact, she's the *only person in the whole world* that I know who *has ever* worn out a stove! Seriously! She's the best cook in Edgecombe County, North Carolina! (Okay, I'm biased – you may beg to differ, if you must! It's okay!) Most folks could hide Christmas presents in their stoves in July and few would ever know it 'til Christmas! Rita even *acts like* Mom – I'm not kidding! My sister is a "cause champion!" If she feels strongly about something, she'll take up arms about it, and go to war *with the drop of a hat*…she usually wins! Oh, and did I mention? *She sounds like Mom! I mean, just like her!*

In fact, when I get to missing Mom *really badly,* I call my sister, and I will say to her, "Just talk, Rita. Say something – I don't care what. I just need to hear Mom's voice!" And we'll spend an hour catching up on each other's busy lives. I love talking to my sister, and I love spending time with her, as rarely as that is, given our busy schedules… in our retirement. Smile.

Rita was immediately and duly concerned for me when she learned I was having serious health issues, this having occurred *before* Mom's passing, of course (one year prior). I begged her to *please not tell Mom and Dad* what was happening. I did not want my beloved parents worrying about me unnecessarily. I hoped it would be over before they ever found out. She consented to my plea but insisted that *if it continued,* I would eventually *have to tell them* myself.

When I wasn't feeling well, she would spend hours on the phone with me, trying to encourage me and to protect and enhance my feeble and fading sense of self-worth. She would listen for the longest time to me detailing my atrocious symptoms, my outlandish worries, my unimaginable fears of highly improbable, but *easily conceivable* disastrous outcomes and possibilities. She would hear me describe day after day after day the hollow in my chest, the burning sensations on my skin, the torture in my soul. And then, she *would always* respond with hope and faith and confidence *that I would get through this!* That my life and ministry *wasn't over!* That the outcome *eventually would* be favorable even though I couldn't see or believe it at the moment.

> That *this health issue* **wasn't too big for God!**

Never, ever once did she fail to encourage me and pull me "up and forward" in our conversations. Next to my wife, she was my *most consulted* supporter – there were others whose names I'll eventually mention, but none so close, concerned, and compassionate as my wife and baby sister.

That's what I call her, "Baby Sister." And sometimes,
"Sweetie" or "Shug" (Sugar). We always teased each
other about being Mom and Dad's favorite. In fact, when I
preached Dad's funeral, I teased her in the sermon that even
though our family boat had been named after her, "The Rita
Kay," *I had a yacht* docked in Morehead that she never knew
about…that Mom and Dad had willed to me. We all laughed,
because we *all knew* it wasn't true. I'm protective of her, more
now than ever. She's in my prayers always, and we talk a lot,
sometimes daily, depending on what's happening in each of
our lives. She sacrificed a lot during this dreadful stretch of
my life, because *it didn't end quickly.* And it certainly didn't
end before Mom and Dad finally had to know.

When that happened, she *then had three persons* to console.
Myself, our mother, and our father. So then, *they* were on the
phone a lot, and Mom was constantly asking, "What's wrong
with Wayne? Why *doesn't* he feel well? I *don't understand*
chemical imbalance. What in the world is that?" And Rita
would solace Mom, Dad too, of course, *but Mom primarily,*
assuring her that I was going to be okay, and that it was just
taking time for the medicine to do its work.

Rita had a "tough row to hoe" propping us all up. *But she
did it*…and she did it well.

What would I have done *without* my "baby sister?"

The Lord *only* knows…

Chapter 12

A Mother's Love

Our mother was an exceptionally strong, *and generous, woman*…in so many ways. Daughter of a tenant farmer raised in a very small home in a rural community, Mom was one of seven girls and two boys, third from the youngest. Her mother, Addie Lucindy Batts, and my father's mother, Julia Pollard Flora, were two very strong influences in our family's coming to faith in Jesus Christ.

Our father was a building contractor who spent 35 years in the industry, building small, ranch-style homes in the Edgecombe County community, and when Dad moved his young family out of our four-room rental home into Mom's "mansion" of 1300 square feet in 1963, it must have *slightly* changed Mom's image among her siblings. *Because,* on the day of Mom's funeral, I learned from her sisters that all her siblings had come to know her as "the rich sister!" (I'm still humored with this remembrance!) Don't mistake me, we weren't, but anyone living in their *own new, brick home was rich!* Dad's becoming somewhat financially independent made it seem that way.

Most of mom's siblings were themselves tenant farmers and lived in *someone else's* small four-room houses and tended *someone else's* small farmlands. And because Mom *didn't have to work,* and was a "stay-at-home" mother, living in a nice, new house – she was "rich!" But I must say, she *was, indeed, rich* in so many ways!

She loved her sisters, most of whom never learned to drive and never got their licenses. So, it wasn't uncommon for Mom to go by and pick up each of her sisters any given day (if they weren't working in the fields) and take them shopping or out to lunch, or simply to just sit around and visit at one or the other's home. And she would not *uncommonly slip them $15 or $20 each* and just let them enjoy splurging as they shopped.

How we miss those days! How precious it was that those seven sisters (and occasionally one or the other of the brothers) would just sit together and rock energetically in their old wood-slat rockers! And they could carry on four or five conversations at the same time, while the kids would sit around and listen, amused that everyone could talk at the same time, yet know *what everyone else* was saying! Or perhaps we kids would just be out playing in the dirt!

Let's not forget the lunch they'd spread either – home-rolled chicken pastry, collard greens, corn on the cob, mashed potatoes and gravy, and fried chicken – *that's how I knew I was called to preach!*

She loved her youngins, all three of us. And it is a fact of matter that when I got sick and Mama feared my illness might be a *"sickness unto death"* (Is. 38:1; KJV),[45] she undoubtedly had Ronnie on her mind a lot in that stretch of

---

[45] *The Holy Bible, King James Version* (New York: American Bible Society, 1611, 1999). "¹In those days was Hezekiah sick unto death" (Is. 38:1; KJV).

days and weeks before she understood what I was *actually* experiencing.

Our older brother, Mom and Dad's firstborn, had died at age 42 (turning 43 less than a month later) in a single vehicle automobile accident. I remember so well heading to Macclesfield where Mom and Dad lived after we got that fateful call at 10:30 pm, September 8, 1994. My brother-in-law, Eddie Drake, had placed the call.

> "Wayne, I've got some bad news. Your brother was just killed in an automobile accident not far from home, and you need to come as soon as you can."

"Are you sure, Eddie?" I appealed. "Yes, it's been confirmed. Your dad was there and saw the scene himself. Be careful driving, but you need to come."

I got off the phone and spent 10 minutes walking the floors, bawling, yet praising God (woefully, but *not at all easily*) for His goodness and mercy…and *comfort now in this difficult moment,* declaring His sovereignty in all things, especially when bad news comes to loving families. Then I called a dear friend, a prayer warrior, who knew just the right words to say when someone was hurting, Barry Warren, to please come to my home and drive me to Macclesfield. He was more than willing to oblige my earnest cry. He was truly a Christian who had a "servant's heart."

I recall arriving in Macclesfield (from Winterville where we lived, 26 miles) and *not believing it had really happened* until I saw all the cars lined up and down the road at my old homeplace. When I went into the house to see my parents, Mama was on the floor squalling like a baby, inconsolably distraught. The room was full of tearfully supportive and sympathetic family, friends, and neighbors, but I greeted no one.

Who could *ever* *forget* the imprint of an experience like that on the conscience of his soul?!

I fell to my knees, grabbed my grieving mother up in my arms and held her like a little girl rocking her doll, and literally swayed with her back and forth, back and forth, to the rhythm of her sobs, whispering sorrows and sentiments and sincere prayers in her ears 'til she calmed down and regained composure.

I am absolutely sure my being sick with an inexplicable illness, an undetermined diagnosis, disturbed her greatly, and she would NEVER be content that her second child would ever recover *until she got a handle* on exactly what was happening inside my body…and with my chemistry. Consequently, Mom would call me every day! I mean, every *single* day! Not a day went by that my phone didn't ring and Mom would talk to me for hours, trying to understand, hoping to hear good news, meaning to reassure me…but not knowing how.

The conversation would always begin with, "How do you feel today, Wayne? Are you feeling any better?" Hey, I couldn't lie to Mama! I rarely ever had before (I *didn't say,* *"Never!"*). This was a lady who could read my soul – she could look right through my glaring, guile-glinted, devious eyes and see deceit in the core of my being! I could *never* get away with anything with Mom – she was too discerning and perceptive to let that happen.

Let me pause to say, I got my fair share of beatings – yes, beatings – old-fashioned, "behind-the-barn," belt-lashing, switch-thrashing whippings that parents today would go to jail for! Mama didn't care what Dr. Spock advised! She always said that if she didn't whip me *while she was angry, I wouldn't get what I deserved!* And I have to say, there were times *I thought the wrath of God was falling upon me*, waiting on Mama's anger to subside! I KNOW I got what I deserved, nothing spared. And you MUST hear me say in conclusion to this tear-jerking story that *I think* I turned out all right! It was good for me! But let me move on…it's making me nervous just thinking about it! I don't need another panic attack to happen while I write this book!

Then after Mom had quizzed me up one side and down the other about *how I felt*, she would "cross-examine" me over and over again, probing me to *please explain to her* in a way she could understand, "Wayne, what *is* a chemical imbalance? What does that mean? What caused it? Why is it happening? Why can't the doctors help you? Why aren't you getting better?"

> **"Wayne, *what is* a chemical imbalance?"**

In as honest, straightforward, *but guarded* manner as possible, I would answer, "Mom, I'm so sorry to say that today isn't a good day. The night was tough, and my symptoms are intense. I'm really struggling. Please keep praying for me. If God hears anybody's prayers, Mama, I know He hears yours! He honors the affections of a mother's love, and He knows how much you love me! I'm so glad you do and I'm glad you called. It *does make me feel some better, Mama.* Let's just keep talking for a little while – it helps me to hear your voice."

And when the daily quiz popped up, I'd try to answer *again* as aptly as possible. "Mama, I really don't understand it. It has something to do with the chemistry in my body, my brain, my hormones. Everything's just 'out of whack' and the doctor says it may take a while to get it under control. It's a slow process, and as difficult as it is, I just have to be patient and let the medicine work."

This became the daily ritual…but I was glad it did. I could always count on that one predictable phone call, just about the same time, mid-morning every day! I didn't care how long it lasted, even on my worse days when I didn't feel well at all, because Mom's voice was medicine to me. Hearing her speak and say over and again how much she loved me and how earnestly she was praying for me brought such comfort to my spirit even as my body ached with brutal pain.

Finally, one day when I felt things were improving (on the timeline of this story, *later than* these last few chapters), Mom pushed all the right buttons, and asked all the right questions, and cornered me in *just the right way*, and I gave in and told her *exactly what she needed and wanted* to hear. I said to her, "Mama, what I'm actually experiencing is an *'old-fashioned' nervous breakdown.*"

She laughed hysterically, right out loud, deep and gullied and bellowing, "Aw, that ain't nothing! I've had plenty of those! I know *exactly what that is! What that's like!* You're gonna' be all right, Wayne! You can handle this! It ain't no big deal! You're gonna' be okay *after all!*"

"That's all it is… just a nervous breakdown."

It was *then* that I realized what she said was true, for I remembered the panicky instances, *and there were many of them,* when Mama would get upset about something and then get "fainty-feeling," as she called it. And would start breathing short, rapid breaths, turn flush in the face and neck, and say, "she felt funny all over." Then she would insist at a moment's notice, "I need a nerve pill!" And she would run to the medicine cabinet and pop one. It never really dawned on me *then* exactly what was happening. I understand now.

And from that day 'til the day she died, September 29, 2007, Mama had peace about her son's sickness and somehow knew, providentially perhaps, or maybe *experientially,* that I was going to be okay. Because finally, she understood what I was going through.

GENETICS...PROMINENT, *AREN'T THEY?!*

Chapter 13

The Caring, but Candid Physician

Hardheaded as I was – and *I was* – I eventually accepted the reality that my situation *was not improving…at all!* I was imprudently pushing the envelope of treatment I *really needed*, only serving to delay the inevitable, and *day by day,* was simply making matters worse. Whatever was happening in my body, the Xanax® wasn't touching it, and I really wasn't getting better. I was now three weeks out from our first visit with the doctor, and while we were returning weekly, as insistently instructed, things *really had* gone from bad to worse, and now it was beginning to affect my family.

My wife had always been so loving and compassionate about my health crisis, and as best she knew how, she tried to comfort and encourage me. But for now, she *herself* was beginning to wear thin. The crisis was taking a toll on her. She was losing so much rest, my wandering about the house, crying out to God all hours of the night. And she was worried I might open the door and just walk away to *who knows where* and possibly endanger myself. She knew I was suffering, and she knew I wasn't thinking clearly at all anymore! By now, *no more than I,* was *she* holding out hope that an *immediate turnaround* would happen *any time soon.* So, she began to *beg me to please* follow my doctor's advice and accept the necessary treatment to arrest this out-of-control crisis.

Allow me to interject at this point that it is so important for anyone reading this book to understand how critical it is that *caregivers take care of themselves.* They need their own support group, I can attest, especially now, looking back! That Lou *was* such a devoted companion to her husband, I was attentive enough to realize I was *inadvertently shoving her* to the edge of *my cliff.* Several times, we teetered there together…feebly standing, unsteadily swaying, and both liable at any moment to drop off the precipice!

And we did drop to the floor several times and lay there together most of the day, weeping, and praying, and asking God for His help in our pitiable condition. It is certainly highly possible that Lou's *own chemistry* was disturbed and challenged throughout the duration of *my* horrible health crisis. It was getting completely out of hand. And besides my own family's appeal for me to receive help, the medical professionals in our church were urging the same.

> ## TREATMENT?
>
> No one saw a way out of this without proper medical treatment.

So, on Wednesday, June 21st, we made our weekly visit to the doctor's office. Only *this week,* I was so distraught and so traumatized by the lack of sleep, lack of nourishment, and loss of weight – *and* the sheer exhaustion from fighting back the pain, fear…*and tears* – that I entered the clinic that day like a five-year-old child, starting Kindergarten, reaching up to tightly hold his mother's hand, terrified of what was about to happen.

My eyes were gaped and glazed. My voice was trembling. My body was shaking. I looked shell-shocked. And yes, my heart was racing wildly, and my blood pressure was off the chart! It was obvious by now that Dr. Ribeiro was seriously concerned and *was right before* making his "final recommendation" concerning my health – *referral!*

By now, he no longer asked *me how I felt* or *what I was experiencing*. Besides, I didn't want to see *or talk*…to *anybody, anyway* – and he knew it. I loved him dearly, but I didn't want to be there. He focused his attention on Lou's update and her restrained but desperate cry for help, compassionately keeping me in the corner of his eye. Like a chastised child with his hands folded in his lap, I sat there, trembling like a nervous, untrained puppy about to be scolded for having peed on the floor.

My nerves were on end. My emotions were shot.

My mind was wrecked. He had besought me *each visit the last three weeks* to please accept long-term treatment and let him write the necessary prescription to begin the regimen. And I had refused. He sternly warned me that I was complicating *and delaying recovery* by refusing to accept help. He had never been so terse, so stern with me as he was that day. When he turned to me, and pulled up into my face, took both my hands into his, and looked right into my eyes – no, *my soul* – I knew this was it, the end…either of my dogged, mulish stubbornness *or* his capacity to offer any further help. I dreaded what was coming, what he was about to say.

He said it candidly, but compassionately. "Pastor Flora, I understand your reluctance…and why. I'm a pastor, too, so

I'm sincerely empathetic for how you feel. But you're very sick, and pastors are human beings just like the congregants they serve. And you need help…*right away.* We can't delay any longer. Your symptoms are worsening; you need treatment. We both know God *can heal you, yes,* but sometimes He chooses to do that with the help of medicines and medical professionals. You're tying my hands, so I must tell you, here's where we are: If you do not trust me and *Christ in me* and are not willing to do as I say, I have no choice but to refer you to a psychiatrist right away. That may be exactly what you need, and it would be totally acceptable and appropriate for you to come under a psychiatrist's care."

My eyes flooded, my lips quivered, my heart pounded out of my chest. I looked at Lou – she was *pleading with me* through those tearful, loving, but sunken, hollowed eyes. I knew she was at wit's end, and I was putting her through hell. I realized it could only get worse. My smitten faith had met its match and reached its own ultimatum. I was now given the opportunity to learn an aspect of faith I had never experienced (nor ever cared to) – perhaps *totally inconsistent with,* or at least, *antithetic to,* all prior convictions about my understanding of faith – *the blessing of human suffering and the grace to trust God for my healing through the use of medicine!*

I was tested *at this moment* to do the right thing – to trust God by trusting my doctor and his expertise in medicine.

I gave up my right *"to be right."* My faulty **I tearfully relented.** opinion of what true faith was, my mistaken concept of what God expects of me, or even what I thought He required of me *to truly please Him.* I conceded, nodding my head with assenting approval, and weeping softly as Dr. Ribeiro hugged me and held me…and loved me as only a Christian physician and peer minister of the Gospel could, empathetically understanding all the reasons for my holdout and hesitancy to accept treatment. He didn't rush his embrace as my wife, just to his side, *took her own needed time* to sob with relief in this turnaround moment of dimly lit hope and breaking optimism.

It was now quiet...and moving...and sacred.

Having now gathered every detail of family history, Dr. Ribeiro said to me, "Pastor Flora, your mother is on Lexapro[46] for depression. Your sister is on Lexapro for fibromyalgia. Your father is on Lexapro for sleep disorder. It is highly likely that *this particular medicine* will work for you. I'm not a psychiatrist; I can't treat you as one. But *I can treat you* for sleep disorder. I'm writing your prescription for this medication and you need to get it filled right away and start taking it today."

"Yes, sir," I complied. He continued, "Lexapro is a light industry standard best, but it is an antidepressant, so you need to understand how it works. It will take about two weeks for you to even notice it is in your body, four to six weeks for it to begin arresting symptoms, and probably two to three months before you begin to truly feel better, more like yourself again. You can't toy with this medication; you

---

[46] "Lexapro," Sanjai Sinha, MD, reviewer, *Drugs.com,* Dec. 14, 2018, sec. "What Is Lexapro?" https://www.drugs.com/lexapro.html (accessed on February 8, 2020). Lexapro is the brand name for escitalopram. "Lexapro (escitalopram) is an antidepressant in a group of drugs called selective serotonin reuptake inhibitors (SSRIs). Escitalopram affects chemicals in the brain that may be unbalanced in people with depression or anxiety."

must take the dosage I recommend. Do not skip the dosage on days you think you feel better, and do not increase the dosage on days you think you feel worse. Stay consistent with the treatment, and your wife will help to monitor how it affects you." "Yes, sir," I consented.

"Furthermore," he instructed. "I'm keeping you on the Xanax®. Begin to take it as needed while the Lexapro tempers in your body. As the Lexapro begins to take over, I will begin to wean you from the Xanax®, perhaps four to six weeks out. Do you understand my instructions?" "Yes, sir," I replied. "And do you have any questions?" he asked. "No, sir," I responded. "I have no questions."

Dr. Ribeiro then invited, "I want to pray for you, Pastor Flora." "Yes, sir," I welcomed. He laid his hands upon me, as *we ourselves would* in the tradition of my own faith, on my forehead and on my shoulder, and prayed the most earnest, sincere, and compassionate prayer I have ever heard. He besought the Lord on my behalf for guidance and help, for hope and peace, for patience and grace.

He also prayed so tenderly for my wife, that God would give her the courage and strength she needed to support me through this dark and dismal season of our lives. He expressed confidence that God was hearing our prayers and that He would answer them. He praised the Lord for His love for us and His hand upon us, even in these difficult times. He ended the prayer, "In Jesus' name. Amen." Together, Lou and I said, "Amen."

And of course, he scheduled our *next appointment* for the *next week, then we* left his office and filled the prescription...*right away.*

Chapter 14

Trip to the Beach

The beaches of eastern North Carolina are absolutely beautiful! Aside from the 200-mile stretch of barrier islands called the Outer Banks that extend from southeast Virginia down through most of North Carolina's coast line, *our family* especially enjoyed the southern stretch of "outer banks"[47] that runs from Fort Macon State Park over to Emerald Isle, all in Carteret County. There are plenty of places to park your RV, pitch a tent, rent a lodge, or stay in motels up and down this stretch of land…Atlantic Beach, Pine Knoll Shores, Indian Beach, and Emerald Isle.

The week of June 18 – 25 was the week my sister and *her family* were enjoying their annual beach vacation down at Emerald Isle…which was always a really big deal! In fact, that had become quite the family tradition for our parents' nuclear family through the years, typically planned with *exacting detail* by my baby sister, Rita. And when possible, Mom's sisters would often go and "man the kitchen" – and why not let 'em?! After all, they loved to cook! So, *we never felt guilty* about giving them "culinary control."

---

[47] This stretch of land is *not formally considered* a part of the Outer Banks proper, *although* they are yet "outer" barrier islands separated by Bogue Sound in the western stretch and Back Sound in the eastern.

The usual two-story, four-bedroom, three-bath, beachfront home was a *place of peace…and lots of laughter* for *everyone* staying the entire week *as well as other* family members popping in and out to visit a night or two. You've never really known what fun is until you've shown up at our family "beach parties!" Listening to Mom's sisters sharing their growing-up stories, playing card games, catching *(cleaning and cooking)* our own fish caught fresh in the surf, watching the children play in the sand, collecting shells up and down the seashore – oh, *the enchanting memories* that resonate even now as I recall those cherished days!

I always thought it was so calming to lay on a bed nearest a back window closest to the beach and listen to those waves crashing on the nearby shoreline. Surely this was *one of the places* on Planet Earth that God did "therapy classes" for His busy children, stress-ridden and

There was something unusually curative about that experience.

overburdened from service to a needy world! And as busy a pastor *as I was* all those 34 years in pastoral ministry, 26 years at one church, this was a rare but welcomed respite from the hectic pace I usually kept, leading a growing congregation.

That was the week I visited my doctor (June 21), and it *was not* a good week, *at least*, the start of it wasn't. It was that week I began my new medication. In fact, I remember so well taking that first 10mg Lexapro and asking myself, "How in the world is this little white pill ever going to make me feel better?!" The first time it touched my tongue, I thought it tasted so bitter and nasty! I didn't feel good about starting this regimen…

It was *also that week* I couldn't attend church on the 25th. I was miserable. Everyone in my family knew it. *Rita knew* I wasn't doing well, for she was in touch daily. And she knew things *seemed to be* declining rather than improving. She was aware I had conceded to the doctor's wishes and that I was starting my antidepressant that very week. So, in the gracious and generous manner she always did, she besought – well, actually *insisted – that we please come down* to the beach to visit with them by end of week. Of course, that would mean Lou had to get off work…and *I would have to leave home.*

Now then, as a side note, let me mention that when *some people* suffer similar health issues such as I was experiencing, many feel the need to be *in company with* others, to feel surrounded by persons who care…*I did not.* I felt the need to be alone in my "deep, dark, black hole" all by myself. My wife understood this, and we were both concerned about whether we should answer Rita's kind, but compelling invitation. In this situation, however, my sister was not just "being nice" – she loved me dearly and felt I *really needed* a break, away from our castle-like "dungeon of darkness" I *thought* I was dying in. Her appeal was authentic and sincere.

So, on the very day that I took my first 10mg Lexapro, we packed our luggage and headed down to Emerald Isle. I quite remember how kindly and compassionately welcomed we were by the family. Rita's two children, unmarried at that time, *always made much-to-do about* "Uncle Wayne." They loved me as much as Eddie and Rita themselves did. They enjoyed bragging on "how smart Uncle Wayne was" and teasing about Rita and me being siblings and wondering if we *really had the same parents,* suggesting that maybe one of us was adopted. [I know which one, Baby Sister!]

I highly suspected that Rita had "lectured" everyone before we came concerning how incredibly *sensitive I was* at this time in my life, not feeling well and all, and had instructed them that caution should be observed not to say anything that might trigger my symptoms. I don't know this to be true, and I've never asked, to be frank, but the "delicate touch" of affection and care we received when we arrived prompted me to think so. Everyone was so excited to see us and so welcoming of our visit!

I had told you earlier that my sister was a hoot – well, I must say, the apples in her lineage didn't fall far from her tree! Her son, Brandon, and her daughter, Leslie, are just as comical and funny as she. Almost anything they say is totally

> To be honest, it seemed good to be among family that Lou and I loved so much, as together we felt "safe" in their company.

original, good-natured and humorous, but just as rib-tickling and sidesplitting as can be!

In fact, at that time, Brandon was a top-notch car salesman at a regional dealership in the city of Rocky Mount, just down the road from their home in Pinetops. One afternoon, he overheard my pitiable groaning about having purchased the Toyota Sienna at this untimely interval in our lives, and my grievous woes of being upside down with our new home and new car, desperately sounding like I was being buried alive in eternal debt. I just simply couldn't stop fretting about it!

Brandon so humorously entered the conversation on one occasion and amusingly asked, "Hey, Uncle Wayne, do y'all have GAP[48] insurance on that car?" "Yes, we do, Brandon...why?" I replied. He wittily responded, "Don't worry about it, Uncle Wayne! I'll take care of it for you – just leave the keys in the car one night, *and I'll make it disappear!*" We all rolled with belly-busting laughter! He was quick on his feet like that *all the time,* and I must admit, it *was, indeed, good medicine!* The Scriptures attest this in Prov. 17:22, "A cheerful heart is good medicine...!"[49] Of course, *we all knew* he didn't mean it...*or did he?* Smile!

Even to this day I feel I "ruined" my sister's and her family's vacation that week. It could not possibly have been as exciting and pleasurable for them *as it had been* in prior years. I would sit on the back porch and watch them play in the water, fish from the surf, build sandcastles, and gather shells. They would ask me to come and join them,

---

[48] "GAP Insurance," *Wikipedia, The Free Encyclopedia,* Updated Nov. 2, 2019, para. 1, https://en.wikipedia.org/wiki/GAP insurance (accessed on February 10, 2020). Okay, I'm not a fan of *Wikipedia,* but this definition of GAP is quite thorough: "Guaranteed Asset Protection (GAP) insurance (also known as *GAPS*) was established in the North American financial industry. GAP insurance protects the borrower if the car is totaled by paying the remaining difference between the actual cash value of a vehicle and the balance still owed on the financing. GAP coverage is mainly used on new and used small vehicles (cars and trucks) and heavy trucks. Some financing companies and lease contracts require it."

[49] It is interesting that the antithesis in this verse, Part B, reads like this: "but a crushed spirit dries up the bones." I was experiencing the "drying up" of my bones, *it seemed,* so this well-placed bit of humor was welcomed, indeed!

but I didn't feel like it. They would invite me to put on my
swimming trunks, which we *had brought,* hoping perhaps
a brisk dip in the ocean waves would refresh my love of
life and wash away some worry. But *I never did.*

We would sit together at mealtime around a table of my
sister's finest cooking – old-fashioned recipes that she had
learned, perhaps, from Mom and her sisters. The table would
be spread with food enough to feed our neighbors on both
sides of the lodge...*and I couldn't eat.* Not a mouthful. I was
repulsed by it but would sit there with the family simply to
be cordial and not completely spoil their table time together.

Brandon would ask me, "Uncle Wayne, why aren't you
eating?" And I would answer, "I'm sorry, Brandon – I can't,
but I really don't know why. I feel
like *if I did eat,* I couldn't keep it
down. I'm just not hungry." I
was later told that "my endocrine
system was emptying into my
digestive system and spoiling my
appetite."[50] I doubt that was an apt

> By now, four weeks since
> the onset of my health
> concerns, I had already
> lost 35 pounds and was
> "disappearing" fast.

---

[50] Will Boggs, "Appetite Changes Reflect Distinct Subgroups of Depression,"
Psychiatry and Behavioral Health Learning Network, July 5, 2018, para. 11,
https://www.psychcongress.com/news/appetite-changes-reflect-distinct-
subgroups-depression (accessed on February 10, 2020). I can't recall who
offered this explanation, and it's probably best I don't – I'm not sure how
accurate it is. However, this may be accurate to some extent, according
to *Psychiatry and Behavioral Health.* Dr. W. Kyle Simmons, participant
in research concerning increase vs. decrease of appetite with chemical
imbalance, states the following: "...the endocrine, immune, and metabolic
changes happening in the bodies of people with depression may lead
to changes in brain activity that regulate appetite when they become
depressed...For some people, depression may be relatively more associated
with increased stress hormones – and those folks may experience appetite
loss." It is noted that depression can lead to *increase* in appetite as well.

explanation of what was actually happening, but it
sounded reasonable enough to me.

Eddie Drake, my brother-in-law and very dear friend,
a devoted leader in many capacities at the Baptist church
where he has worshiped all his life, would sit for hours
with my sister, Rita, and encourage me, quoting Scriptures,
offering prayer, answering questions, hearing my heart. It
seemed they never tired of it, though I felt I was wearing
them out and consuming the quality family time they
could be spending with their children.

Those few days spent at the beach were invaluable to us,
probably more so to my wife, Lou. She really hadn't had a
decent break tending to me *at all* for days on end now, and
she was extremely exhausted emotionally. At least, for a little
while *now, someone else could distract* her husband from his
over-exaggerated worries and woes. *Someone else* could hear
him drone on and on for hours and hours about his grief
so profound and anxiety so intense. It was true that I was
constantly repeating myself over and over and over. Looking
back, I realize how taxing and tiring that must *surely have*
been for anyone who cared enough to listen.

I DIDN'T HAVE A CLUE! I understood that my new meds
would not really begin to take effect until
two weeks out, but in my case, I began to
notice an *immediate effect* right away. I had
always heard that the adjustment period between *when* an
antidepressant was begun and *when it finally began arresting*
symptoms could be quite horrifying and unbearable.

I had wished for my wife we had slept separately, because
I felt I was seriously disturbing her sleep…as always, but *now*
more than ever. Not only were my symptoms getting worse

and worse, but now I began to think thoughts I had *never ever* considered before, thoughts of self-extinction that I never shared with my family until way later and well into my recovery.

My sister had placed a small oscillating fan in the room to help us sleep: 1) for the flow of air over our bed, and 2) for the sake of noise to *simply distract me* from my lurid and alarming thoughts. But it didn't help. I don't know how many times I got up those several nights, panicking horribly, excessively sweating out, horrified by my fears and imaginations, and went to the restroom to wash my face. I remember staring time and again into that mirror at the shell of a man I had become and crying, almost wailing – trying *not* to awaken anyone – and thinking, "I *don't* want to die, BUT I don't want to live *like this!*"

I COULDN'T GET THOSE THOUGHTS OUT OF MY MIND. ANY ATTEMPT TO PRAY SEEMED FUTILE.

I was beginning to *feel that maybe* God *had abandoned* me, that He wasn't listening anymore, and that He certainly wasn't answering. I asked Him over and over again why He was letting this happen to me, what I had done to make Him so mad at me, and why a life so promising and hopeful was ending this way.

As I stood at that mirror, I could imagine myself forcing the blade of a really sharp butcher knife through my heart and mused over and over again how easy that might be, and how quickly it would end my pain. I knew where the knives were, and I knew they were easily accessible. But in each instance, when I'd rehearse this in my mind, I would conclude by imagining how devastated that would leave my family, *more than they already were,* my being so sick. And I pondered how they might fear I had gone to hell and missed heaven after all. I just couldn't leave my children, my mom and dad, my sister, and especially my wife with such despair and hopelessness in their hearts! It could destroy their own lives and decimate any promise of a future at all for them.

While both days and nights *had been toilsome* at home, at the beach I did *at least feel* that break of day got me past that alluring "song of the Sirens"[51] and brought me some much-welcomed, morning cheer. I knew my wife would be close, and I knew I was surrounded by family who truly loved me.

And they were willing to listen...
and pray. Lots.

---

[51] Adam Augustyn, et al., "Siren, Greek Mythology," *Encyclopaedia Britannica,* Amy Tikkanen, revised and updated Dec. 19, 2018, https://www.britannica.com/topic/Siren-Greek-mythology (accessed on February 11, 2020). "Siren, in Greek mythology, a creature half bird and half woman who lured sailors to destruction by the sweetness of her song... In Homer's *Odyssey,* Book XII, the Greek hero Odysseus, advised by the sorceress Circe, escaped the danger of their song by stopping the ears of his crew with wax so that they were deaf to the Sirens. Odysseus himself wanted to hear their song but had himself tied to the mast so that he would not be able to steer the ship off its course." PLEASE NOTE that my reference to Greek mythology *in no way* infers my *belief in* mythology. I simply allude to this grade school story to *accentuate* the "sense of danger" I felt contemplating the thought of self-extinction.

Chapter 15

Adjustment Phase

Adjustments can be difficult. Life is full of them. Starting kindergarten. Changing schools. Welcoming a new sibling to the family. Moving to a new home. Going to high school. Going to college. Getting married. Becoming parents. The list is endless. Sure, some are easier than others, but all of them can be quite scary and intimidating.

Some seem impossible. Adaptation to new circumstances can be met with apprehension, fear, resistance, *even* defiance. Or, depending on the nature of the adaptation required, some changes in life can lead to a sense of despair, hopelessness, inability to cope, leaving one feeling as if, "This is the glaring paradigm shift I can't make – *this is the rut* (or *grave*) I'll be stuck in for the rest of my life, what there is left of it." This is *how I felt* as the antidepressant medication began "tempering" in my body.

Change isn't easy! EVER!

I've often wondered why we place medicines in our mouths whose label warnings *are longer than* their lists of expected benefits. I'm often amused at television commercials that introduce these new meds – the images are most frequently pleasantries and enchantments about a better quality of life, and then in the last few seconds, the announcer lowers his tone of voice, speeds his speech to cite an "incapable-to-be-understood" list of *fair warnings* announcing what dangerous side effects this medicine can cause. Then, of course, all these dangerous caveats dash rapidly across the screen in tiniest print so that no one can possibly read them!

Antidepressants have their cautions as well. One must know *before and while* taking antidepressants that halfing or doubling dosages *without a doctor's advisement and monitoring* can be quite dangerous!

The human body is delicate and its many systems function in well-coordinated and proper balance.

When malfunction occurs and medications *are prescribed* to correct imbalances, *it takes time*…plain and simple.

That said, it is needful to know that while medical science may not *know exactly why* (or *perhaps they do…* only supposing) antidepressants may cause thoughts of harming one's self, it is a fact of matter that *they can.* Therefore, while it may seem immaterial to this conversation (or at least, uninteresting – if so, *skip it*) to "share the facts," I consider the following statistics from the American Psychological Association to be quite intriguing:

- 12.7% of the U.S. population over age 12 took antidepressant medication in the past month, according to an analysis from the National Center for Health Statistics. Most antidepressants are used to treat depression, while some are prescribed for other conditions.

- 64% was the increase in the percentage of people using antidepressants between 1999 and 2014. In 1999, 7.7 percent of the population took the medication.

- 19.1% of older adults (over age 60) took antidepressants in the past month. Antidepressant use increases with age. These medications are used by 16.6 percent of people ages 40 to 59, 7.8 percent of those ages 20 to 39, and 3.4 percent of adolescents ages 12 to 19.

- 2 times – Women are twice as likely as men to take antidepressant medication (16.5 percent compared with 8.6 percent). Women are more likely than men to take antidepressants in every age group.

- 16.5% is the percentage of non-Hispanic white Americans taking antidepressants, about three times as much as any other race or ethnic group. By comparison, 5.6 percent of non-Hispanic black Americans, 5 percent of Hispanic Americans, and 3.4 percent of non-Hispanic Asian-Americans took antidepressants in the past month.[52]

Immediately, I see some disturbing patterns emerging in Western Culture as I read these (and other) stats:

- Depression or anxiety disorder is *no respecter of persons!* Gender, age, and ethnicity seem not to

---

[52] Lea Winerman, "By The Numbers: Antidepressant Use On The Rise," *American Psychological Association* 48, no. 10 (November 2017): 120, https://www.apa.org/monitor/2017/11/numbers (accessed on February 11, 2020).

matter *entirely*. Over 1 in 10 persons in our country use antidepressants (12.7%, some say higher).

- Youth are affected with this health concern, ever more so in our "latch-key" society. This percentage is alarmingly increasing with the fragmentation of family and values.

- A horrific spiraling effect is happening in our culture; increased usage is rising *rapidly!* A 64% increase in usage happened between 1999 and 2014 – we're going "off the charts."

- For whatever reason, women are twice as likely to take antidepressants than men. I do not think this speaks to *fragility of women* as much as does to *diffidence (reluctance) of men* to seek help.

You will notice that religion is *not mentioned* in these statistics. You know why? Everyone is susceptible! Personal faith certainly plays an important part in one's attitude about and hope for recovery, but it is *not a preventative*.

In other words, people of faith *are not exempt!*

For my ministry peers *and me*, it is important to also note that ministers *are highly susceptible* to suffer anxiety disorder, in fact, "at far greater risk for depression than individuals with other occupations." In 2008, it was found that the rate of depression among clergy was *double the national rate!* "'Pastors may have created a life for themselves that is so strongly intertwined with their ministry, that their emotional health is dependent on the state of their ministry,' said Rae Jean Proeschold-Bell, the

Clergy Health Initiative's research director, and assistant research professor at the Duke Global Health Institute."[53]

Let me pause here for a minute, *just for my peers in ministry,* to sincerely and empathetically acknowledge – *I know what you're going through!* I really do! The world of ministry has become quite a "spinning top" with absolutely

 dizzying effects that sometimes leave us reeling and roiling! Friends, we're not the "pillars in the community" that we were 40 years ago, and the steeple on the church is no longer the center of town or the moral point of reference. In our post-modern, *post-Christian* world, the pastor's voice is no longer the respected voice of authority it used to be.

A Gallup poll in 2018 suggests only 37% of Americans even consider ministers ethical and honest anymore.[54] Further, our congregants – *not intentionally,* of course – sometimes fail to realize that we "are people, just like everyone else…broken people who live in a broken world.

---

[53] Duke Today Staff, "Clergy More Likely to Suffer from Depression, Anxiety," *Duke Today,* Aug. 27, 2013, para. 8ff., https://today.duke.edu/2013/08/clergydepressionnewsrelease (accessed on February 11, 2020). "A number of factors were found to be powerful predictors of depression and anxiety, most notably job stress. Clergy engage in many stressful activities, including grief counseling, navigating the competing demands of congregants, and delivering a weekly sermon that opens them up to criticism. The strain of these roles is further amplified by having to switch rapidly between them, which other studies have shown to exacerbate stressful experiences. Furthermore, the study found that pastors' sense of guilt about not doing enough at work was a top predictor of depression, and that doubt of their call to ministry was a top predictor of anxiety. Pastors with less social support – those who reported feeling socially isolated – were at higher risk for depression."

[54] David Crary, "Stress Over Violence, Other Issues Multiply for Clergy," *The Daily Reflector,* February 23, 2020.

Sometimes we need help too."[55] It is believed by many that pastors are "somehow above the pain and struggles of everyday people," and "we are the ones who are supposed to have all the answers. But we do not."[56]

Further, somehow pastors are expected to be superhuman.

But "they're human beings who are going to feel the same kind of fear and numbness and depression that other people do." One dear pastor put it this way, "They don't understand that I get tired like they get tired. They want you to be at their constant beck and call...I know what depression is. You have to sit in your car when you drive up in the driveway of the church and get your game face on to go in there. I have contemplated walking away many times...There's a wearing-down effect, a sense of frustration and malaise..."[57] This pastor says it's easy to think, "I've spent all these hours with people trying to do good things, and I'm just getting nowhere."[58]

---

[55] Ibid., *Reflector*. Greg Laurie, pastor of a California megachurch, is quoted here. He is also a prolific author and global radio host. Natalie Neysa Alund, "Pastor, Mental Health Advocate Jarrid Wilson Dies by Apparent Suicide, Wife Reports," *USA Today*, Sept. 11, 2019, https://www.usatoday.com/story/news/2019/09/11/jarrid-wilson-suicide-apparent-death-after-mental-health-tweets/2284793001/ (accessed on March 8, 2020). Senior Pastor, Greg Laurie, serves at the Harvest Christian Fellowship in Riverside, California, where his Associate Pastor, 30 yr. old, Jarrid Wilson, took his life on September 9, 2019, one day before World Suicide Prevention Day. Jarrid had struggled with depression most of his life, and he and his wife, Juli, "founded Anthem of Hope (2016), a nonprofit [intended] to better equip churches to help those with mental health issues like depression, anxiety and self harm."
[56] Ibid., *Reflector*. Laurie quote.
[57] Ibid., *Reflector*. Rodney McNeal, 54, an Army veteran and social worker in a local hospital offers these quotes. He pastors the Second Bethlehem Baptist Church in Alexandria, Louisiana.
[58] Ibid.

Okay, I'm a witness! I easily attest to and agree with this research – my personal life is a testimonial of it (if it can be called *a testimonial*). But folks, don't hear me "excusing myself." I'm simply licking my wounds and solacing myself that *I'm really normal!* AND, that I'm *really not* alone concerning this matter of chemical imbalance! Furthermore, *you're not alone either*, if you happen to be one of those persons who is suffering this health issue.

Enough data. My adjustment phase was horrible. It is a fact of matter that many people never make it through the adjustment phase because the side effects can be so unpleasant, so awful, so unbearable that the "patient" removes himself from the treatment (itself a problem). However, I was so sick going into treatment that I felt I had no choice but *to trust God, to trust my doctor, and to trust the medicine.* It wasn't easy, and I look back now and wonder how, except for God's gracious goodness, I ever made it through my "long dark night of the soul."

I'm certain my wife was terrified in this stage of my treatment. I remember so clearly sitting with her at the corner of the table in our breakfast nook one morning and bemoaning my health…well, at least *I was.* I had this strange

> I was reticent to say what I felt to my wife, but I sensed I had to do it to process my anguish.

and peculiar feeling that day, a false sense of "knowing," I guess, a most *unfamiliar conviction* that had arisen in me that I didn't know how to explain.

My eyes were glassy and my soul seemed "remotely recessed" in the darkest depths within them. She was horror-struck when I spoke these words:

"Honey, I don't understand why I'm feeling this way, but *I feel like* the equilibrium of the world cannot be corrected until I die." "Horror-struck" is *really a limited description of* the shock she felt. She had already asked me one morning as she left for work, "Are you going to be okay today?" And I had responded, "People who hate themselves *hurt themselves.*" Her concerns were now seriously heightened.

Please know I've never been one to "play on" peoples' emotions. I feel that is manipulative and scheming. It is a selfish and deceitful way of deliberately causing someone else pain to elicit a sympathetic (or perhaps, reactive) response of pity and commiseration. I simply didn't know where the "lines" were anymore...lines of discretion and prudence, discipline and tact, perception and judgment. I never meant to hurt my wife or make matters worse for her, but I was simply crying out for help, and didn't know *how or what to ask!*

She was the *only person* I could talk to this way!

This stretch of my health crisis was the worst of all. I was about to face the greatest challenge to my faith I had ever experienced, and I wasn't sure I would survive it. For now, *it seemed* the devil was playing tricks with my mind. And in the eyes of God, *I felt* I was being "weighed on the scales and found wanting" (Dan. 5:27).[59] I sincerely felt

---

[59] This text references how the wicked Neo-Babylonian king, Belshazzar, son of Nebuchadnezzar, had flaunted God and dared to desecrate the gold and silver vials and vessels from the temple in Jerusalem, and had them

God was judging me *here and now* on this earth before I ever stood before His Great White Throne (Rev. 20:11-15).[60] I not only felt I was losing my life – I now felt I was losing *my soul*...and I didn't know why.

BEING SICK WAS ONE THING...
FEELING LOST WAS ANOTHER.

---

brought in to be used in a drunken orgy of worship to his false gods with his wives, concubines, and nobles. In mid-air, God, with his own finger, wrote a message to Belshazzar on the wall, and no one could interpret the message but Daniel the prophet. When the message was read, it announced to the king that God had numbered the days of his reign and brought it to an end, and that he had been weighed on the scales and found deficient. Further, it stated that his kingdom had been divided and given over to the Medes and Persians. That very night, the kingdom was overtaken by the Medo-Persian empire and Belshazzar was killed (Dan. 5).

[60] "[11]Then I saw a great white throne and him who was seated on it. The earth and the heavens fled from his presence, and there was no place for them. [12]And I saw the dead, great and small, standing before the throne, and books were opened. Another book was opened, which is the book of life. The dead were judged according to what they had done as recorded in the books. [13]The sea gave up the dead that were in it, and death and Hades gave up the dead that were in them, and each person was judged according to what they had done. [14]Then death and Hades were thrown into the lake of fire. The lake of fire is the second death. [15]Anyone whose name was not found written in the book of life was thrown into the lake of fire" (Rev. 20:11-15). I acknowledge unbelievers *(not believers) will stand* before God in judgment. *But at this time in my life, I feared* this might be where I would see Him "face to face."

Chapter 16

Danger! Danger!

V1 – "Commit to fly." Decision speed. That's the speed *beyond which* a pilot is committed to fly and no longer has sufficient runway to safely stop his craft from leaving the ground. Vr – "Rotation speed." That's the speed at which the pilot enters control input to "rotate" the nose upward into flight altitude. V2 – "Takeoff safety speed," (V2$_{min}$ – *"minimum* takeoff safety speed") is the speed at which a craft may safely leave the ground *even with* one failed engine…"best climb rate," as it is known by some pilots. This is all determined by weight and performance capacity of the craft, runway configurations, and flight conditions (weather, wind speed, direction, temperature, etc.).[61]

Using these standards of flight craft takeoff speeds as an analogy for my situation, I *feel I was past* V1 and Vr. I *actually feel* I was past V2 and had "left the ground" with *at least*

---

[61] Marty McFly, "Insider Series: A Day in the Life of a Pilot – During the Flight," *The Points Guys,* Oct. 1, 2017, para. 6, https://thepointsguy.com/2017/10/what-pilots-do-during-the-flight/ (accessed on February 12, 2020). John Cox, "Ask the Captain: How do pilots decide when to take off?" *USA Today,* Sept. 29, 2013, https://www.usatoday.com/story/travel/columnist/cox/2013/09/29/takeoff-speed-v1-v2-rotate/2885565/ (accessed on February 12, 2020). "V Speeds," *Wikipedia, The Free Encyclopedia,* Updated Jan. 9, 2020, https://en.wikipedia.org/wiki/V speeds (accessed on February 12, 2020).

one crippled engine, maybe more…if that is possible. I was "in the air," but not flying very well. I had lost control… *complete* control, *it seemed.* I was flying aimlessly – No! – *flailing! Actually,* floundering, "flapping my wings" like a wounded pheasant, shot from below, and dropping to the ground…*fast!*

Falling downward. No lift. No resistance. I *sensed* when I should hit, I would hit hard, and it would hurt… *really badly,* possibly even kill me…end my life. I felt hopeless. Completely despaired. Lost. Utterly lost. And *it seemed* this whole situation was unconditionally irreversible.

REALITY!

Impressions are very real. In fact, I have always said that truth is "reality as it appears" – *apparent* – particularly from one's angle of view. I have since learned that truth is *actually* "reality as *it is,*" as God sees it, or as He *knows it to be.* So, please understand as I share my story that I am conveying to you what *I experienced – my current reality* at that time. It may not *have been* exactly as I describe it, but that is *precisely* how it *"appeared" or seemed to me!*

No one could have told me different. Some tried, but I couldn't hear them. My ears were stopped by the, "Bong, bong, bang! Bong, bong, bang!" *as well as* the many imaginations[62] of my mind, racing through the cranial matter

---

[62] I simply *must* "come up for air," and, at least, *give you time* to catch your breath as well. I knew the Scriptures, for I had studied them from a youth, but they seemed "silent" to me in this season of my life. I was having a difficult time "hearing God's voice" in them – I knew it was there, but my hearing was dull. Nevertheless, this Scripture has since become precious to me – I'll share it now to give you *some hope* for me in this situation: "⁵Casting down imaginations, and every high thing that exalteth itself against the knowledge of God, and bringing into captivity every thought to the obedience of Christ" (II Cor. 10:5; KJV).

in my head (or the ethereal "conscience" of my soul, maybe?) at lightspeed, considering every conceivable, ignominious end result possible. Shamefully disgraced. Despicable. Desperate. My life was a fiasco, a farce really.

> A scathing, scornful, disgusting embarrassment to God!

And the whispers *of the enemy in my ear*...did I mention him? Oh, you already *sensed* he was near, didn't you?! I never fought a spiritual battle like the one I was fighting now...for my *very life* and eternal destiny, *it seemed!* Oh yes, he *was* near. We wrangled rancorously – struggling spiritually, fighting physically *(it seemed)*, viciously going 'round and 'round in scuffles and skirmishes that lasted for hours and days on end, sparring for my soul – God's possession, really. And I wondered every day who was going to win out and top the other – me, *I hoped* – and give back to God what *rightfully belonged* to Him...or not.

All my life I had been a "militant" prayer warrior. I was trained in my holiness upbringing to pray out loud. To use the Scriptures in my mouth as the "sword of the Spirit!" To hold forth my "shield of faith"[63] in defense – and to "stand firm" – resolutely, steadfastly, with unwavering devotion and

---

[63] "[14]Stand firm then, with the belt of truth buckled around your waist, with the breastplate of righteousness in place, [15]and with your feet fitted with the readiness that comes from the gospel of peace. [16]In addition to all this, take up the shield of faith, with which you can extinguish all the flaming arrows of the evil one. [17]Take the helmet of salvation and the sword of the Spirit, which is the word of God. [18]And pray in the Spirit on all occasions with all kinds of prayers and requests. With this in mind, be alert and always keep on praying for all the Lord's people" (Eph. 6:14-18).

loyalty to my Savior and Lord! And to know that as I did, *He* would fight my battles for me! *He* would come to my rescue! *He* would deliver me!

But *it seemed* I was fighting this battle alone. *It seemed* God had left *me* to decide the outcome of this conflict by myself. I really wasn't sure anymore *who* was on trial – me? For my soul? Or God? For my loyalty? We often speak of the "trials of Job," but it is *my opinion* that it *wasn't Job* who was *really on trial – it was God.* Satan was saying to God "behind the scenes," in a sense, "You just let me touch Job, take his possessions, ruin his health, kill his children, and I guarantee you, *he will curse you* to your face – he will turn his back on you and stop serving you! In fact, the only reason Job serves you, God, is because *you bribe him with blessings;* you stoke his worship of you with your goodness to him. But if you *let me touch him,* I will prove you are guilty of bribery."[64]

This was honestly my spiritual take on this entire health

> **UNFAIR FIGHTING!**
>
> I didn't know where the "battle grids" were drawn.

crisis, but *I didn't know* how Job managed, how he fought back, how he outlasted Satan and eventually won. At age 49, this was all new to me. I had "met"

---

[64] "[8]Then the Lord said to Satan, 'Have you considered my servant Job? There is no one on earth like him; he is blameless and upright, a man who fears God and shuns evil.' '[9]Does Job fear God for nothing?' Satan replied. '[10]Have you not put a hedge around him and his household and everything he has? You have blessed the work of his hands, so that his flocks and herds are spread throughout the land. [11]But now stretch out your hand and strike everything he has, and he will surely curse you to your face.' [12]The Lord said to Satan, 'Very well, then, everything he has is in your power, but on the man himself do not lay a finger.' Then Satan went out from the presence of the Lord" (Job 1:8-12).

Satan before, but I had never fought him as I did when I got sick. In fact, I could no longer distinguish between what was spiritual *oppression* and what *might be* physiological *depression.* I highly suspect both were happening at the same time.

As this medication was wreaking havoc in my body, mental-emotional and spiritual chaos was wreaking havoc in my mind. I was going crazy! I just knew I was! What a miserable way for a Christian, a believer in Jesus Christ, a man of God, a *minister* nonetheless, to finish his life, to leave his legacy, to end his journey, and to close the last chapter of his time on earth!

None of my thoughts were clear and focused anymore. None of my emotions could any longer be trusted. None of my attempts to "snap out of it" worked, and none of my former "antics" to fight previous battles proved any worth. None of my prior victories mattered. And none of my "laurels" pinned *for any* ministry accomplishments throughout 45 years of Christian experience meant *anything at all to me* in this loathsome, pitiable condition that I found myself. I had truly come *to the end* of myself. And my rope...and I couldn't even find that last knot to cling to!

Did I pray? Yes, I prayed *all the time!* It may be the only time in my entire life that I *really* "prayed without ceasing" (I Thes. 5:17; KJV). Yes, *out loud!* I learned that *"he who hurts most prays best!"* And I came to realize *through* (key word) *this crisis* what a life of prayer truly resembles.

BUT *IT SEEMED* MY PRAYERS WEREN'T SUCCESSFUL.

Consequently, I began to question my position with God and whether I had lost my relationship with Him in some way, for some reason. For James says that "the prayer of a righteous person is powerful and effective" (Jms. 5:16). I still like the *King James Version* rendering of this verse better: "The effectual fervent prayer of a righteous man availeth much." If my prayers weren't heard and answered, then it stood to reason I was no longer in right standing with God. He was no longer available to me. He *really wasn't listening, it seemed.* And He no longer cared.

On one occasion, I had the most horrifying experience trying to pray through this morass of muddled confusion and disorder. In the middle of the night, I was upstairs squalling my eyes out and begging God to help me...or kill me. And *it seemed to me,* in my mind's eye, I could see the devil standing there in front of me, sneering, jeering, hissing like a serpent and chiding my faith, hooting and heckling, daring me to *believe that God even cared!* He was taunting and teasing me, trying *with demonic persuasion,* as demons can,[65] to convince me that it was over and that I was going to die *a slow and painful, pitiable, pathetic, doleful death,* and *then* I was going to *go straight to hell!*

I *have never* experienced fear so alarming as what I experienced that night! Not before...and not since! And it didn't end there. In my **Not before... and not since!** efforts to speak, barely able to even quiver my lips, *it seemed,* I tried to resist Satan, as the Scriptures instruct.[66] But the words wouldn't

---

[65] "¹The Spirit clearly says that in later times some will abandon the faith and follow deceiving spirits and things taught by demons. ²Such teachings come through hypocritical liars, whose consciences have been seared as with a hot iron" (I Tim. 4:1, 2).
[66] "⁷Submit yourselves, then, to God. Resist the devil, and he will flee from you" (Jms. 4:7).

come. I felt paralyzed, petrified as one might in a nightmare facing a fire-breathing dragon, or some ghoulish creature from the underworld, or some spiritless, macabre, cadaverous beast about to attack. I felt locked into a time-space capsule, "vacuum-packed" and bound in my body like a statue in stone.

"Fight or flight" adrenaline was rushing, *but I couldn't move...*

Then with a lurch so swift I could hardly see the motion, and a recoil so strong I could feel the blunt force blow of it, the devil thrust his hand into my chest, and grabbed my heart and started squeezing so tightly I could hardly breathe. The pain was horrendous, but the terror was tormenting, and I held my breath until I couldn't any longer. I thought he was going to pull my heart out of my chest. I crashed to the floor and lay there in a fetal position – I don't know how long – sobbing, moaning, dreading my death, shrouding my face…wondering when the searing flames of hell would begin.

Hours passed. I slipped in and out of restless sleep, troubled deeply by this experience. ALL in my head. My imagination. My brain. My soul, maybe? My spirit? I don't know. It was real to me…or surreal, perhaps. Bizarre, weird, dreamlike. And I lay there, grieving from the shock of the experience, admitting to myself that *I was insane.* Deliriously insane. Now I realized I was *not only hearing things* – I *was seeing things as well!*

I was smitten, stricken. There was no esteem left. I had been conquered. The battle was over, and I had lost. There was nothing left *now* but death itself. And that was coming,

I was sure. For the next three weeks – I lie not! – symptoms intensified and imaginations ran wild: the night by night, "Bong, bong, bang! Bong, bong, bang!" funeral dirge continued, torments of approaching hell anguished my soul, and the smirky images of the devil's face in mine mocked my faith.

I had walked the floor so much that Lou *made me promise* to stop getting out of bed. She simply couldn't rest knowing I was wandering about the house all night long! I consented, but reluctantly, and continued to suffer every waking moment I lay there. I panicked and cringed from each new break of day. I hated daybreaks now, because they reminded me of what I no longer had – light, life, hope. I was empty, lost, "dark," and lifeless…or so *it seemed.*

WORST STILL, LOU WAS LEAVING ME...EVERY DAY!

Every working day, she would leave me. Alone…in this haunted house we had bought that I now so despised and detested. I was imprisoned…awaiting execution, *I felt.* But just didn't know when it would happen.

I was afraid *to be* alone. I didn't trust myself. On several occasions when I couldn't stand it any longer, I would call Lou at work and implore her to please come home, that I didn't feel safe to be by myself. I didn't have to beg. She understood. She always came. Her supervisor was a wonderful Christian person who so compassionately consented to each request, knowing what Lou was dealing with and always offering sincerest prayers. She would never return to work on those days.'

I'm certain Lou was deeply troubled in her spirit for me, and her own emotions were wracked and restless. Thinly worn herself, she daily lived with open-ended apprehension about what to expect when she got home. One day in particular, she opened the door and quietly entered the house. She heard nothing. She didn't call my name, perhaps hoping I was praying, or resting and had fallen asleep. When she entered the master bedroom, there I lay on the floor, sprawled face down in an awkward and bulky form, somewhat fetal but ominously corpsy.

She was jolted by the sight...and breathless. She approached me silently, fearing the worst, then slowly extended her hand and touched me. She was relieved when I stirred and lifted my head, then reached up to welcome her into my arms. We embraced for the longest time, weeping softly together...and praying. She lay down in the floor with me, and there we spent the rest of the day, crying and praying, petitioning the Lord for His help.

Throughout those three miserable weeks, I would resist the impulse to call Lou home. I knew she couldn't take off work indefinitely and certainly couldn't accomplish her work assignments leaving early every day. So, I began to sit in one of our two reclining Queen Anne Chairs we had situated in our master bedroom, lain back, meditating, no – pining, pouting, sulking – languishing away. Grieving.

Wishing this would end. Begging God to let me die.

I thought of Jonah sitting under the leafy plant in the hot, blazing sun just outside the city of Nineveh, pitying himself, angry with God that Nineveh had repented and not been

judged for their harsh treatment of Jonah's ancestors –
and begging God to let him die.⁶⁷ I rehearsed with Elijah his
victorious conquest of Jezebel and her false prophets on Mt.
Carmel and his sulky, self-righteous claim to God that he was
the *only prophet* in the land who had not bowed the knee to
Baal. I remembered how God had rebuked him, insisting
7,000 other righteous persons yet remained in the land.
And Elijah wanted to die.⁶⁸

I was there. I began to sink deeply into thoughts of
suicide, "self-extinction," ways to help God make up His
mind what He wanted to do with me. And here was the
greatest challenge of all this harrowing and horrendous
story! "To be, or not to be: that is the question:"⁶⁹

> Whether 'tis nobler in the mind to suffer
> The slings and arrows of outrageous fortune,
> Or to take arms against a sea of troubles,
> And by opposing end them? To die: to sleep;
> No more; and by a sleep to say we end
> The heart-ache and the thousand natural shocks

---

⁶⁷ "⁷But at dawn the next day God provided a worm, which chewed the plant so that it withered. ⁸When the sun rose, God provided a scorching east wind, and the sun blazed on Jonah's head so that he grew faint. He wanted to die, and said, 'It would be better for me to die than to live'" (Jonah 4:7, 8).
⁶⁸ "³Elijah was afraid and ran for his life. When he came to Beersheba in Judah, he left his servant there, ⁴while he himself went a day's journey into the wilderness. He came to a broom bush, sat down under it and prayed that he might die. 'I have had enough, Lord,' he said. 'Take my life; I am no better than my ancestors.' ⁵Then he lay down under the bush and fell asleep" (I Ki. 19:3-5). *I consider it interesting that every time a prophet of God felt sorry for himself, it seems, he sat under a bush in the shade and sulked...just as I.*
⁶⁹ William Shakespeare, "Hamlet, Act III, Scene I [To be, or not to be]," 1564-1616, *Poets.org.*, https://poets.org/poem/hamlet-act-iii-scene-i-be-or-not-be (accessed February 12, 2020).

> That flesh is heir to, 'tis a consummation
> Devoutly to be wish'd. To die, to sleep;
> To sleep: perchance to dream: ay, there's the rub;
> For in that sleep of death what dreams may come
> When we have shuffled off this mortal coil,
> Must give us pause: there's the respect
> That makes calamity of so long life...[70]

My wife and I had owned an *unregistered*[71] .22 caliber, snub-nosed pistol her mother had given us for "self-protection" when we married. I couldn't for the life of me tell you *now* what brand it was. I've never been a gun enthusiast, so I never paid attention. However, throughout *most* of our 31 years of marriage (at that time), we had "casually" argued about whether that pistol should be loaded with live rounds or blanks. My wife contended we should keep it loaded with live rounds so we could defend ourselves in the event of a break-in. *I maintained* it should have *blanks,* because we had kids in the house and they could possibly find the gun and accidentally harm themselves, or worse.

And around it went – live rounds? Or   Live rounds?
blanks? Live rounds? Or blanks? She'd   Or blanks?
change them out, and I'd change them back. She'd change them out, and I'd change them back.

I couldn't get my mind off that pistol. Over and over and over, I rehearsed in my mind how easy it would be and how

---

[70] Ibid.
[71] If you're in law enforcement, don't even think of it! I can't tell you where that pistol is – *my wife either dispensed or disposed of it completely from my access or ever again finding it!* So there!

quickly it would be over. One shot. Right in the temple.
And it would all end. Just that simple. I would clutch the
arms of that Queen Anne Chair and literally "hold on for
dear life." I don't know if it was the antidepressant toying
with my chemistry or the devil toying with my soul, but *I
DO KNOW* that even though *I didn't want to die,* I-DIDN'T-
WANT-TO-LIVE-*LIKE-THIS!*

I begged Christ to *please rise up within me* and to *be strong
for me!* I confessed to Him that, of myself, I was nothing, and
that I desperately needed Him. And that IF He *didn't come to
my rescue...soon,* I would not survive this menacing ordeal.
I quoted Scriptures attesting to His Holy Spirit indwelling
believers in Christ, His imminent and manifest presence to
His children in time of need, His power, victorious and
overcoming in believers' lives...[72]

Pause...

[72] "[29]He gives strength to the weary and increases the power of the weak"
(Is. 40:29). "[4]Ye are of God, little children, and have overcome them: because
greater is he that is in you, than he that is in the world" (I Jn. 4:4; KJV). "[18]For
the message of the cross is foolishness to those who are perishing, but to us
who are being saved it is the power of God" (I Cor. 1:18). "[13]I can do all this
through him who gives me strength" (Philip. 4:13).

Yes, Pause. Reflect. Ponder.[73]

> *"Every man has his secret sorrows which the*
> *world knows not, and often times we call a*
> *man cold when he is only sad."*

Henry Wadsworth Longfellow[74]

---

[73] Wayne Cordeiro, *Leading on Empty, Refilling Your Tank and Renewing Your Passion* (Minneapolis, Minnesota: Bethany Publishing House, 2009), 46-50. Mother Teresa and Rev. Brian Kolodiejchuk, *Mother Teresa: Come Be My Light* (New York: Doubleday, 2007). Gilbert Thomas, *William Cowper and the Eighteenth Century* (London: Ivor Nicholson and Watson Ltd., 1935), 131-132. Charles Spurgeon, *The Minister's Fainting Fits* Lecture XL, retrieved from www.the-highway.com/articleSept99.html. Darrell W. Amundsen, "The Anguish and Agonies of Charles Haddon Spurgeon," *Christian History* 10, no. 29 (1991). Authur Brooks Lapsley, ed., *The Writings of Abraham Lincoln, Vol. 1, 1832-1843* (New York: The Knickerbocker Press, 1905), 235. Bear in mind that some of the greatest persons who ever lived suffered depression, not just Bible characters: 1) Mother Teresa lamented, "I am told God loves me – and yet the reality of darkness and coldness and emptiness is so great that nothing touches my soul…I feel just that terrible pain of loss, of God not wanting me, of God not being God, of God not really existing." 2) William Cowper, famed hymnist, hospitalized for depression, co-wrote these words (with John Newton), "God moves in a mysterious way, His wonders to perform; He plants His footsteps in the sea, and rides upon the storm." 3) Charles Haddon Spurgeon stated that his success "appalled [him]" and "cast [him] into the lowest depths." Of this experience, he said, "I would go into the deeps a hundred times to cheer a downcast spirit. It is good for me to have been afflicted, that I might know how to speak a word in season to one that is weary." 4) Abraham Lincoln pined, "I am now the most miserable man living. If what I feel were equally distributed to the whole human family, there would not be one cheerful face on the earth. Whether I shall ever be better I can not tell; I awfully forebode I shall not. To remain as I am is impossible; I must die or be better, it appears to me." 5) Martin Luther King, Jr. would admit that the struggles of his life would plunge him into deep doldrums and become "preoccupied with death." 6) Henri Nouwen, a Dutch Catholic priest and author of over 40 books, struggled to "reconcile his depression with his Christian faith."

[74] "Henry Wadsworth Longfellow Quotes," *Your Dictionary*, LoveToKnow Corp., 1996-2020, https://quotes.yourdictionary.com/author/henry-wadsworth-longfellow/ (accessed on April 2, 2020).

On May 25, 1979, "Friday afternoon, Memorial Day weekend, American Airlines Flight 191, a Los Angeles-bound DC-10, takes off at 3:03 p.m. from Chicago-O'Hare International airport with 271 aboard. As Flight 191 raised its nose during the initial stage of the takeoff, an engine under the left wing broke off with its pylon assembly and fell to the runway. The aircraft climbed to about 350 feet above the ground and then began to spin to the left, continuing its leftward roll until the wings were past the vertical position, with the nose pitched down below the horizon. Moments later, the aircraft crashed into an open field about a half-mile from its takeoff point, killing all 271 people aboard and two others in a nearby trailer park."[75] "A report less than three months later detailed the '10-billion-to-1 long shot' that caused the plane to fall from the sky. An improperly repaired engine mount gave way under the 40,000 pounds of pressure, and compounding the problem, it smashed the forward edge of the wing, severing the hydraulic lines controlling that wing."[76]

Until 2001, this was "the worst domestic air crash in U.S. history."[77]

---

[75] History.com Editors, "Worst Air Crash in U.S. History," *History: This Day in History,* Mar. 3, 2010 A & E Television Networks, pub., Updated July 28, 2019, https://www.history.com/this-day-in-history/worst-air-crash-in-u-s-history (accessed on February 12, 2020).
[76] Stephan Benzkofer, "Worst Plane Crash in U.S. History," *Chicago Tribune,* May 25, 2014, para. 2, https://www.chicagotribune.com/news/ct-1979-ohare-crash-flashback-0525-20140525-story.html (accessed on February 12, 2020).
[77] History.com Editors.

Last Words from American Airlines Flight 191 ATC

03:02:38 sec.	Cleared for Takeoff.
03:02:46 sec.	Under way.
	At some point between Takeoff and Liftoff, the left engine breaks away from the pylon and flips *over* the wing, tearing out hydraulics (control) and electrics (communication). The last word heard from the cockpit was the First Officer.
First Officer:	Da##!
03:03:34 sec.	Liftoff (32 sec. to crash).
Tower:	LOOK AT THIS! Look at this! He blew up an engine. Equipment. We need equipment. He blew an engine.
Nearby Cessna Pilot:	Oh sh##!
Tower (03:03:52 sec.):	Alright American ah…191, heavy. You want to come back and to what runway?
Tower:	He's not talkin' to me.
Tower:	Yeah, he's gonna lose a wing. Look at him. [Flight 191 stalls and rolls over.] There he goes! There he goes!
03:04:05 sec.	Crash. [Sound of crash impact][78]

---

[78] "American Airlines Flight 191 ATC Recording, May 25, 1979," http://www.planecrashinfo.com/lastwords.htm and http://www.planecrashinfo.com/MP4%20AA191.htm (accessed on February 13, 2020). Laura Zumbach, "The Legacy of Flight 191: When An Engine Ripped Off A DC-10 At O'Hare It Killed 273 People, And Changed Air Travel Forever," May 23, 2019, *Chicago Tribune*, http://graphics.chicagotribune.com/flight-191-anniversary/ (accessed on February 13, 2020).

Remember V2? "Takeoff safety speed" – "the speed at which a craft may safely leave the ground *even with* one failed engine?"[79] *Typically,* pilots should be able to safely fly a craft with one failed engine, circle the airspace, and land for disembarking and engine repairs.

However, on May 25, 1979, Flight 191 had *not only* lost its left-wing engine, it had *also lost* all hydraulics (control) and all cabin communications (contact with Air Traffic Control). Had the pilots *known* what had failed, they *might could have* made necessary corrections and saved the plane. But 32 seconds from liftoff to impact wasn't enough time *for anyone to discern and adjust anything!* Flight 191 was doomed from the moment the pylon broke and the engine fell off.

I felt I was *way* past saving. Beyond V2. Liftoff and engine loss – yes! But *no discernable communications* (answers to prayer) and *no obvious control* (will to live). *Flailing. Floundering. "Flapping my wings"* like a wounded pheasant, shot from below, and dropping to the ground...*fast!*[80]

---

[79] Repeated from paragraph 1 of this chapter.
[80] Repeated from paragraph 2 of this chapter.

STATISTICS[81]

Anxiety-Related Loss of Life

- Suicide claims more lives than *war, murder, and natural disasters* combined.

- *Every day, approximately 129 Americans* take their own life.

- Currently, suicide is the *10th leading cause of death* in the United States.

- Suicide is the *second leading cause of death* for persons between the *ages of 10 - 34 years* in the United States.

- There are *3.54 male suicides for every female suicide*, but *twice as many females as males attempt* suicide.

- More Americans suffer from depression than coronary *heart disease, cancer, and HIV/AIDS.*

- Over *50 percent of all people* who die by suicide suffer from major depression. If one *includes alcoholics* who are depressed, this figure *rises to over 75 percent.*

- Depression affects *nearly 5-8 percent* of Americans *ages 18 and over* in a given year.

- Depression is among the *most treatable of psychiatric illnesses.* Between *80 percent and 90 percent* of people with depression *respond positively* to treatment, and *almost all patients gain some relief* from their symptoms. But first, depression *has to be recognized… through early detection, diagnosis, and treatment…*

---

[81] "Suicide Claims More Lives Than War, Murder, And Natural Disasters Combined," *American Foundation for Suicide Prevention,* 2015, 2020, https://www.theovernight.org/?fuseaction=cms.page&id=1034 (accessed on February 20, 2020).

Chapter 17

Word from Above

I know the voice of God. It is familiar to me. It *should* be. For Jesus said in the story of the Good Shepherd, John 10:2-5, that His sheep *know His voice.*[82] In fact, He insisted that they *would not follow* a stranger because "they do not recognize his voice" (5). Consequently, they would *run from* the stranger!

I was *trying* to run. I just didn't know what direction. It was deep and dark in that pit, claustrophobic and constricting. I couldn't move...*literally.* I felt pressure *just to breathe,* let alone run. I didn't know what to do.

And yes, *I listened...intently.* But I heard nothing. Nothing at all. Even though God's voice was familiar to me, I didn't hear it. It was gone. The "airwaves" were silent. I wondered why.

I read the Scriptures, for I know *they are God's voice,*[83] one of several compelling revelations of His Son, Jesus Christ, to

---

[82] "²The one who enters by the gate is the shepherd of the sheep. ³The gatekeeper opens the gate for him, and the sheep listen to his voice. He calls his own sheep by name and leads them out. ⁴When he has brought out all his own, he goes on ahead of them, and his sheep follow him because they know his voice. ⁵But they will never follow a stranger; in fact, they will run away from him because they do not recognize a stranger's voice" (Jn. 10:2-5).

[83] "³⁹You study the Scriptures diligently because you think that in them you have eternal life. These are the very Scriptures that testify about me, ⁴⁰yet you refuse to come to me to have life" (Jn. 5:39, 40).

us! Aside from His *general revelation* to all mankind attesting that *there is a God* – nature, order in the universe, man's sense of "moral oughtness, conscience"[84] – there is *also specific revelation*…His Son made known in history, His Word spoken by the Holy Spirit through prophets, priests, and kings. And yes, these are *reliable words from God, verbally inspired, "God-breathed!"*[85] Human beings can count on these words for information, instruction, and accuracy in their quest for right relationship with God and *for guidance to eternal life!*

My faith in this truth was being tested *as never before in* my entire life *until now!*

As best I could, I clung to this truth, *and all truths* from God's Word I held dear from a child, though without "backup," *it seemed*…without reciprocated confirmation, without rescue.

I loved His Word immensely and sincerely. I was a student of it. I had read it devotionally, preached it fervently, taught it passionately. But for whatever reason in this dark season of my life, *it seemed* it wasn't speaking. It was mutely hushed, unnervingly quiet, like the thick lay of heavy fog in an old cemetery on a windless night. And it haunted me why it wasn't speaking. I was sickly troubled in my soul that

---

[84] "[18]The wrath of God is being revealed from heaven against all the godlessness and wickedness of people, who suppress the truth by their wickedness, [19]since what may be known about God is plain to them, because God has made it plain to them. [20]For since the creation of the world God's invisible qualities – his eternal power and divine nature – have been clearly seen, being understood from what has been made, so that people are without excuse" (Rm. 1:18-20).

[85] See a fuller study of the word "inspiration" in footnote #122 in Chapter 28.

I was hearing *so many other things*, destructive to my being, but I couldn't hear God's Word that I loved so much.

And I prayed in every way at all times (quietly, mentally, meditatively, in spoken words, conversationally, loudly, militantly), but in vain, *it seemed.* I felt so alone, so broken, so lost, and so hopeless.

> Not since high school had I weighed 165 lbs, but I did now. And I still couldn't eat. I was fading fast.

Into the fourth week of taking my new med, I wasn't sure it was right for me. If it was working yet, I couldn't tell it, at least, not in correcting my chemistry, not in a restorative way. The sleepless nights with rampant symptoms continued. The long days of grief and woe, wailing and whining before God, begging to die, didn't abate. I was miserable.

Then one day, I approached God from another angle (if that's possible). I first cried out, "What have I done to make you so mad at me? Why are you punishing me in this way? Why don't you hear my prayers? Why don't you come to my aid?" And I began repenting *twice of everything* I could remember I had *ever done* to possibly offend God, to upset Him, even the slightest of misdeeds. Literally. I went back to my earliest memory of my conscious childhood and started there – the list was long.

I repented of stealing candy from Taylor's Grocery Store in Macclesfield as a six-year-old youngster, cramming my pockets full and stealthily sneaking out of the store. I would have made restitution, if possible, but by now, the store had been torn down and Mr. Taylor had passed away. I repented of sneaking cigarettes when but a junior in grade school and smoking them behind the barn, in the fields, in the ditches.

I repented of lying to my parents about severing the tendon in the first joint of my index "guitar" finger of my left hand. I told them I had been making a reed whistle, but not until I was saved at age 14 did I confess that I had lied – I *had actually* been making a corncob pipe! Kid you not! My best friend was with me that day, and when the knife slipped, I said, "Dang! I cut my britches!" He said, "Dang nothing! You cut your finger!" And blood was flowing freely everywhere! Mammy, my dad's mother, dressed the wound that day, and my finger healed nicely...*except... the tendon was still severed!* And I could no longer play the guitar. I felt badly when Mom and Dad had to schedule surgery to repair the tendon.

"Dang nothing! You cut your finger!"

I repented of everything...honestly, that I could *think of,* at least. Some of the things I did as a youth and repented of are unmentionable. I can't say them here. God wouldn't want me to. Let's just say, I should have had my hide tanned, at the very least (my "tail tore up," Mom would say), or *gone to jail,* at the most. I'm so glad that modern day drugs were not available *in my day* as a youth. I might not have lived to get grown. After repenting of things I *could remember,* I repented *of everything else* that I *couldn't remember!* I don't think I left anything out.

Stricken with guilt and groveling in shame, I pitied myself before the Lord, as beaten down and badly broken as I could possibly be, *I felt.* Then just as clearly as I had *ever heard God's voice before in my past, He spoke to me!* In my spirit. Within my belly. Originating *outside and beyond myself,* from that other

world where God in His manifest glory dwells! By His sweet
Holy Spirit, beginning in the seat of my emotions, the "heart"
of my being, then surfacing with the strength of a sapling oak
breaking through earth…no, *concrete,*
to meet the rising sun on the dawn of
a new day! It came up from the
center of my being to my smitten
conscience and frazzled mind! And
the words *were clear, crystal clear,*
indisputably, undeniably *clear…*

It was light in
darkness and
love in lostness
and hope in
despair!

distinct, succinct, yes, and *"clear" – unmistakably and clearly
recognizable!* It was the sound of a voice I knew and *knew well!*
It was the tender entreaty of my "Abba"[86] Heavenly Father!
"My very own dear father!"

I was the lost sheep on the craig of eternity and
the Good Shepherd reached out with the crook of His
shepherd's staff, and gently pulled me to safety! He picked
me up (figuratively) and held me in His arms, and yes, He

---

[86] Romans 8:14-16 records one of the most beautiful passages of Scripture
I've ever read, *and love:* "[14]For those who are led by the Spirit of God are
the children of God. [15]The Spirit you received does not make you slaves, so
that you live in fear again; rather, the Spirit you received brought about your
adoption to sonship. And by him we cry, 'Abba, Father.' [16]The Spirit himself
testifies with our spirit that we are God's children." Anna Wierzbicka, *What
Did Jesus Mean? Explaining the Sermon on the Mount and the Parables in
Simple and Universal Human Concepts* (New York: Oxford University Press,
2001), 232. Anna Wierzbicka offers as the meaning for "Abba" this most
intimate expression: *"My very own dear father!"* Archibald Thomas
Robertson, "Romans 8:15," *Word Pictures in the New Testament* (Grand
Rapids, MI: Christian Classics Ethereal Library, 1930-1933), 1462. As
Robertson poses, "'a sort of affectionate fondness for the very term that Jesus
himself used' (Burton) in the Garden of Gethsemane." Note also Gal. 4:6,
"[6]And because ye are sons, God hath sent forth the Spirit of his Son into your
hearts, crying, Abba, Father" (KJV).

spoke softly, but surely, to me! And these were His words –
the first I had heard in days, now approaching at least two
months: *"What you are experiencing has nothing to do with
personal sin; I am simply reshaping you for my own purposes.
Let me do my work in your life as I please."*

I was speechless! But I wasn't at all dry-eyed! I wept, but
not bitterly. I wailed, but not woefully! I worshiped the Lord,
and I expressed my love to Him! I thanked Him for His voice
to me! It was like bread to a hungry traveler or water to a
thirsty soul! It was true company to a lonely heart!

I had heard the Lord speak to me once again, and He reassured
me that I was in His plan, in His thoughts, on His mind, in
His heart! The swells and billows of pain and anguish were,
at least, momentarily overwhelmed – even vanquished – by
the power and the impact of God's precious presence in my
life! And as a good friend once shared with me, the timely
lesson for this moment came back to my mind: I was *"In* His
will – *On* His Wheel!"[87] The Lord *had not* forgotten me, and
He certainly *had not abandoned me!* He was there, imminently
and manifestly present with me, and declaring it so with a

---

[87] This friend, Susan Stancill, was once my secretary at University Church
of God. She is a very gifted and studious teacher of the Word! This apropos
analogy references the beautiful text of Jeremiah 18 where the prophet was
instructed to go to the potter's house to learn an important life lesson about
God's purpose in the believer's life. There he saw the clay collapse in the
hands of the potter. But he noticed that the potter *did not throw away the
clay!* He simply began refashioning it again "as seemed good to the potter
to make it" (Jer. 18:4; KJV). "⁴But the pot he was shaping from the clay was
marred in his hands; so the potter formed it into another pot, shaping it as
seemed best to him. ⁵Then the word of the Lord came to me. ⁶He said, 'Can
I not do with you, Israel, as this potter does?' declares the Lord. 'Like clay
in the hand of the potter, so are you in my hand, Israel'" (18:4-6).

voice so clear. The phone ringing or the door knocking hadn't been clearer!

And *what He said* was just as important to me as the fact that He said it – my pain, this trial, my health issues *had nothing to do with personal sin!* Immediately, the guilt I had been fighting left me! The gravity of *personal responsibility* wherewith I had assigned myself blame lifted, and it seemed for the first time in two months, *I could breathe!* I could rest! I could relax and enjoy the resonating and lingering afterglow of God's gracious glory and personal presence with me in that hour. I spent the rest of the day weeping and worshiping, praising and praying – effectively, *it seemed* – and feeling better that God had a purpose for my life, a plan in place that I could soundly trust!

I thought of the beautiful Scripture where God spoke to Israel and reassured His beloved of His well-thought-through intentions for them and their descendants: "'[11]For I know the plans I have for you,' declares the Lord, 'plans to prosper you and not to harm you, plans to give you hope and a future. [12]Then you will call on me and come and pray to me, and I will listen to you. [13]You will seek me and find me when you seek me with all your heart. [14]I will be found by you...'" (Jer. 29:11-14).

I welcomed it, I cherished it, and I believed it. Indeed, it was so.

And *for now,* it was enough.

Chapter 18

S-A-D: Crying in the Chapel

Human beings are emotional creatures. God made us that way. However, we *don't always* pay close enough attention to our emotions to learn from them and benefit by them.

Emotions are important. They *inform sound judgment how to act or behave.* When emotions *"race past"* sound judgment (or rational discernment, we might call it), we "act out" – sometimes badly, hastily maybe – or perhaps even, we *overreact.* That's when we end up regretting things we've said that we can't take back. Or perhaps, worse still, we end up *doing things* that can't be undone.

Bells rung can't be "unrung." Statements made in angry bursts cannot be "unsaid." Sure, we can say, "I'm sorry," but really, *it's too late – it's already been said.* What came up *came out!* Jesus said that, "A good man brings good things out of the good stored up in his heart, and an evil man brings evil things out of the evil stored up in his heart. For the mouth speaks what the heart is full of" (Lk. 6:45).[88] *And* shots fired can't be retrieved. Consequently, emotions *can be* dangerous!

---

[88] "⁴⁵For out of the abundance of the heart the mouth speaketh" (Mt. 12:34; KJV).

The Scriptures are emotional...in fact, *God is!* He loves "with an everlasting love" (Jer. 31:4), He grieves (Is. 53:3), and He gets angry (Ex. 32:22). Jesus was "moved with compassion," and that compassion prompted action on His part – He taught and fed (Mk. 6:34ff.; KJV), healed (Mt. 14:14), forgave and delivered (Mt. 18:27). He saves, then *rejoices* (Mt. 18:11-13; KJV), and He feels and empathizes (Heb. 4:15)! The Kingdom of heaven is righteousness, peace, and joy in God's Holy Spirit (Rm. 14:17)!

> No way around it – emotions are a part of our unique and complex makeup as human beings.

And I, like everyone else, am an emotional creature. Sentimental even. Some people aren't, but I am. *I feel deeply!* Empathetically. I always have. But I never knew that could be a problem for me.

When I completed CPE in 2000, I learned something about myself I had never known before then. CPE is a very engaging and strenuous program of clinical pastoral education, "on-the-job" training actually, designed to enhance pastoral care, especially in clinical settings. It requires close examination of one's own personal mental and emotional challenges. It involves the "unpacking of baggage," you might say, so that both supervisor and peers can help to assess "your problems" (growth challenges), analyze them, and *then* help determine how to address them. *But this is primarily so they don't reappear (or hinder authentic care) in critical ministry experiences later in life.*

I say it's like *taking your guts out,* laying them on the table, and letting your buddies pick around through your entrails until they learn what you're made of and what makes you tick...*and particularly, why you shy away* from certain ministry challenges and opportunities. You know what I learned in CPE? I learned that I had a serious "fear of intense feelings!" Go figure. I'm Pentecostal – Wesleyan Holiness Pentecostal – *and I have a fear of intense feelings?!* That's funny, isn't it?! But we validated the claim and found it to be so! And was it hindering my ministry in a really big way?! You bet! But before then, I never knew why!

One day when I was assigned to the cancer ward, I was visiting an elderly gentleman who was angry about his diagnosis. He motioned for me to come close to him. I really expected a moving moment of personal ministry. "I've got this," I thought. "I'm about to say something really spiritual to this man that will help him transition to his new home in heaven." Instead, he grabbed me by the nape of my neck, pulled me into his face, and with the fieriest eyes and fiercest outburst of anger I've ever experienced (that *up-close and personal,* at least), he shouted in my ears, "Why is God letting this happen to me?!" I was terrified! I jerked away, screamed back at him as I raced for the door, "I don't know!" And ran out of the room! I missed a serious ministry opportunity that morning, and of course, when I returned to my CPE session that afternoon, we had some *serious debriefing to do as well!*

On one occasion, I was removing my lab jacket, clocking out, and leaving the pastoral services office when the phone rang. A very simple but sincere message was requested to be

> "Why was God letting this happen to me?"

sent to the PICU[89] to the family of "the one-month-old little boy with a hole in his heart." "Tell them we are praying for him," the caller said. I felt that was so touching and thoughtful. This wouldn't take long, I assumed. I wrote down the message on a sticky note, put my jacket back on, headed upstairs, and looked for that family. They were nowhere to be found. I checked with the charge nurse, and she told me they had gone to dinner. "Just leave the note on the door of the child's room," she instructed, so I did exactly what she said.

I had no sooner gotten back to pastoral services when the charge nurse rang me from upstairs, *screaming in my ear (why do they do that?)*, "You'd better get up here right away! This family has returned and they said *they don't know anything* about a hole in their son's heart!" I turned flush red in the face. Hot nervous energy surged through my body, and my heart started racing. By the time I got to PICU, I was perspiring and quite panicky! The charge nurse put me in a private room with this family and didn't mince words instructing me!

"You'd better explain yourself, and it had better be good!"

I first had to calm the family down...*imagine that!* The mother was hyperventilating. She was so distraught! Then, as best I could, I told them that I had simply delivered a message from outside the hospital from caring friends in a distant town. I assured them [BY FAITH, *I promise you!*] that I had heard *no medical professional* make any statement *whatsoever* about their son's diagnosis. I apologized for mishandling the information and upsetting them, and again

---

[89] Pediatric Intensive Care Unit.

reassured them that unless their medical team had told them otherwise, the message sent was *misinformation.* It worked.

But I hysterically cried myself back to the CPE office. The CPE supervisor, having gotten the call by now, demanded to see me immediately! *I knew I was in trouble!* I could already see my name in lights in the evening news, "Pitt County Memorial Hospital Sued! Chaplain Wayne Flora Goes to Jail!"

Chaplain Wayne Flora Goes to Jail!

I threw my jacket on my supervisor's desk and told her I was quitting! In a very terse and commanding voice, she hollered back at me (*there we go again!*), "YOU sit down right now! You don't quit until I say you quit! Do you understand me?!" "Yes, ma'am," I meekly, but blubberingly responded. Then she made me sit there for an hour, snorting and snotting, recounting the story, and rehearsing what I had done wrong and what I *should have* done differently.

Then finally, when I had calmed down, she said to me, "Wayne Flora – this *moment of grace* is for you! You pastors are so good at dispensing grace, but *so pathetic at receiving it!* I had just called PICU when you walked into my office and I happen to know that the child *doesn't have* a hole in his heart. God just gave you a wonderful gift of great grace – do you realize that?" So relieved, I burst into tears, replying, "Yes, ma'am! I do! Thank you!" Then she shared with me how *she herself,* in *her CPE training,* had taken a birthday cake *with lit candles* to an 80-year-old man…*under an oxygen tent!* She said that as she was about to pass it to him under the tent, the

Holy Spirit spoke to her and said, "I wouldn't do that if I were you!" Wow! What a life lesson!

It was *ultimately determined* that I was fearful of intense feelings *within myself* and *in others*. What an embarrassing limitation for a believer in Christ, *but especially for a minister!* My supervisor and peers concluded my Type A personality was likely the culprit – my "controlling perfectionism" – the need to "regulate" circumstances, situations, *even individuals,* and prevent unexpected, "unanswerable" surprises! Okay, I get it...*now* – but *I didn't* then!

I could never calculate the worth of my CPE training to the quality of pastoral ministry that eventually ensued because of this profound pastoral coaching and education! No way! BUT, neither could I have known how *the intensity of my emotions* would wreak havoc in my body whenever my hormones and endocrine system would eventually go awry!

> Yes, I had heard my first word from the Lord, and the burden of guilt was lifted, gone. *But the pain wasn't!*

And the symptoms continued. As the Lexapro began to take effect, as slowly but surely it did, a prominent emotion began to emerge: S-A-D![90] I don't know why, but it became more and more pronounced as each day passed.

Everyone's chemistry is different, and while there are some aspects of my experience that may seem similar to others', there are likely *many* that are not. Some people

---

[90] This very prominent emotion that I experienced at this time, "S-A-D," is *not to be confused with* the "SAD" diagnosis of *Social Anxiety Disorder.*

experiencing what I did may feel dejected, devalued, dismally downcast. Others may feel suspicious, distrusting, paranoid. Some may feel perturbed, distraught, frustrated. Still others may feel resentful, angry, maybe vindictive, even *violent*. That can be *quite a challenge,*

S-A-D!

But at this point *in my recovery,* however, all I began to feel was *one emotion, and one only: S-A-D!*

indeed, for the caregivers and support team of a person so sick with chemical issues!

You will likely humor this next story, *as looking back I now do.* It is a most extreme example of this predominant emotion taking over my pity parties and showing up to derail the day every waking hour during this stretch of my recovery. One day our children had come to enjoy a meal with us. And there we were, gathered around our dining room table together, eating the sumptuous meal my wife had prepared. I felt so somber, so sad, so sorrowful... almost *as if* someone had passed away, and we hadn't properly grieved yet. My wife asked, "Honey, what are you thinking? What are you feeling?" Tearfully, I replied, "I miss my children so badly," and I began to weep. They were *all appalled* and wondered what in the world I could possibly mean by those words. "What are you saying, Wayne?" Lou asked. *"Here they are sitting around this table, right here in front of you!"* But I continued to pine, "I know, but they're not kids anymore – and I miss them so much!"

And indeed, it truly felt that somehow, someway, I had *really awakened* from a long life of loving family and devoted ministry into this nightmare of sadness and sorrow and had *missed seeing my children grow up!* I despaired that 20, maybe

30 years, had passed like an eclipse in a moment of time –
and there I was, standing in rushing rapids with swirling
tows and undercurrents right at the brink of a huge
"Niagara…" and was about to *go over the edge.*

No, I wasn't grieving anymore that I had failed God – and
yes, that was a weight off my "spiritual shoulders" – I didn't
anguish any longer in prayer that God might be upset with
me. That agony had ended. But I was still sad, always S-A-D,
and couldn't understand why.

Folks, I *sincerely thought* I loved Jesus before this health
concern happened. But now, I was not only questioning my
personal *faith in Him,* but my *personal love for Him* as well.

I BEGAN TO REALIZE THAT MANY OF MY PRIOR EXPRESSIONS OF
LOVE FOR HIM HAD PROBABLY BEEN PLATITUDES AND CLICHES.

I'm *so embarrassed* to admit that. But I'm being really honest.
So, during this period of extreme sadness, I began examining
my heart to know it truthfully. I kept hearing the Scripture in
my mind, "²³Search me, God, and know my heart; test me and
know my anxious thoughts. ²⁴See if there is any offensive
way in me, and lead me in the way everlasting"
(Ps. 139:23, 24).[91]

Consequently, I would literally lay for hours and say one
phrase per breath as sincerely and truthfully as I knew how,
"I love you, Jesus. I love you, Jesus. I sincerely and dearly

---

[91] "²³Search me, O God, and know my heart: try me, and know my thoughts:
²⁴And see if there be any wicked way in me, and lead me in the way
everlasting" (KJV).

love you, Jesus." I would speak with soft, slow, moving tones, giving Christ plenty of time and opportunity to "examine me," to study me, to know my heart. I kept saying in my mind that we are "naked and opened unto the eyes of him with whom we have to do" (Heb. 4:13; KJV). As stated another way, "Nothing in all creation is hidden from God's sight. Everything is uncovered and laid bare before the eyes of him to whom we must give account" (NIV).

I knew I was "undressed" before the Lord, and that there was nothing about me or within me that He *did not know!* Even my thoughts were exposed to Him: "You have searched me, Lord, and you know me. You know when I sit and when I rise; you perceive my thoughts from afar. You discern my going out and my lying down; you are familiar with all my ways. Before a word is on my tongue you, Lord, know it completely" (Ps. 139:1-4).

So, I would confess for hours *and days* incessantly, "Jesus, you know my heart – as sincerely as I know how to express myself to you, I say to you, Lord, 'I love you, Jesus. I truly and deeply love you, Lord. I love you, Jesus. I love you. I love you…'" Until I would either cry myself to sleep or speak until I could hardly say another hoarse word. I would continue expressing my love to Him until I felt *He was convinced* how sincerely I really did.

> I would "breathe" out love to Christ, desiring so much to "know *that I knew*" that I truly loved my Savior!

It was a sort of coming "to the end of myself" and examining my heart with such scrutinous "spirit eyes" and introspection, such soul-searching and critical analysis that there was *no way* I could "get past God" without loving Him sincerely, authentically. ALL façade stripped away. All nakedness exposed. Bare in my soul and my spirit before the Lord God Almighty, the Judge of all the earth!

When Lou would come home, I would cry some more and confess some more. On our bed, in her arms, on her lap. She would softly stroke my hair, gently swipe my face, and sweetly wipe my tears…and weep with me. For hours and hours. She would listen to me describe how I felt, as I repeated myself redundantly, looking out through blurred eyes, watery and glassy, swollen and red – and she would never complain…but just weep, and tell me how much she loved me, and how she believed everything was going to be okay.

I felt so safe in Lou's arms, being near to her, feeling her touch me with affection and tenderness. She was so understanding, so caring…and of course, so concerned. I ultimately became so attached to and possessive of her that I *absolutely felt I had to be where she was,* no matter what. But she couldn't quit work or take a leave of absence – we had no idea how long this would last, and we had no way of knowing how long I could continue pastoring in this *virtually dysfunctional condition* I found myself. So, like a duckling would its mom, I began "following her" to work. What else could I do?

She worked in the neonatal department at Pitt County Memorial Hospital, now Vidant Medical Center, ultimately serving there (neonatal) for 23 years (total 30 at Vidant now). Many of her peers and supervisors were Christian people who felt deeply empathetic for Lou and sincerely concerned for *her and her husband's* well-being. She asked her employer if

I could stay in *the neonatal chapel, literally just down the hall* from her office. It was rarely used except when hospital chaplains would need it to visit with grieving families whose newborn had just passed away or to counsel families whose child's medical status had taken a turn for the worse. Her supervisor graciously consented, and for many days after that, *when I could,* I would spend most of the day, from the hour Lou clocked in until the hour she clocked out, in that tiny, chilly chapel...near my wife, the only place in the whole wide world that I felt safe while these medicines were adjusting my chemistry and arresting my symptoms.

I could lie down on the sofa in that chapel and rest...and pray...and worship as I cried and wept before the Lord for the sadness I felt. Confessing softly, slowly, tenderly my love for Him. Whispering quietly, gently, breathily with every exhale, "I love you, Jesus." Frequently during the day, Lou would open the door and visit with me, offer prayer, touch my face, and reassure me she was near. I loved her for that and looked forward to those visits. I was disappointed when the door opened, and *it wasn't Lou.* And though the chapel wasn't "mine," I had claimed it. Any time anyone else opened the door needing it (which was rarely), I felt like they were imposing, disturbing my rest, and shoving me out.

I'm sorry, but that's just how I felt in this skewed, exiled season of my life! When all I yearned was the desire *to know* how sincerely *I truly loved* my Lord.

And all I felt during those long, dark, dreary days... was S-A-D.

Chapter 19

That Still Small Voice

I've acknowledged to you that my faith heritage is Wesleyan Pentecostal. I've enjoyed a lifetime of service and ministry celebrating my faith in the context of the Church of God, Cleveland, Tennessee.

I'm quite an "excitable" preacher of the Gospel, animated and dramatic. I enjoy sharing my faith with others. I truly and sincerely *do love Jesus* and *do love God's people – all people – all races, ethnicities, faiths, and people groups.* And I am quite an enthusiastic (en – "in;" theos – "God")[92] worshiper! *Rarely, very rarely* does much "silence" happen in a full Gospel worship service, at least the ones *I've been in!*

We're not very good at "silence." But we're working on it. You know, prayerful meditation. Quiet and solitude. Just "being still before God."[93] I am yet learning to do this myself.

---

[92] "enthusiasm (n.)," *Online Etymology Dictionary,* Douglas Harper, 2001-2020, https://www.etymonline.com/word/enthusiasm (accessed on February 20, 2020). "c. 1600, from Middle French *enthousiasme* (16c.) and directly from Late Latin *enthusiasmus*, from Greek *enthousiasmos* 'divine inspiration, enthusiasm (produced by certain kinds of music, etc.),' from *enthousiazein* 'be inspired or possessed by a god, be rapt, be in ecstasy,' from *entheos* 'divinely inspired, possessed by a god,' from *en* 'in' (see en- (2)) + *theos* 'god' (from PIE root dhes-, forming words for religious concepts)."

[93] "¹⁰He says, 'Be still, and know that I am God; I will be exalted among the nations, I will be exalted in the earth'" (Ps. 46:10).

And I must say, that at my age, the *treasure* of solitude
and quietness is becoming more and more sacred to me,
especially as I also suffer tinnitus…loud noise seems to
make it worse.

That said, however, *too much quiet* makes many of us
a little nervous. Remember how it was when your children
were very young? When things got a little *too quiet,* we had
a good idea they *might be into something they shouldn't* – playing in the toilet, unrolling the tissue, emptying the soft soap, or maybe even *taking off a dirty diaper!* All those things have happened to us! The background noise of their playtime chitter-chatter, though rather "subconsciously" noted, still gave ease that everything was okay.

> But when the chitter-chatter stopped and it became as quiet as "kids in a cookie jar" – well, *they probably were!*

Perhaps you've heard the expression, "deafening
silence." That's how it can "sound" *when it seems* that God's
not speaking, you know, when "the heavens are brass?!" And
God's not "talking back?!" There's an old adage that suggests
most people had rather be "slapped than ignored." I suspect
there's some truth to that!

Why? Because all of us need affirmation, company,
fellowship, interaction…*some attention,* at least. And in long
periods of time when it seems God has left his "prayer booth"
and isn't "taking requests" or "accepting appointments
today," *we usually get a little nervous about that too!*

I'm *so grateful* I heard that *first* encouraging word from
the Lord – remember? That He wasn't mad with me? That He
wasn't punishing me? And that my sickness had nothing to

do with personal sin? That He was fashioning me into a better person, one who could be more effective for His use and glory in the kingdom? That was quite a relief to my spirit! And it certainly affected my prayers and my worship! It encouraged my faith and gave rise to hope! It was *then* I began to understand that God *had a plan* bigger than I could grasp or "wrap my mind around." So, yes, my faith was bolstered, and I experienced a paradigm shift in my conviction *just enough to deepen my trust in God* and express greater confidence in an eventual, favorable outcome.

However, that *one word* did not make me well. I'll say this more than once – because you need to hear it!

IT DID *NOT IMMEDIATELY* END MY HEALTH CRISIS!

In fact, *it didn't dampen or diminish my symptoms at all!* I'm sorry to disappoint anyone who feels my faith should have ended my crisis right then and there! But…it didn't.

Yes, I had some serious reexamination of my theological rationale for human suffering to review as well, so throughout this ordeal, I *did considerable study* of the Scriptures…that is, when I felt well enough to. It took quite some time to "give back to God" the divine prerogative that belongs *only to Him* – His doing things as *He wished,* as *He knew best,* and as *He only* had the wisdom and power to do! Undoubtedly, that was all part of His master plan!

Then eventually when *I did begin* to "notice" the antidepressant having *some bit* of positive effect on my chemical imbalance, I would *also begin* to express *bits and bits* of hope – not *huge "chunks"* of it, but "little bits…" little bit by little bit! (Unentangle your tongue and say that again!) I came to realize that hope is the "supernatural confidence that things *will get better*" (Honestly, *Flora definition*, forged out through my sickness!)! It is "faith on tiptoe" or "forward-looking faith!" I had spent so much time looking back that I had begun to plow "a crooked row."[94] In fact, the "current reality" for me at that time was nothing but grief and heartache about *all the mistakes* I thought I had made *in my past* by that stage in my life!

As my symptoms continued, there were yet long nights that I had to wrestle through – no longer worried that God was upset with me, true – but *very worried* about *how much longer* this was going to last! When in the world would it ever be over?! That's why I needed to hear from the Lord again.

So, one evening when I was "a quarter inch" from asking my wife to please take me to the hospital, knowing full well to which end of the facility I would be admitted, I sat on the edge of the bed and rocked and cried, rocked and cried. And moaned and groaned. And whimpered. "Let's go," I said. "No, not right now; give me a few more minutes." "Yes, let's do," I repeated. Lou started to get up. "No, not just yet," I restated. And then I began to pray to God in a deep form of *soulish supplication*, pleading with pitiable petitions for God to *please make me like I used to be!* "Please, please, God!" I cried. **"I don't want to be like this – I want to be like I *used to be!*"**

To my utter amazement and unsuspecting surprise, God answered! But I wasn't expecting His reply, and *certainly not*

---

[94] "'62Jesus replied, 'No one who puts a hand to the plow and looks back is fit for service in the kingdom of God'" (Lk. 9:62).

specifically what He said! Just as I had "heard His voice" in the prior instance when He released me from guilt and unburdened my soul from the anguish of self-blame, I heard it again! Crisp, clean, clear – like a phone call from heaven! Like an uninterrupted telegram right from the heart of God sitting on His throne!

Again, it originated from *outside myself, it seemed,* forming the semblance of a tiny snowflake, materializing in the seat of my being, then merging and commingling with others falling rapidly from the sky into my spirit. Until it shaped into a small ball that *then began rolling "downhill," getting larger and larger and larger.* It swelled through my being, rising to my cognizance and opening my mind to the words of God so distinctly spoken! It would have been easy to mistake them for ambient sound in my bedroom as if someone had entered unbeknownst and suddenly spoke up!

And this is what I heard, "Do you *really want to be just like you used to be?!* Never taking care of yourself?! Never eating right?! Never going to bed on time?! Never slowing down?! Never saying, 'No?!' Never asking for help?! Always trying to fix everybody?! Everything?! Every situation?! *Is that really what you want?!"*

I was stunned! Appalled even!

And utterly amazed that God had spoken to me again, *but especially with what He had just said...OR ASKED, REALLY!* I was speechless. The words were echoing in my spirit as upon the hollows and valleys of a great canyon. I felt so small, but so *significant* before God that He would even care to speak to me, as awesome and as mighty as He is!

I began to weep profusely and cry uncontrollably, answering Him all in the same breaths, "No, God! That's *not what I want!* I don't want to be like *that again!* I don't want to experience that again – I can't handle that anymore! But I need you, Lord. I want your help! I need to have your hand upon my life! I'm pitiful and helpless without you. Help me, Lord! Please help me!"

Again, He responded, and *all He said* was, "Okay, then. Let me handle things *my way, my time!* And stop complaining to me about *how I want to do it!*" "Yes, Lord," I relented. "I will. I will stop complaining."

> "And I will accept your purposes and your plan in my life."

Then I lay down, crying with concession to the will of God in my spirit, weeping worshipfully before the Lord *simply that He had touched me and spoken to me personally.* Again extending my hope beyond that night into a brighter future, *His future, "plans to prosper [me] and not to harm [me], plans to give [me] hope and a future"* (Jer. 29:11).

From that night to this day, I have *never made that request of God again…*to make me like I used to be. And I have *never since complained* about who or how I am. I like how He made – actually, *re-made me…*and I *accept how* He did it.

I shared with Lou what I had heard. Then we fell asleep…weeping…together.

Chapter 20

Days in a Row

Day one, two, three – click! Day one, two – click!
Day one, two, three, four – click! Day one – click! Day one,
two, three – click! And that was the pattern! Well, not *quite* a
pattern, but sort of a *predictability*. It seemed not to make any
mathematical sense exactly, having no recognizable, *rhythmic
pattern* to it, per se; but it was becoming rather obvious and
ordinary…almost an expected nuisance, I guess I'd say.

Oh, you're wondering, "What?" Oh yeah, of course you
are – you know, *the SWITCH – the malfunctioning switch* that
had broken inside me, remember? Or at least, it had seemed
to no longer be working properly. Well now, it *seemed like* it
was *beginning* to work again, a little…along…with some
degree of predictability.

It seemed to be turning on (or off) for several days,
now…*in a row!* That's kind of how I knew the medicine was
starting to take effect and beginning to work in my body.
And why I began to express some measure of *hope* that I
really was, at long last, getting better.

No, I wasn't completely well. It would be a long time
before I would be. And no, that *one most encouraging word* I
had heard from the Lord didn't fix everything all at once, but
it certainly did reassure me that God was in control –

sovereign, "all reigning" in *my life* – and had me on His radar! He truly was providentially "working things out for my good..." *just like He promised!*[95]

Now, don't misunderstand me...I'm not saying that I *ever completely grasped* what was happening to me (or *in* me), but I was *beginning to feel* that *there was* a "method to the madness," if you will, a means to an end, a favorable and *determined outcome!* One that God Himself was fully aware of, and had not forgotten, even since the beginning of time.

See, *I believed* and HAD PREACHED *all my life* that God had a purpose for each of us. I had already concluded that none of us was merely a randomly-made or -placed "figurine" in His beautiful galaxy of galaxies simply to adorn Himself with beautiful ornaments so He could *brag to somebody else* about how awesome a God He was!

After all, who could He brag to?!
There *was* no one else! For He Himself
was the only true God *there ever was!*[96]

---

[95] "[28]And we know that in all things God works for the good of those who love him, who have been called according to his purpose" (Rm. 8:28). I *still like* the King James rendering of this text that I learned from a youth, "[28]And we know that all things work together for good to them that love God, to them who are the called according to his purpose" (KJV).

[96] See "34 Bible Verses About No Other is God," *New American Standard Bible* (La Habra, California: The Lockman Foundation, 1960-1995), *Knowing Jesus,* https://bible.knowing-jesus.com/topics/No-Other-Is-God (accessed on February 19, 2020). "'[10]You are my witnesses,' declares the Lord, 'and my servant whom I have chosen, so that you may know and believe me and understand that I am he. Before me no god was formed, nor will there be one after me'" (Is. 43:10). "'[22]How great you are, Sovereign Lord! There is no one like you, and there is no God but you, as we have heard with our own ears'" (II Sam. 7:22). "'[32]Well said, teacher,' the man replied. 'You are right in saying that God is one and there is no other but him'" (Mk. 12:32).

And I believed that purpose was "the original idea for the creation of a thing…what made the Maker make it." In other words, for anyone to understand the purpose of any invention, he must "meet" its maker and hear *from the maker* what the *intent* for that specific design or invention was! Without hearing from the inventor what the purpose of a weed eater is, one could do himself (or someone else) great harm…using it to mix batter, trim hair, or discipline a child! *I had met "the Maker,"* and had become convinced that from the foundations of the world, *God knew me!* He had purposely designed me *in His mind* before I was ever conceived in my mother's womb. And He had already decided with prophetic intention what my destiny should be…*if I would only cooperate with Him* in that plan.

UNTIL I GOT SICK, I THOUGHT I *HAD BEEN* COOPERATING!

And *not until* I got sick had my faith in Jesus Christ *ever been tested* like it was during this desperately dark season of my life! As my reader, you have already been through a lot just hearing me tell my story, so I think it's time I gave *you* a little hope, offer you some optimism! In fact, *I hope* it has dawned on you that the author of this book *probably survived* this traumatic experience. If it hasn't, I'm offering you a hint *without prompting* you to "cheat" and turn to the back of the book to see how the story ends. Smile!

You may remember that I had said I preached nine of 11 double-AM services to a church of 225 persons every Sunday morning throughout this entire stretch of time. No sleep the night before. It's true. I don't know *how now,* but I really did.

My wife still marvels that we never had to call 911 because I had collapsed in the pulpit. I probably should have – but I began to feel that *the second safest place* for me on Planet Earth, *next to* the neonatal chapel…near my wife while at work, *was the pulpit.* I can't explain it, except to say that when I stepped into that pulpit, something marvelously supernatural happened! God sustained me. He helped me. He "showed up." And sometimes, He "showed off" – I'm Pentecostal, remember?! Smile.

But *before* those services and immediately *after* those services, I was sick…frail, weak, and scared. While all my life I had been a very extroverted person with a chipper personality who *always greeted everyone* in my congregation, *guests especially* (as well as said goodbye), *during this period of my ministry*, I did not. I couldn't. I came in late, almost on the hour, or "hid away" in my office. When church was over, I left.

We got out of there as quickly as we could because I didn't feel sociable, nor did I want to be.

I went to the office some days during the week, late morning usually, *but I closed the door* and hid my face. I usually just sat in the dark…and prayed…and worshiped…*and wept.* My Administrative Secretary of ten years, Barbara Reaves, a sweet and talented woman, retired from AT&T, having spent most of her life in the Washington, D.C. area, was so compassionate toward me and so understanding of my condition. She had suffered these same health issues, with some degree of variance, of course, and she herself had survived. She knew *how and when* to approach me, and she seemed always to know exactly what to say to cheer me. She offered prayer for me and comforted me with encouraging words that only a person who really identified could offer. Thank you, Barbara, my dear friend for always!

By now, I had resigned being MIP (Ministerial Internship Program) Coordinator for the Church of God in eastern North Carolina. This "switch thing" was too erratic for me to trust. I couldn't possibly manage our 10-month intensive training program for this next year. My Assistant Coordinator for MIP and my good friend, Mike Wells, stepped up and took the bat. He capably led our board and ministry development team through the next two years of MIP.

> **I absented myself. I simply couldn't handle it.**

After accepting my resignation, our Administrative Bishop announced in Camp Meeting to an audience of 1800 persons that we were *"killing our best and strongest leaders in the state"* because we were overusing them and expecting too much of them. Whoa! That was jolting and telling! I could hardly believe the confession I was hearing before that entire congregation! Keep in mind that any service in state leadership offered by a local pastor *was above and beyond* what was required to lead and pastor a healthy, growing church.

Bishop Harold Downing, who offered those kind and sincere sentiments, requested to speak with me privately after that meeting. He advised me that I needed to listen to my doctors and that taking medication to correct my chemistry was not an embarrassment…and certainly not an indication of a *lack of faith*. Then he confided in me that *he himself* was on an antidepressant, in fact. I would never have known it *had he not said so!* I was so comforted by his own admission and by his personal encouragement that *I was not displeasing God nor defaulting my faith* to come under a doctor's care. He only cautioned me that I should be wary of "overmedicating" and suffering a consequent *personality change.* He advised that treatment was available *and possible* to help me get well without changing the gifted leader and loving pastor he thought I was. I will *ever be grateful* to him for that solace!

As you recall, Mom was calling me daily, and I was glad I could say to her *on occasion,* "Mom, I slept better last night, and I feel better today. In fact, I've felt better the last three days. I know God is answering your prayers, Mom! He knows how much you love me, and He understands the heart of a caring mother."

> "Keep praying, Mom – I feel myself improving day by day."

So, it seemed that as I was improving, I began to recognize the "on" switch and the "off" switch in my chemistry. I still didn't have *any control* of it, for it seemed to be operating on its own. However, I knew to expect it *to function intermittently* as the Lexapro took over – because Dr. Ribeiro had instructed me to expect it and to realize that as it happened the medicine *was, indeed, working!* And so, I did. It brought me hope…

BUT it also brought me despair! "Off" – I was "up." "On" – I was "down." And I would say to Lou, "Oh, Sweetheart – it's over! The switch has turned off, and it's been off for three days now!" I would have such hope that the nightmare had ended. Then, *all of a sudden,* I would "feel" that switch "click" inside my body, and here we'd go again! What a letdown!

And this happened over and over before I was ever confident the switch was finally working properly.

My sleep patterns were still messy, leaving much to be desired, I must say. Up all night many nights. Up half the night others. The symptoms were still occurring, but they *came and went* with the "click" of the switch. Strange, isn't it?! Almost sounding like I was some sort of mechanical robot needing a "tune-up!"

Or the Tin Man, perhaps, from Dorothy's magical land of Oz, who simply needed to borrow the *famed oil can* to grease my rusty switch!

That's probably why Dr. Ribeiro decided I should see my high school friend, Dr. Almond Jerkins Drake, III[97] (my brother-in-law, Eddie's, first cousin), a lead specialist in endocrinology, diabetes, and metabolism, *as well as* a scholarly physician and educator in internal medicine at the Brody School of Medicine here in Greenville, North Carolina. My mother had been a patient of Al's herself, given her thyroid health issues (among others). She loved him dearly and agreed seeing him was a good idea.

How incredibly providential was it that Dr. Ribeiro would recommend that I see Dr. Drake?! He felt he should do a complete work-up to be sure nothing suspicious was happening with my thyroid…or any other aspect of my

---

[97] Al was the 1975 class valedictorian of South Edgecombe High School in Pinetops, North Carolina (I was salutatorian…smile). By now, he had retired from the U.S. Navy as Captain after having practiced at the Bethesda Naval Hospital in Annapolis, Maryland (The Walter Reed National Military Medical Center), where he had treated several presidents as well as a number of congresspersons.

endocrine system. Al is a wonderful Christian man whose personal faith in Jesus "goes with him." He respects protocol, but he doesn't "check his faith at the door" – he *lives* and serves by it! I felt very comfortable making this visit.

So, my wife and I went to see him. He was already fairly well-informed, for Eddie had been in touch with him on a regular basis, and Al had "monitored" my progress via Eddie's periodic reports...*at a distance,* of course. Further, my wife had called him numerous times "behind the scenes," seeking guidance, appealing advice, hoping for answers.

To this day, I remember that first visit with Al, for I recall asking him a *very silly question* prodding for answers to my health crisis. As he gathered specimens for blood and urine analyses, I offered my question: "Al, do you think this wristwatch is the problem?" I held it up for him to see. "Can you see how corroded it is on the bottom? Is it possible that chemicals from the watch have entered my bloodstream through my skin and *poisoned my body?*" Quite sincere, though trepidatious as could be, I was desperately grasping for straws!

AT THAT POINT, I COULD EASILY HAVE BELIEVED ANYTHING!

Looking back, I imagine Al was humored! He responded, "No, Wayne. That's not the problem. Your chemistry is likely fouled right now, and we have to study your blood and urine samples to see if we can determine what's causing it. It may be stress-related or genetic, or both. But I'll be checking your metanephrines and catecholamines to see if anything is amiss

with your endocrine system."[98] [Yeah, I thought that too –
what in the world is he talking about? Smile!?] He carefully
examined my thyroid to be sure it wasn't tumorous or
swollen. I'm certain he ran many more tests than I could aptly
understand (or explain here), but he found nothing of
concern to indicate what was causing my symptoms.

However, he *did suggest,* after reviewing my meds, that
I might request Dr. Ribeiro to switch my shorter half-life
Xanax® to the *longer half-life Ativan.*[99] This became somewhat
a significant turning point in my recovery because, as you
remember, the Xanax® was supposed to help me rest *while
the* Lexapro tempered in my body. But I was continuing to
awaken in early morning hours with rebound anxiety and
still wasn't getting any *significant rest* at all!

---

[98] Donna Freeborn, PhD, CNM, FNP and Chad Haldeman-Englert, MD,
reviewers, "Metanephrine (Urine)," *Health Encyclopedia,* University of
Rochester Medical Center, sec. "What is this Test?" https://www.urmc.
rochester.edu/encyclopedia/content.aspx?contenttypeid=167&contentid=
metanephrine_urine (accessed on February 17, 2020). "This test measures
the amount of metanephrines in your urine that your body makes over
a 24-hour period. Metanephrines are made when your body breaks
down hormones called catecholamines. These hormones are made by
the adrenal glands. Catecholamines help your body respond to stress.
They are sometimes called 'fight or flight' hormones. They also include
epinephrine, norepinephrine, and dopamine…Pheochromocytomas are
found in the adrenal glands. Paragangliomas are found outside the adrenal
glands. Signs and symptoms of pheochromocytoma or paraganglioma
include: high blood pressure, paleness, headaches, sweating, heart
palpitations, and tremors."
[99] "Drugs and Medications, Ativan," *WebMD,* sec. "Uses,"
https://www.webmd.com/drugs/ 2/drug-6685/ativan-oral/details (accessed
on February 17, 2020). "This medication is used to treat anxiety. Lorazepam
belongs to a class of drugs known as benzodiazepines which act on the brain
and nerves (central nervous system) to produce a calming effect. This drug
works by enhancing the effects of a certain natural chemical in the body."

Upon dropping the Xanax® and starting the Ativan, my sleep patterns began to improve almost immediately. I commenced sleeping *most of the night* when I switched to this new med. I have to say, when I realized how "miraculous" it was, it began *to taste like candy on my tongue,* and I looked forward to taking my evening dosage each night *just so* I could get some decent, uninterrupted sleep!

I must mention that it was in this season of my recovery that my stepmother-in-law, Betty Smith, called me one morning when, although sleeping better, I was yet plagued with despair to face each new day. On this particular day, when my phone rang and I answered, Ms. Betty (as I affectionately called her) said that she had been praying for me and that the Lord instructed her to share a "message with me." I was pleased to listen to Ms. Betty, because she was a very meek-spirited and quiet person who rarely volunteered any advice to anyone. I knew the mere fact that she called was itself a miraculous indication of the authenticity of her message to me.

"YES. MA'AM."

"I thank you so gratefully, Ms. Betty, for obeying the Lord. This is just what I needed to hear, *and I'm climbing out of bed right now!"*

"Yes, ma'am," I graciously responded. "I'm listening, Ms. Betty." She replied, "Wayne, the Lord is instructing you that it is time to get out of that bed and start your day! And I believe He wants you to greet each new day with hope and courage that He is healing you and that everything is going to be okay."

She felt encouraged for me that I had received her message so willingly and was obliged to respond with such favorable acceptance. I was beholden to her, and especially now as I look back, I will ever be appreciative that she called. Ms. Betty has since gone to be with Jesus, and this instance of her love for me will always be a fond memory of what she means to my family and me!

I was on my way to being my new self! In fact, I was having some really good days now and then…*all in a row!*

Day one, two, three, four, five – click! Day one, two – click! Day one, two, three – click! *Uh oh! Here we go again!*

Chapter 21

The Waking Word

My restless nights were also Lou's. Although she was terribly exhausted "processing" my grief and dealing with my symptoms, it had become quite difficult for Lou to get a good night's rest at all anymore, even though the medications had begun to work. The "switch" was beginning to "toggle" in the right direction by now, favoring my recovery and affording us more good days than bad. However, I doubt seriously Lou got any decent REM[100] sleep during those first several months. I felt badly about that.

---

[100] William C. Shiel, Jr., MD, FACP, FACR, "Medical Definition of REM Sleep," *MedicineNet,* Dec. 27, 2018, para. 2, https://www.medicinenet.com/script/main/art.asp?articlekey=8677 (accessed on February 21, 2020). "REM [rapid eye movement] is characterized by a number of other features including rapid, low-voltage brain waves detectable on the electroencephalographic (EEG) recording, irregular breathing and heart rate and involuntary muscle jerks." "REM Sleep and Our Dreaming Lives," *ResMed,* 2015, https://sleep.mysplus.com/library/category3/REM Sleep and Our Dreaming Lives.html sec. 4, "A Time for Mental Recharge," (accessed on February 21, 2020). REM sleep is considered healthy because it is "…closely linked with mental recharge. During its time in REM throughout the night, your brain refreshes and restores itself. This is one reason why REM sleep is so important, and why a healthy sleep routine with sufficient amounts of REM sleep is essential to feeling mentally and emotionally well, and to performing at your best during your waking life."

Lou had almost always slept on her back with her hands folded over her chest, much as we funeral directors would "pose a body in an open casket" (humor – remember, *I am a funeral director now*, but *only because* my daughter *married one!*). In fact, she had scared the living daylights out of me (well, actually "nightlights") on several occasions when I would awaken and see her postured that way, and hear nary a breath emitting from her nostrils…nor see any faint indication of the rise and fall of her chest. I've held my breath and touched her softly to be sure she hadn't passed away in her sleep and left me to figure out the rest of life all by myself.

However, during these dreary days of our lives, she had begun to sleep on her side, facing me, watching me sleep…that is, when I did. When my symptoms were unbearable, she would put her hand on my chest and calm my nerves and slow my respiration and heart rate, almost like magic! That very close and intimate point of contact became for me a soothing sense of reassurance that God was present, and someone He loved very much was there *as His personal agent* of comfort to remind me of that.

Lou and I both clearly recall that on one particular morning, she had already awakened and was "watching me" sleep. It brought her peace to see me resting.

That morning, *as I awakened*, I did so, easing gradually out of a very moving and convincing experience with God, a dream perhaps, but nevertheless *realistic*.

I was weeping as I awoke, and I was speaking to someone in echoes of repetitious responses. I was stirred with emotion as

I kept reiterating, "Yes, Sir…(sob), yes, Sir…(weeping profusely). Yes, Sir. Yes, Sir…(crying liberally), yes, Sir."

When I had consciously aroused, Lou asked me, "Honey, who were you talking to?" Continuing to snivel and sob, I replied, "It was the Lord." My response was faint but emphatic. "What was He saying?" Lou asked. I answered, "He asked me, 'Do you believe I love you?' 'Yes, Sir,' I replied. 'Do you consider me trustworthy?' 'Yes, Sir,' I answered. 'Do you believe I can handle this?' 'Yes, Sir…yes, Sir, I do.' 'Are you willing to let me do it *my way in my time?'* 'Yes, Sir. Yes, Sir.'" Then together Lou and I wept and thanked the Lord that He had been so personal with me – *with us* – again!

This was now the *third time*[101] that the Lord had instructed me to permit Him to do *His work in my life – His way, His time!* I was convinced the Lord had me in the palm of His hand (John 10:28, 29).[102] And I knew now, more than ever, that He truly loved me! He was making it perfectly clear to me that *I wasn't* a pawn on a "chess board game of the gods!" No, He wasn't playing games with me at all – He was "re-forming" me, for higher purposes than I understood at that time,[103] into a vessel of greater value and use to His kingdom and calling.

---

[101] "**16**…every matter may be established by the testimony of two or three witnesses'" (Mt. 18:16).

[102] "**28**I give them eternal life, and they shall never perish; no one will snatch them out of my hand. **29**My Father, who has given them to me, is greater than all; no one can snatch them out of my Father's hand. **30**I and the Father are one" (Jn. 10:28-30).

[103] "**8**For my thoughts are not your thoughts, neither are your ways my ways,' declares the Lord. '**9**As the heavens are higher than the earth, so are my ways higher than your ways and my thoughts than your thoughts'" (Is. 55:8, 9).

Mentally and emotionally, and *certainly* spiritually, the Lord Jesus was gradually restoring my strength and stability, my hope and confidence, making *absolutely sure* that I clearly understood *Who God was*...and *who I wasn't!* Never again could I pride myself in what I had accomplished nor what I had become. Because now, I was a *different person!* God was changing me from *less the man I was* to *more the man of God* He wanted me to be. Sober, solemn, and sold-out, I now had nothing to boast *except Jesus* – that I might truly know Him in His sufferings, His power, and the glory of His resurrection![104]

After all, that was precisely why I had started this journey years ago at age 14 when I gave my life to Jesus Christ, wasn't it?!

Perhaps my vision had since clouded, and the clarity of the road signs had dulled a bit...

But now, *it seemed*, everything was coming back into sharper focus, and I was beginning to see clearly once again.

> **However it happened that He "healed my spiritual eyes," I am grateful that He did...*and I shall always be!***

---

[104] "**7**But whatever were gains to me I now consider loss for the sake of Christ. **8**What is more, I consider everything a loss because of the surpassing worth of knowing Christ Jesus my Lord, for whose sake I have lost all things. I consider them garbage, that I may gain Christ **9**and be found in him, not having a righteousness of my own that comes from the law, but that which is through faith in Christ – the righteousness that comes from God on the basis of faith. **10**I want to know Christ – yes, to know the power of his resurrection and participation in his sufferings, becoming like him in his death, **11**and so, somehow, attaining to the resurrection from the dead" (Philip. 3:7-11).

Chapter 22

Dad, You're Boring!

Ouch! That stings!

That's the last thing in the whole world…well, other than being S-A-D, that I would ever want to be. I think I *really am* a fairly pleasant blend of Types A and B personalities. Those kinds of persons *just aren't* boring!

But oh dear, at this point in my life as I was recovering from very serious health issues – "I was boring!" My daughter, Rhapsody, said so! And Rhapsody always tells the truth…*just like her mama!* And to be honest with you, if you don't want to know the truth, *don't ask Lou* or *Rhapsody!* They will both say it *the way they see it!* But you will never cut your feet "walking on eggshells around them!"

As I began to feel better, I became a little more open and conversational with my children. I had actually tried to hide most of my feelings. Of course, that was impossible! How can anyone hide the "king with no clothes," standing in the middle of the street in the open market?! I mean, everyone knows a zebra when he sees one, right?! You can't possibly confuse those bold black stripes with the dull, gray coat of a jacka…donkey! Can you?! (Hey, it's in the Bible!)

Rhapsody's my baby girl. I call her, "Lovely" all the time. But then, I call all the girls in my life, "Lovely" – Lou, Rhapsody, Hannah, Bethany, Kylah, and Kendall. That's the birth order of the girls in my family...but the list stops there! Because if I call any other lady I know, "Lovely," my wife is going to get suspicious. Believe me, I know the boundaries!

And Rhapsody truly is lovely in every way! She is a talented person with the most cordial and complimentary personality. Her name means, "ecstasy, praise, exuberance," and she is every whit that! She is an absolute joy in everyone's life and loves Jesus as enthusiastically as anyone I know. And *she is a worshiper!* Besides that, she's knockout gorgeous! It's hard to believe that Lou and I gave the world such a stunning and attractive young lady! But we did! How incredibly genius God must be to mix two batches of DNA and get that result! Absolutely amazing! Breathtaking even! There *really is* a God!

Rhapsody is a neonatal nurse at Vidant Medical Center and worked as a clinical instructor for three years at Pitt Community College...*and is now a stay-at-home-mom* who homeschools her three children. Figure *that one out,* if you can! She is married to Justin Russell Smith, owner-operator of Smith Funeral Service & Crematory here in Greenville as well as Edwards Funeral Home & Cremations in Kinston. He owns Carolina Crematory and Carolina Pet Crematory as well. He began his businesses at age 26! He is a prince of a gentleman with a sharp mind and remarkable business savvy! Everybody loves him *and* Rhapsody as they have made such a favorable impression in our community and the eastern North Carolina region in such a short time to be so young. I've often said of Justin (not Rhapsody…smile!) that he is smarter *than I was* at his age. However, I have recently conceded to the fact of matter *and* brazen reality that he is *actually smarter* than I am *at THIS age!* That's hard to admit, but what can I say?

Justin and Rhapsody have given to us *our three youngest,* beautiful grandchildren: Kylah, 11, Karsten, 8, and Kendall, 3. Kylah is mature beyond her age and interacts with adults as if she *were one,* a quite gifted communicator, I might say. Her name means, "beautiful, graceful, lovely." She certainly is. Besides that, she's a wonderful big sister. She helps Mommy out a lot with baby sister, Kendall. Karsten means, "Christian!" What an appropriate name for a handsome young man who loves Jesus! Karsten's the "engineer" in our family – he has a creative mind and is always thinking of something "to invent." I'm absolutely sure he's going to be rich and famous one day and end up sipping Kool-Aid in Acapulco! Isn't that what all rich and famous people do?! And Kendall means, "royal valley." Uh huh! She's free-spirited enough to be that! She could easily rule the world (smile). Or her own home – or, *at the least,* she takes *no junk* from her big brother!

Okay, you've met my daughter's family… let's get back to the story. Since during my sickness I could no longer "be objective," it was quite a concern to me during my recovery *how* I was being perceived by others. I was kind of monitoring the *progress* of my "return to normal," and hoping that folks were no longer *noticing* how sick I was (or had been). I sat down with Rhapsody one day and had a low-

Since…I could no longer be objective.

key, but frank conversation with her. I really wanted to
know *how I was coming across* to my family as my medicines
did their work…and I did mine. "Rhapsody," I asked. "Can
you be honest with me and tell me *exactly how you feel* about
me right now? Can you tell me *how I impress you?* What
would you say is the dominant aspect of my personality
this very moment as I recover from this sickness?"

She really didn't think long. She didn't have to. After
all, she *is her mom!* In so many ways! Without hesitation,

she said, "Dad, you're boring!" Then
laughed right out loud! I couldn't believe
it! I thought I could take it "on the chin,"
but man, "that smarted a bit," maybe
even *bruised* my ego. I didn't really know

it was *that bad!* "Are you kidding me?" I asked. "No, Dad –
you asked; I'm telling – you're boring right now!" And she
laughed again!

Well, I wasn't completely well yet, so I felt I could, at
least, give myself *that much* benefit of doubt. But I'll tell you,
IF I was boring, I sure didn't want to stay that way! I've been
called many things throughout my life and ministry –
prideful, conceited, egotistical, perfectionist, even bossy
(I'm not really!) – BUT NOT BORING!

So, I guess this whole conversation is about image.
That's always been important to me! I didn't say "status!"
That's a very different thing…horse of a different color! And
status has *NOT been important* to me. I have no concern with
needing to impress anyone in the matter of *status.* In fact, I
think Jesus has done quite an effective job *dealing with the*

pride in my life – He has surely forced me to my knees more than a few times!

But *how people perceive me* has always been a matter. Again, not at all that I feel the need to impress anybody! But, certainly because I have never wanted to reflect poorly on my Lord and Savior, Jesus Christ! And neither have I ever wanted to cast ill light upon the churches I served, especially University Church of God (26 years), knowing that the Church (capital C) is the "body and bride" of Christ Jesus!

Okay, but I have on a few occasions likely blown it – I may have learned a bit too late "in the game" that I really shouldn't take politics with me into the pulpit. And several times, I did. And I might *likely have* divided the camp on those given Sundays (not drastically…just slightly). I'm sorry – those sermons bombed. And because I'm so animated *and passionate* when I preach, I *may have* gotten a bit too enthralled in my preaching *now and then* such that my descriptives and depictions were *a little too crass…too blunt*, maybe. Don't mistake me – no one *ever* fell asleep when I preached, but some did drop their jaws and hold their hands over their mouths as if to ask in disbelief, "Did Pastor Flora just say that?!" Yeah, I confess. I resemble that. But folks still loved me. They knew I was human too. Smile.

Perhaps it had something to do with my rather *legalistic* background and upbringing, I don't know, or my restrictive understanding of holiness in my younger years (hair, dress, makeup, etc. – you know, "appearances"). Or maybe it was my ministerial training and my guarded intentions *not to let*

The "image" thing was a matter of deep disquiet and uneasiness for me during my sickness.

"my good be evil spoken of" (Rm. 14:16; KJV).[105] I'm really not sure, but somehow I felt when I got sick, I HAD FAILED GOD MISERABLY!

I hope I don't sound *too much* like an extremist to say what I'm *about to say*, but *it is* a matter of fact that I have often said these words – ask my wife how many times she's heard them. I have declared without reservation and sincerest intent that, "I'd rather die and go to heaven *early* than to ever *fail God miserably.*"

And when I got sick, I THOUGHT I HAD!

Why? Because I was a Christian and I had preached "faith" all my life...and *tried to live it.* I'm sincerely supposing NOW that *when I got sick at age 49,* I had not yet faced up to my own mortality – I was not yet ready to die! I am now. Whoa! Stop right there -- I didn't say *I wanted to,* but just that *I'm ready to!* Big difference! And I had apparently developed the impression that pastors and preachers *can't hurt!* Or at least, they ought not to! It seemed a conflict in interest to me that I would preach the Word of God and tell *other people* how to have faith and how to trust God – and *not do that myself!*

So, all kinds of questions raced through my head during my illness. What will people think of me now? What kind of faith *does he really have?* How can he possibly stand up there and tell *me* what to believe and how to live if *he can't even do that himself?* Why can't HE trust God for a miracle like he

---

[105] "16Therefore do not let what you know is good be spoken of as evil" (Rm. 14:16).

encourages US to do? How can we afford to listen to him anymore? And on and on it went! Second-guessing EVERYTHING I ever believed *myself*, having to determine what really mattered and what didn't. Deciding what I was actually *willing to die for* (and live for!) and what I wasn't! Every single conviction that had ever happened in my heart, in my belief systems, was examined, cross-examined, then re-examined again! I truly felt that not only was my body suffering, but my mind *also* certainly was!

I dug deep to discover (or should I say, "re-discover") who I was in Christ and what I believed about my faith. I had to resolve that IF I REALLY WASN'T willing *to die for* what I believed, then I certainly wasn't ready *to live for* what I believed. I said, "I dug deep…" *but really,* I think God, *through His Holy Spirit,* was the One doing the digging.

And He was mining for gold…

BORING, HUH?! Not anymore…*not for a minute!*

Thanks, Rhapsody! I love you, "Lovely!" Dad.

Chapter 23

Shhh! Wayne's Whistling!

I love whistling! I really do! I always have! *And I'm pretty good at it!* It has always tickled me pink trying to teach my grandchildren how to whistle and seeing them blow and blow until they *almost hyperventilate!* I can't really aptly instruct someone how to do it without *almost having to stick my fingers in their mouth* to properly shape and place their tongue! So consequently, most of my grandkids can't whistle!

That said, my enjoyment of whistling has virtually been a nuisance to everyone else, especially my kids! Not because I don't do it well – but *because I do it too much!* Unconsciously! Kind of like someone smacking chewing gum when he doesn't realize he's doing it and it's getting on everyone else's last nerve! That's right, I whistle when I don't even realize I'm doing it!

In fact, once on a flight to Seattle, Washington to board a cruise to Alaska, I was having such a grand and glorious day...whistling, as was typical for me in my usual good mood. Without any attempt to courteously greet us initially, this very rude and snarky traveler sitting in the seat just ahead of me snappily spun around and said to me with a not-so-polite tone of voice, "Hey, Buddy – would you please stop the whistling?! You're getting on my nerves!"

First of all, *I didn't realize I was whistling!* Second, I really thought he could have made his request of me in a more congenial manner! I was jolted – quite shocked really! *And I really didn't think* about sharing my bubbling faith in Jesus in that perturbing instance! *What I did think about was*…well, you *really* don't want to know. Let's just say that I suffered a momentary "lapse of faith" and felt carnally-inclined, for *just the flash* of a fleeting second, to say to him…well, use your imagination. Okay, okay, *I didn't do it* – I didn't want to be *totally* classless!

My children and I have always teased about *why* I whistle! *I say* it's because I'm happy! When I feel especially pleased with life and have a cozy sense of contentment and well-being, *I whistle!* Oh, and did I mention, I also rock to and fro, back and forth when I whistle? I don't know why – maybe because in the deepest seat of my emotional being, it reminds me of how Mom rocked me in her loving arms when I was a baby?! Maybe?

However, *my children* say that when I whistle and rock, it's for another reason…you know, a little "off my rocker," maybe?! Perhaps they are right… a little bit, at least; and at long last, their speculative theorizing has proven true! In any event, they have tolerated my whistling *most of their lives*. Not so infrequently, either one or the other would say to me, "Dad, would you please give us a break?" And I would say (with a rather dumbfounded look), "What?!" "Whistling, Dad! *Give us a break!* Would you please let it rest for a while?!" And I would concede, although reluctantly. I can't explain it –

"Dad, give us a break!"

when I feel good, I want to whistle! Feeling good and whistling just simply go well together, you know, like "peanut butter and chocolate, apple pie and ice cream, popcorn and butter" – some things simply fit well together! And *feeling good* and *whistling* really do! [By the way, you *ought to hear me* whistle the theme song to Andy Griffith!]

When I got sick…I *lost* my whistle. It left. It was gone. Not only had laughter and cheer forsaken me, but my whistle had as well! Even as I recount this story, I know *now* how *sorry for myself I felt then,* kind of like how Paul must have felt when he was telling Timothy some of his dearest friends had departed his company when the going got rough: "At my first answer no man stood with me, but all *men* forsook me: *I pray God* that it may not be laid to their charge" (II Tim. 4:16; KJV).

And the grief of it all was, I hadn't even realized my whistle was gone!

BUT my mother did! You know, no one knows a child like his loving mother. There is something instinctively wondrous about a mother's "intuition," her ability to "read" her child like a book. And as I've mentioned earlier, my mother could. In fact, she missed my whistle before I did! I don't really think my children ever minded that I had lost it – *the whistle itself, that is* – they *may* have been quite pleased, in fact! Smile.

I can't really say exactly when this happened, for as my health began to improve and when I no longer felt hopelessly lost, I stopped journaling. Especially after I had received *three personal encouragements* from the Lord Himself! I didn't stop making *mental notes,* per se, but I did stop writing down

my thoughts in a dated document. In any event, I'm fairly
confident this profoundly enlightening experience occurred
in the fall of that year when my entire family was visiting
with Mom and Dad in Macclesfield.

My dad was always good at catching, cleaning, then
cooking the fish he caught...remember? And if ever (rare as
it was) all of our family could arrange to visit together at

 Mom and Dad's home, all we had to do was call
and ask if Dad could "fry us up some fish tonight?!"
Absolutely nothing made Dad happier than to get
that call, thaw those freshly caught and frozen fish, heat
the grease, and start battering to get the show on the road!

We would all arrive just in time to help him carry those
golden brown, fresh-fried, speckled trout (or white perch,
crappie, brim…), hot fries, and tasty hush puppies from the
shop behind their house to Mom's set-to-eat table! Then we'd
all sit down and feast like kings! And have the most fun in
the world, laughing and cackling about the funniest stories
we could tell of things that had happened to each of us
in the past few days! Oh, how I miss those days! And that
scrumptious, delectable dining! Carolina's finest, right there
in the sweet homeplace where hundreds of memories were
made loving on our parents!

Then after the meal was over, the guys would usually
vacate...kind of deliberately...and let the girls clean up!
And when the kitchen was clean, we'd gather back in the
great room (once two rooms, den and living room), now
reconstructed into one since the housefire of 1989. We'd sit
and talk 'til our hearts were content, catching up on the latest
news, the most recent happenings in our kids' lives, and of

course, how Dad and Mom were managing our mother's declining health. Keep in mind, *all of us* knew how to carry on six or seven conversations at once, *and still know* what everybody else was saying! Smile.

This particular evening, we were all enjoying each other's company (while commiserating together that we had overeaten!), and we were all seated *anywhere* seats could be found...*or made.* Some on the furniture (or the arms of it), some in kitchen chairs brought into the great room, and many on the floor – some stretched out to alleviate the symptoms of "gastric distress." Still others *sitting up* on the floor, but leaning on the sofa or an armchair. And *it was noisy! Almost riotous and rowdy!* Chatter – chatter! Yap, yap, yap! Gossip – gossip! You would never enjoy better entertainment than what my family was enjoying that evening!

Then all of a sudden, my mother from her hospital bed, who we supposed *might not have even* been paying attention, abruptly interrupted everyone – with quite exertive and commanding assertiveness, I might add! *And everybody* (except me) *responded with the deadest silence:* "Shhh!" she said! "Listen! Listen! Wayne's whistling! Listen, ya'll... Wayne's whistling!" And sure enough, before I had even realized it myself, there I sat on the floor near Mom's bed whistling like a mockingbird!

> *"Shhh! Wayne's whistling!"*

All at once, everyone broke out in a spirited cheer, celebrating the return of my long-lost whistle! I, *not least among them,* was moved to tears to realize what was happening, and was merrily – no, *"chirpily"* – encouraged to grasp the implications of this most wonderful rediscovery!

I myself was charmed with the reawakening of that most vital and crucial "spark of life" rekindling in the recesses of my soul! To say the least, *even my children* were pleased that Dad's whistle was back...even though we all knew *I had to learn to keep it under control!* Smile!

I enjoy whistling, *especially now* that I have something so precious...*and priceless* to whistle about – my family, my friends, my faith...*and my life!*

You oughta' hear me whistle!

Chapter 24

A Somber, but Sacred Christmas

Christmas is a happy time…and a *sad time,* for some people…at certain intervals in their lives. Perhaps it's because the much-anticipated, long-awaited traditions of the holiday season imprint our memories so boldly that our family gatherings at Christmas can never be forgotten. Or, maybe it's because *everyone finally slows* down long enough to *think and reflect…and feel!* Or, maybe it's because every year when Christmas rolls 'round, someone whose company we enjoyed *last year* is now no longer with us.

In any event, the nostalgia of the season brings almost instant recall of yesteryear's recollections and experiences during these festive times. And while the bright lights, sparkling ornaments, and glittering tinsels dazzle the minds of youngsters happily anticipating Santa's arrival, for many adults, Christmas is a sad, somber time of year. It *can bring* melancholy and distress to people whose family dynamics have *dramatically changed* since prior years' family gatherings.

Christmas for *my family* was different that year in 2006. Mom was in her hospital bed, requiring of my father more attention and considerable care to meet the needs of her declining health. Her doctors' reports were not favorable as she was now living on 15 percent capacity of her rapidly failing kidneys. She had conceded to the installation of an AV fistula (arteriovenous)[106] for purposes of long-term dialysis (had she *needed* dialysis), but the fistula "had not taken." And she had stated quite emphatically that she *would not be interested or willing* to consider other options (peritoneal dialysis, port installation, etc.)…ever!

Of course, I had been sick, *quite sick,* since the month of May. And I suppose these variables had cast a *slightly shaded tone* of drear and dismal dampness on our spirits that particular Christmas season. We enjoyed the usual merriment we always did, yes, eating good holiday food and opening gifts together, and especially doting on Mom and Dad, my sister and I *both realizing* these later stages of our parents' lives were likely to be the most challenging yet.

But not until Mom asked me, well actually – *charged me with* – a particular appeal did I feel unusually moved that brooded Christmas night. From out of nowhere, it seemed to me, Mom up and asked, "Wayne, will you preach my funeral?" I really wasn't ready for that! Thinking of Mom's

---

[106] "AV Fistula Creation," *Azura Vascular Care,* 2017, 2020, sec. "What is an AV Fistula?" https://www.azuravascularcare.com/medical-services/dialysis-access-management/av-fistula-creation/ (accessed on February 27, 2020). "An AV fistula is a surgical connection made between an artery and a vein, created by a vascular specialist. An AV fistula is typically located in your arm, however, if necessary it can be placed in the leg. With an AV fistula, blood flows from the artery directly into the vein, increasing the blood pressure and amount of blood flow through the vein. The increased flow and pressure causes the veins to enlarge. The enlarged veins will be capable of delivering the amount of blood flow necessary to provide an adequate hemodialysis treatment. AV fistulas are the preferred vascular access for long-term dialysis because they last longer than any other dialysis access types, are less prone to infection and clotting, and can be relied upon for predictable performance."

passing during this stretch of my life, when rarely *any thought I had anymore* was even rational, wasn't really helpful for my recovery. It stoked emotion within me that I didn't want to feel. "Dear Lord," I thought, "I really don't want to deal with this right now!" I responded, "Mom, please don't ask me to do that." She briskly retorted, "But I don't want anyone but you to preach my funeral!" "Mom, please…" I pled. "Okay," she relented. "I won't ask you to promise to preach my funeral, but will you at least promise me *you will try…if you can?*" I realized how important this was to her, so as sincerely as I knew how, I conceded, "Okay, Mom, I promise that *when that time comes,* I'll at least *try.*" She was contented with the earnestness of my "compromised" concession.

…emotion *I didn't want to feel!*

I couldn't get that off my mind for the remainder of the evening. By the time everyone had loaded their cars with opened gifts and generous leftovers to carry home, I felt prompted to offer a devotion with our family before we all parted company. Everyone was obliged to settle down for just a few more moments for us to do that and to take the time to cherish the sacredness of the moment…and of the season.

I read the Christmas story from our favorite texts in Matthew and Luke (Mt. 1, 2; Lk. 2) with brief reference to Jesus' incarnation recorded in John's Gospel (Jn. 1). Then I sensed the Holy Spirit hovering over us as the soberness of dawning reality gripped each of us, and I spoke with the calmest assurance, purest peace, and the tenderest compassion for my family as I shared these words:

This has been a difficult year for our family in many ways. I myself despaired of my faith when it was tested as never before with my sudden sickness. We have all been concerned for Mom and her health needs as well as Dad's exhaustive and devoted care of her.

But we are so blessed to have a Savior who has given His life so that we can be together forever. I'm so grateful for all the members of our family who believe in Jesus and trust Him for their salvation and eternal life. I strongly urge everyone in this room to accept Jesus Christ as your personal Savior, because none of us knows when any one of us might leave this world and meet God to give account of ourselves before Him. In fact, it is entirely possible, perhaps even likely, that someone here tonight *might not be here next Christmas. Yours or mine may* be the empty seat in this house next year this time.

> When I finished speaking, most of us were moved deeply, some to tears.

I sensed we were ready for prayer. So, I led my family in prayer that evening – the "sinner's prayer," a prayer of comfort, and a prayer for grace. And greatly moved by the Holy Spirit, *yes, even during this time of my sickness and recovery,* I heard the Spirit of God praying through me "with groanings which cannot be uttered" (Rm. 8:26; NKJV, or "words and expressions that only the Holy

Spirit knew how to pray," *translation mine*).[107] We all wept together, and pledged ourselves to our love for Christ and our devotion to each other, but especially to our parents in this trying time in their lives.

Mom and I talked on the phone the next day. She said that Dad told her he had been profoundly touched by my words the previous evening and that he hadn't slept a wink all night long. That wasn't usual for my dad. Except for having trained himself to sleep "with one eye open" and an ear bent to Mom's beck and call when she might need him during the night, *he typically slept quite well* under most circumstances. She said he was particularly moved by the thought that one of us *might not be here* next Christmas.

Mom *wasn't there* the next Christmas. Perhaps Dad sensed in his own spirit that Mom would be leaving us…I don't know. But he was certainly sobered by the awe of the occasion and the presence of the Holy Spirit to comfort us with the thought of that pending possibility.

> Mom *wasn't there…*

I preached my mother's funeral the following year on Monday, October 1, 2007 just a few days after her 75th birthday. October 1 was *also* my brother's birthday – Ronnie would have been 56. On that day, I'm confident that Mom and her firstborn son were back together again and were very

---

[107] "26In the same way, the Spirit helps us in our weakness. We do not know what we ought to pray for, but the Spirit himself intercedes for us through wordless groans. 27And he who searches our hearts knows the mind of the Spirit, because the Spirit intercedes for God's people in accordance with the will of God" (Rm. 8:26, 27).

happy to see each other. And I was *so glad* I could answer Mom's request and *I didn't think twice* about it. I was honored to do it and believed she would have been pleased that I did.

I was glad that by then I was *well enough* to do it. Had Mom passed a year earlier, I would not have been. God knew this in advance and readied me for it. I was getting well…gradually, but nevertheless…*getting well.*

Even under the most somber of circumstances.

Chapter 25

Break of Spring

As time passed, the antidepressant began to arrest my symptoms and adjust my chemistry. I completely weaned off the Ativan, quartering down my dosages until there was so little of it, it hardly mattered. As my sleep continued to improve, my glaring, "glassy eyes" restored to their normal, hazel color my Mom used to say looked as pretty as a girl's (she wanted one when I was born, remember?). The gaunt look in my ashen face faded away as my appetite returned and I began to gain weight.

Dr. Ribeiro had concisely described to me how the medication should work, and it was following an almost "prescribed" and predictable path of temperance and adjustment in my body, exactly to the tee. Not *every day* was a good day, but now past Christmas into 2007, there were more *good days back-to-back* than there were bad. That was so encouraging and confidence-building!

About a month before the coming of spring, I received an especially uplifting phone call from my dear friend, Dr. Franklin Hunt. Dr. Hunt is a double-doctorate scholar in counseling and therapy, a peer minister friend of mine, *a mentor and model* whom I highly respect. He was deeply moved by the Holy Spirit as he spoke with me, "Pastor Flora, I have been in prayer for you for the last three days, and today, the Lord gave me a personal word of hope for you!" I listened intently, eagerly anticipating what Dr. Hunt would say. I had never known him to *ever* *"miss it"* when the Lord gave him a word of prophetic hope. He went on to share, "The Lord has instructed me to tell you this sickness will all be a memory come 'break of spring.' On the first day of spring, you will receive assurance that the Lord has touched and healed you, and that the future before you is bright and hopeful."

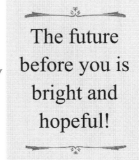

The future before you is bright and hopeful!

I was so moved by Dr. Hunt's words that I came to tears and thanked him so graciously for loving me enough to spend such quality time before the Lord interceding in my behalf. It mattered tremendously to me that people who knew me so well and loved me so much would care to ask God for His favor in my life. He prayed for me over the phone, and we worshiped together. The sense of God's presence was awesome and overwhelming! I was truly convinced this was a miraculous moment in my life and that the word from the Lord I just heard was authentic and accurate! How compelling and impressive God's love for me must be for Him to convey such hope through someone I trusted and respected so highly!

I struggled less and less each day, *it seemed*, as the end of winter (How ironic and symbolic is this?!) brought us closer and closer to the break of spring! Certainly, with confident expectation, I awaited that day – March 20 of 2007. And just as Dr. Hunt had prophesied to me, it happened exactly as he said! By the first day of spring, I was worshipful and ready!

I made a day of quality time with the Lord and loved on Him generously, thanking Him for seeing me through the darkest days of my entire life! Yes, I worshiped...*and wept*, grateful to the Lord for not forgetting me and not forsaking me during those dismal days of torment and horror! I celebrated His presence as I had many times in my distant past, *long before I ever realized* how incredibly precious He really is to me and my family!

I had learned through this whole, harrowing experience

"Fearfully and wonderfully made!"

(Ps. 139:14)

how "fearfully and wonderfully made" (Ps. 139:14; KJV)[108] I really was and *how delicate a creature* my mortal being is. I had been through the "fires of hell," – *and back, in a sense* – and I was glad to have returned... all in one piece, but new – *re-newed*, actually, into "another vessel that seemed appropriate to him" (Jer. 18:4; ISV).[109]

I will share in the close of this book the lessons I learned from this most traumatic and trying season of my life and ministry. But for now, may it suffice to say, I was relieved to be out of that *"deep, dark, black hole."*

---

[108] "**14**I will praise thee; for I am fearfully and wonderfully made: marvellous are thy works; and that my soul knoweth right well" (Ps. 139:14; KJV).
[109] *The Holy Bible, International Standard Version,* (Bellflower, CA: Davidson Press, LLC, 1996-2010). "**4**But the vessel he was working on with the clay was ruined in the potter's hand. So he remade it into another vessel that seemed appropriate to him" (Jer. 18:4; ISV).

Chapter 26

Life Lessons Learned

The questions remain after all this heartache, "Did I learn something? Was I listening? Did I really pay attention? Am I *truly* a better person now? Are there 'life lessons' I can carry with me the rest of my days? *Better still,* is there *any counsel* I can share with you *to help you through* your life experience right now?"

I believe so. But first of all, let me say that *my wife says* I'm a better person – she's lived with me almost 45 years – she should really know! And family and friends who *know me best* and *love me most* say the same thing. So, yes…I *guess* it must be so!

Beyond that, however, there *truly are* some invaluable lessons I have learned that I *could not* have learned any other way! They didn't happen in educational venues, classroom settings, seminar sessions, *nor even* the transformative engagements of one-on-one mentoring. And I've had lots of exposure in these areas. They only came through the crucible of suffering, the "purging" of pain, the agony of angst – indeed, the seasoned "proving" of personal faith!

How appropriate is that after all?! For Peter says, "These trials will show that your faith is genuine. It is being tested as fire tests and purifies gold – though your faith is far more precious than mere gold. So when your faith remains strong through many trials, it will bring you much praise and glory and honor on the day when Jesus Christ is revealed to the whole world" (I Pet. 1:7; NLT).

I would like to cite for you some of the most significant life lessons I've learned from this "deep, dark, black hole" experience.

• Lesson #1: God truly is faithful!

Not at all that He *ever wasn't!* However, more now than ever, I *realize it!* I am soundly convinced of the faithfulness of God in my life! I have greater confidence in His love for me and His purposes for me than I ever had *before* I suffered my health crisis. Why shouldn't I? He proved Himself to me, didn't He? And He was *very personal with me* when I needed Him most – His "voice" to my heart was *and is* crystal clear. I cannot mistake His voice for another's. His love for me is overwhelming, and truly, His "mercies endure forever" (Ps. 136).[110] James' words in *The Message* concerning God's faithfulness read like this: "There is nothing deceitful in God, nothing two-faced, nothing fickle" ['no change nor slightest hint of change' – *translation mine*] (Jms. 1:17).

REMEMBER, HE IS ALWAYS WITH US, EVEN
"TO THE VERY END OF THE AGE" (MT. 28:20).

---

[110] *The Holy Bible, New King James Version* (Nashville, Tennessee: Thomas Nelson Publishers, 1982). You simply must read Psalm 136 for yourself as *every single verse* repeats this phrase. This is likely a worship song that was sung with a choral refrain repeated by the congregation, emphasizing the covenantal love of God for His people.

- **Lesson #2: Authentic, heartfelt empathy for suffering humanity matters!**

I *only thought* I "cared" for others before I suffered; I sincerely *do care* now! God used the crisis of suffering to enhance my empathy for others' pain.[111] However, the depth of my emotions *now* for human suffering is almost *surrogate… substitutionary.* It's as if I can sense the pain of

> *I've always been a sentimental and deeply emotional person, as earlier stated.*

others "vicariously" and *feel with them* as they hurt. How appropriate this is as the word for "sympathy" in the New Testament means "to feel with." This is so Scriptural, because Paul says we should, "Rejoice with those who rejoice, and weep with those who weep" (Rm. 12:15; NKJV).[112]

- **Lesson #3: Family and friends are integral to one's health and well-being!**

I am so grateful for family and friends. Maybe it's my age…do you reckon, that I am so sentimental about family now? Or, is it simply that one's quality of life actually *increases in value* once "tried by fire" and purified as gold?! But this is especially true when family members *place a*

---

[111] "³Praise be to the God and Father of our Lord Jesus Christ, the Father of compassion and the God of all comfort, ⁴who comforts us in all our troubles, so that we can comfort those in any trouble with the comfort we ourselves receive from God" (II Cor. 1:3, 4).

[112] James Strong, "4834 – sumpatheo," *Strong's Exhaustive Concordance of the Bible* (Nashville, Tennessee: Abingdon Press, 1890). The New Testament's use of the word "sumpatheo" (sympathy) means "to feel *with.*" In the English language, "empathy" carries more this concept of "feeling *with,*" while "sympathy" implies more a "feeling sorry *for.*"

premium on quality of life, and extend authentic care and tireless support to the hurting member of a nuclear family!

I am convinced I would not have survived without a loving wife, caring children, and real friends! "One who has unreliable friends soon comes to ruin, but there is a friend who sticks closer than a brother" (Prov. 18:24). Do you remember the "good wife, favor of the Lord?" It's worth mentioning again: "11Her

"A friend loves at all times, and a brother is born for a time of adversity" (Prov. 17:17).

husband has full confidence in her and lacks nothing of value. 12She brings him good, not harm, all the days of her life" (Prov. 31:11, 12).

I dare not say one cannot survive anxiety disorder *without* a strong support team of family and friends, but the prospects are certainly much greater when they are compassionately and attentively present to the situation. This is implicitly understood in Solomon's words here in Prov. 18:14; NLT: "The human spirit can endure a sick body, but who can bear a crushed spirit?" Who is there to heal the wounds of the broken spirit *if not* caring family and friends?

- **Lesson #4: Passion is important!**

Do you know how passion comes? Suffering. Its root derivative is "passio" which means "suffering."[113] It is often used to refer to the sufferings of Christ between His last supper with His disciples and His death on the cross. I have

---

[113] "Passion," *Merriam-Webster Dictionary,* 1828, 2020, https://www.merriam-webster.com/dictionary/passion#h1 (accessed on March 13, 2020). "Middle English, from Anglo-French, from Late Latin *passion-, passio* suffering, being acted upon, from Latin *pati* to suffer."

learned that the "energy," the driving force behind my zeal
for and love of life as well as my focus and effectiveness in
ministry *comes from passion.* Before my suffering, I was too
"perfunctory," too mechanical, too "ivory tower." But since
I recovered from my health crisis, *everything I say and do
is passionate!* I no longer waste words…or time – mine or
anybody else's. Life is too short to waste, especially now
that I know its value. I feel deeply, speak passionately, and
serve ardently.

- **Lesson #5: I am frail and I need help!**

I repeat what I confessed to my church the day I tearfully
besought their prayers: "I'm not as strong as I thought I was.
I'm not as good as I thought I was. And I'm certainly not as
spiritual as I thought I was." Point blank. That was *never* a
confession I would have made had I not suffered as I did. I
was not ready nor willing to admit this *until I was shown to be
the weakened human being I truly was!*

Was that easy for me? No. Was it good for me?

Of course, it was. Until I realized my humanity and its
flagrant limitations, I smugly asserted myself (perhaps,
"inserted") into the equation of piety and pretentiousness,
supposing myself to be someone I wasn't – *God saw through
that* and *took the reins!*

Now then, I fault no one for my health crisis *but me…if
anyone* is to be faulted. Certainly not the beloved church I
pastored, the denomination I serve, the peer ministers and
leaders I love, nor the medical professionals who guided me
through this egregious "dark alley" back into "the light" of

health and well-being. Admitting my weaknesses "has made me strong!"[114] It was not until I admitted I needed help that I found grace! ["Now, think about that, Grandpa!" to quote my 4-year-old grandson, Caleb, again!] I now have a "Flora translation" of II Cor. 12:9[115] – it is this: "God can do the *most for me* when I can do *the least for myself."* How incredibly true is that?!

- **Lesson #6: Consequently, it's okay to ask for help![116]**

This may be the toughest lesson of all! Not asking for help... how sad, for help is available. Maybe too many of us suffer needlessly because we are too prideful (or stubborn) to ask for help. Or maybe we simply don't know *what to ask* or *who to ask* to find the right answers. I hope the resources cited at the end of this book or *even this story of my health crisis* can point you in the right direction.

I believe that God took me *this route* through the "minefields of life" rather than "the long way around." I'm grateful He did. But *your route* may be different than mine. Why? Because *every situation* is different, and each person's health crisis may require different forms of treatment.

That said, it is time for me to make a bold statement about the importance of asking for help. Hear me out and ponder my rationale. I need to be absolutely clear stating

---

[114] "[10]That is why, for Christ's sake, I delight in weaknesses, in insults, in hardships, in persecutions, in difficulties. For when I am weak, then I am strong" (II Cor. 12:10).

[115] "[9]But he said to me, 'My grace is sufficient for you, for my power is made perfect in weakness.' Therefore I will boast all the more gladly about my weaknesses, so that Christ's power may rest on me" (II Cor. 12:9).

[116] "[2c]You do not have because you do not ask God" (Jms. 4:2c).

that *some persons* needing help may require *psychological or psychiatric* attention and treatment. *For you in your situation,* that may be exactly what you need and, if so, that is absolutely appropriate! Please understand your medical professionals are servants in the hands of God! Keep in mind that the only Gentile writer in the Bible ("Dr. Luke") was a caring, conscientious physician! That is a significant notation the Lord wants you to remember!

Just because *I was stigmatized by my own self-image* does not mean that I did not need or should not have sought psychiatric attention. Given my own unique circumstances, I just didn't feel I could have…*or it may have* worsened my situation. Remember, after all…I wasn't thinking clearly anyway!

Are these *all* the life lessons I learned? No, but these are the most *prominent ones*…the ones that *I feel* sharing with you would be helpful to your recovery, or perhaps, the recovery of someone you love. Understanding these *settled* truths (actually, *"crisis-sifted"* truths) can help you take *a shorter route home than I did*…maybe.

No need getting lost in the woods with Hansel and Gretel, is it? Or showing up at the home of Little Red Riding Hood's grandmother, if you mustn't? Right? The breadcrumb trail can be hard to follow coming out…if the birds haven't eaten it.

Better still…*stay out of the woods,* if you can. Smile.

Chapter 27

A Good Wife, Favor of the Lord

There were plenty of times she could have...you know, shoved me off the mountain – over the cliff -- and collected life insurance, around a half million dollars in several policies *at that time* (mostly term). No one had known better. We were way past the typical "suicide exclusionary windows" that most life insurance policies require, and no questions would have been asked whatsoever. Had she been *that kind of person,* or had we *truly not loved each other* and *had faith in Jesus Christ* when this onset of major health concerns happened, that might have been the end of this story. And *had that happened,* I would not be sharing it with you because the conclusion of it would have been entirely different.

The Bible says, "He who finds a wife finds what is good and receives favor from the Lord" (Prov. 18:22). I especially like the *New Living Translation* of this passage: "The man who finds a wife finds a treasure, and he receives favor from the LORD."[117] "Treasure" – I like that word. Not that I ever imagined *I would be* a rich person, especially having accepted

---

[117] *The Holy Bible, New Living Translation* (Carol Stream, Illinois: Tyndale House Publishers, Inc., 1996, 2004, 2015).

the call of God upon my life as a young person and spent the whole of my life answering that calling. But simply that I have learned that "treasure" is not *what you have*, but *who you have!* I have much treasure...lots!

In fact, Solomon, the next wisest man who ever lived (second only to Jesus), said these words, and I would like to share the most of it here: "¹⁰Who can find a virtuous and capable wife? She is more precious than rubies. ¹¹Her husband can trust her, and she will greatly enrich his life. ¹²She brings him good, not harm, all the days of her life" (Prov. 31:10-12; NLT). Did you notice that? "...can trust her." The *King James Version* says, "...*safely* trust in her." Safety – how important *was that to me* in this most desperate time of my life?! Did you see what else? "She will greatly *enrich his life!*" Wow! Looking back now, it's hard to imagine we went through what we did...and survived.

BUT IT WAS BECAUSE I WAS "WEALTHY" – I *HAD* A GOOD WIFE!

Proverbs 31 goes on to say, "²⁵She is clothed with strength and dignity; she can laugh at the days to come. ²⁶She speaks with wisdom, and faithful instruction is on her tongue. ²⁷She watches over the affairs of her household and does not eat the bread of idleness. ²⁸Her children arise and call her blessed; her husband also, and he praises her: '²⁹Many women do noble things, but you surpass them all.' ³⁰Charm is deceptive, and beauty is fleeting; but a woman who fears the Lord is to be praised. ³¹Honor her for all that her hands have done, and let her works bring her praise at the city gate" (25-31).

Should I need to expound every aspect of this text? Or does it speak quite clearly for itself? "Faithful instruction is on her tongue" (26). My dear friend, King James says, "…in her tongue is the *law of kindness.*" That describes my wife, Lou. There really should be a picture of her right beside the opening of this most beautiful passage in the Proverbs! In my mind, her photo *is there!*

Lou sometimes thought she was wearying me to constantly repeat these ten words over and over and over: *"It's okay, Honey! Everything is going to be all right!"* I heard them lots – they weren't trite platitudes and put-offs – they were *sincere expressions of faith!* Because my wife *has such* faith and *truly believed* that somehow, someway, *some day* – everything REALLY was going to be all right…

she confidently trusted God for that ultimate outcome! And I would ask her to please say it to me again!

"Honey, please say it again! I need to hear it *one more time!*"

Hey, this is the girl I married when we were both 18 years of age. You heard me – 18! And barely more than four years prior to that, *right before* I gave my heart to Jesus, she had told her best friend, Judy Baker, during recess one day, "You see that guy out there on second base?" "Yeah," Judy said. "I'm going to marry him," Lou insisted. "No, you're not!" Judy retorted. "Yes, I am!" she confidently replied. That was before I even got saved and ever dared to look her way! I have to tell you, when Lou gets a word from the Lord, you can pretty much "take it to the bank." It's already been deposited in God's storehouse of divine intention!

Lou has great faith, and she exercised it during one of the longest, toughest stretches of her entire life! Nothing has (yet) challenged the intensity and severity of it...*before or since*. She lives by it all the time! I'm glad she does, because except for Jesus, *nobody knows me* like my wife does. And *still, she loves me!* If she ever *had to prove to me* (which she doesn't) that she loved me, she already has.

Now approaching 45 years of wedded bliss on July 31 (well, *maybe* a *tiny tad* of exaggeration about the "bliss" thing), we have enjoyed one of the most wholesome, healthy, endearing, and devoted marriage relationships we have ever witnessed or known. Our parents' model marriages gave us good reason to hope *our marriage* could be healthy as well (her parents, 49 years and my parents, 57).

I will say – without any disparagement *whatsoever* toward anyone who feels differently – we agreed when we married that the words, "I do...until death do us part" were binding before the God of all creation, and we meant it! We *never viewed* Christian marriage as a contract, but *as a covenant!*[118]

---

[118] Gerard Van Groningen, "Covenant," *Baker's Evangelical Dictionary of Biblical Theology,* ed. Walter A. Elwell, 1996, para. 6, https://www.biblestudytools.com/dictionary/covenant/ (accessed on February 21, 2020). It is my understanding that the *primary* distinction between a contract and a covenant is that a contract is bilateral, but a covenant is *unilateral.* That is, when God covenanted with man, *He set the terms,* and never withdraws His commitment to it. As Groningen states, "Persons are recipients, not contributors; they are not expected to offer elements to the bond; they are called to accept it as offered, to keep it as demanded, and to receive the results that God, by oath, assures will not be withheld." In other words, God *never walks away* from His "part of the bargain." He *intends* for marriage to be unilaterally binding in this same way – each party committing himself/herself *before God...to the other* with no intentions of default...ever!

We also agreed that the word "divorce" should never be a topic of conversation concerning *our* marriage relationship. Please understand these are *our personal sentiments!*

We both concur that there is a quality of love that *no couple can know* until they've lived together many years as companion friends, true lovers, *beyond* the typical short-lived charade that *our culture* calls "marriage." I say with as sincerest regard as I can muster and as modicum of flippancy as I possibly can that *Elizabeth Taylor never experienced this kind of love!* No denigrating disrespect intended. It is simply a fact of matter that *no one lives long enough* to experience THIS kind of commitment but *a few times, at most* – and only *once, at least!* You are blessed – and rich – if *you have found* a wife like mine! I feel *I am truly* the blessed one!

Statistics prove (and they *don't lie!*) that "75% of couples dealing with chronic disease *end in divorce.*"[119] That saddens me immensely. This suggests that *after having said, "I do,"* many companions part company when they *actually need each other most!* What kind of culture does that give our world? What kind of values does that give our kids? And perhaps the crucial question is, "What kind of impact does this have on the mental-emotional health of one or both parties?" And does that "pass along?" Does it "convey" into the *next relationship?* It *certainly has the potential* to affect it, at the least, no doubt about it!

> **75% of couples dealing with chronic disease *end in divorce.***

---

[119] Alexandra Sifferlin, "Divorce More Likely When Wife Falls Ill," *Time,* May 1, 2014, para. 3, https://time.com/83486/divorce-is-more-likely-if-the-wife-not-the-husband-gets-sick/ (accessed on February 14, 2020).

Don't mistake me – I'm not merciless and I'm glad for "second chances" – but *no one ever* "gets a second chance to make a *first impression…*" Ever! I was taught in seminary (1979-1983) by Dr. Robert Crick, Director of Field Ministries for the Church of God School of Theology at that time (Pentecostal Theological Seminary now), that *by the time* his students would enter ministry as full-time pastors, 75% of their local churches *would have been* touched by the pangs of separation, divorce, and remarriage. He was well-informed and quite "on the mark" with the churches *I pastored*. So, I have celebrated with my congregations the great grace God gave many to "start all over again," their much appreciated "second chance." I pastored many wonderful *and happy* blended families. I am grateful for that! But I continued to preach the sanctity of marriage (as my *congregations expected)* and what *God's ideals were* concerning the nature of covenantal relationship between a husband and his wife.

Lou and I are thankful for our parents' models, our mentors' training, and our pastors' teachings. What we learned from the Scriptures about "hanging tight in tough times" helped to get us through one of the toughest we have ever experienced!

I could write another whole book *just about her!* Perhaps, I shall! But until I do, I need to hear her *continue saying to me,* "It's okay, Honey! Everything is going to be all right!"

> I can't really say enough about Lou.

Let me close this chapter of my admiration for my dearest friend in the whole world by restating what Solomon had to say *about my lovely wife, Lou.*

[INSERT PHOTO HERE...*OF LOU*. SMILE!] "[28]Her children arise and call her blessed; her husband also, and he praises her: [29]'Many women do noble things, but you surpass them all.' [30]Charm is deceptive, and beauty is fleeting; but a woman who fears the Lord is to be praised. [31]Honor her for all that her hands have done, and let her works bring her praise at the city gate" (Prov. 31:28-31).

I do call her "blessed," and *I do "praise her,"* for "a woman who fears the Lord is to be praised."

I love you, Lou! When you told me *then,* "Everything is going to be all right," I believed you...

And *I still do!*

Chapter 28

Closer Than a Brother

So, *how did* I survive?! I suppose you're asking this question. Obviously, *I did survive* – here I am writing this book…and here *you are* reading it – needing it, *perhaps* – asking, "How possibly did he make it?! How possibly *could he?"* Yeah, I asked the same questions too. Over and over. It was terribly dark in that black, thickened forest; that low, dense fog, *smog, actually;* that "deep, dark, black hole." I was bound to hit a mountain, wasn't I? Or a tall building, maybe? I had to "bottom out" at some point and hit rock bottom *eventually,* right?!

I did. I crash-landed…*but I didn't burn.* I wasn't destroyed![120] Whew! I'm relieved. Are you? I *hope* you are. I mean, after all, the first chapters of this book have been a bit spine-tingling, hair-raising, *really terrifying…even for me,* just recalling it, just talking about it. But *I can now*…talk about it. It doesn't hurt anymore. I don't feel the pain. I've been healed…in so many ways.

---

[120] "**7**But we have this treasure in jars of clay to show that this all-surpassing power is from God and not from us. **8**We are hard pressed on every side, but not crushed; perplexed, but not in despair; **9**persecuted, but not abandoned; struck down, but not destroyed" (II Cor. 4:7-9).

Proof Of Healing
1) Trace it.
2) Face it.
3) Erase it.
4) Replace it.

Dr. Hunt, whom I previously mentioned, offered me this original insight: "Human beings can help you: 1) trace it, and 2) face it – *but only Jesus can:* 3) *erase it,* and 4) *replace it!*" Wow! That's powerful! Think about it! *Only when* you can rub the wound and it doesn't hurt anymore can you know *for sure* you have truly been healed…*then you can talk about it.* That's why I'm writing this book, because I can now "rub the wound," and it doesn't hurt anymore!

But how did I make it? Family. Friends. Faith. That's how. *That's it?!* Yes, that's it! I don't mean it was easy – *it wasn't.* I don't mean it happened overnight – *it didn't.* I *didn't* bounce back…you *may* not either. But I made it, *and you will too!* But you need these: family, friends, faith[121]…*that's so important* to your complete recovery. *You must have them!* And for purposes of *my story,* I'm speaking of faith in Jesus Christ, the one and only Son of the living God. The God of the Bible, His Word and His inspired revelation of Jesus Christ to the world![122]

---

[121] My daughter asked why I wouldn't list my faith as *first.* The reason is because when it "lapsed," my *family and friends* were there to help restore it.
[122] "¹⁶For God so loved the world that he gave his one and only Son, that whoever believes in him shall not perish but have eternal life" (Jn. 3:16). Note: The word "inspiration" means "God-breathed." I say that inspiration is "the superintendency of the Holy Spirit over the sacred authors so that what they wrote *in the original documents* was *without error* and *was not* in violation of their own free wills" (tacit). This is the conservative Christian's understanding of "inspiration of the Holy Scriptures." Not just goose bumps, good feelings, and *certainly not* good luck – but *authentic, actual, and effective* faith in Jesus Christ! This is *my story,* so I declare to you what *my testimony is* without debate. That's my final answer! And I stand by it! Smile! After all, *personal faith* isn't personal UNLESS it's *personal,* is it?! Mine is!

I'm blessed. *I had all three of these...*family, friends, faith. And they were ALL tested, yes, believe me – all! Family, friends, faith – *"tried in the fire"*[123] *even,* and found to be true-blue faithful, loyal, and reliable. Remember my Associate Pastor, Glenn Nichols? He was *one of* my many friends. The Bible says that, "a man that hath friends must shew himself friendly: and there is a friend that sticketh closer than a brother" (Prov. 18:24; KJV). Yes, *I do have many,* for I am (or *consider* myself to be) a friendly person by nature. But I suspect I could count on one hand – *maybe two –* the friends who would go to bat for me, stand in harm's way, shield me from destruction, *even if* their own life depended on it. Glenn would... *and did.*

Really good friends are really, really rare!

Early in the development of my traumatic health crisis, Glenn and I were sitting in my office one day, and as usual, *I was commiserating!* He was listening...*intently,* like good friends do. He was so casual, so calm, "cool as a cucumber," as they say. When the timing was right, he spoke his turn and said, "Pastor, I know exactly what you're going through. My oldest daughter, Mandy, is experiencing the same." I couldn't believe it. Really? Someone that young? He went on to detail

---

Thayer, 287, 524, "theopneustos" ("theo" – God; "pneustos" – breath) is used in II Tim. 3:16 to explain how the Scriptures were revealed to humankind. And by the way, *there are plenty* of *historical and exegetically reliable* studies on this word to substantiate the Scriptures' internal witness for its claim of Holy Spirit inspiration.

[123] "7That the trial of your faith, being much more precious than of gold that perisheth, though it be tried with fire, might be found unto praise and honour and glory at the appearing of Jesus Christ..." (I Pet. 1:7; KJV).

for me what he and his family had been experiencing with *her health challenges*. And I was amazed to hear how *similar they were* to mine.

Not only was she on antidepressant medication, as was I, but it was causing her to *lose her hair*, most of it. That was distressing enough, all to itself, especially for a young woman 18 years of age. Imagine the image issues she likely experienced among her friends in high school, let alone *the chemical issues* happening inside her body. And I couldn't understand what I was experiencing?! How incredibly empathetic *I now felt* for Mandy, Glenn and Sheryl's oldest of two beautiful daughters (Candice is their youngest)!

From that very day, Glenn became my closest peer confidant, and Mandy and I became "best buddies!" So amazing! I could talk to Mandy for hours on the phone (we often did), and she could comfort me as no other friend could. She understood. She identified. Her words made sense to me, and her encouragements spoke hope to my spirit. She was so mature, even at that age, and knew just what to say to cheer my heart and give me courage. I highly suspect there were days I "wore her out," and she probably wished I would give her a break, but she never said so.

Then there was Charles…Charles Brown, Glenn's brother-in-law, Sheryl's big brother. He had experienced the same and "beat the odds." Go figure – same family – *genetics, maybe?!* Charles was about my age, employed in management at his family's business. And was he *so patient* with me?! I kept his cell phone hot, probably discharged, but he never refused my call. And I called him lots. He was, yet again, only one of a *very few persons* who wasn't "anxious" talking with me (how ironic to say that!). It was quite "old shoe" to him, and his reassurances were inspirational and comforting. I'm saddened to say that Charles has since passed away, in fact, shortly after my recovery, but I know the Lord is commending him for having been my friend through the darkest days of my life, and I know he is being rewarded for his kindness to me.

Kay Walston was another caring person who reached out and offered hope. She is my wife's cousin-in-law, very involved in ministry in our home church in Pinetops. She had suffered anxiety disorder and struggled desperately through some of the same types of vexing exasperations I was dealing with. She lent a listening ear…and a caring heart. Kay's a deep-tanned "farm girl" who can drive any of the dozens of tractors and combines they own to do some serious farming. And *they are quite serious* about it – I'm humored to mention the sign on their equipment shelters that warns vandals not to approach: "Trespassers will be shot; survivors will be shot again!" I'd keep my distance, if I were you! Although her family's big farms demanded hard work and long days disking, plowing, planting, cultivating, and harvesting, Kay always made time for me!

Thank you, Glenn…Mandy, Charles, and Kay! And thank you, Ruth Craig, for your weekly cards – they spoke volumes. Ruth, one of my most supportive parishioners, is a home health nurse, the best. And whether she has ever experienced personal health issues like mine, I cannot say. *But* she is certainly one of the most empathetic caregivers I've ever known!

Thank you, Sandra Lee, for your cards as well. Sandra was Linda Byrum's mother. I was Linda's pastor, and she and her husband, Henry, were very concerned for me. Her mother had suffered as I, and Linda kept her informed of my status all the way through my sickness until recovery. Based upon Linda's weekly reports, Sandra made sure each card was the personal touch the Holy Spirit wanted for me that very week. They were like "text messages from heaven," and I looked forward to them. They spoke. They mattered.

The Bible says that "[4]we can comfort those in any trouble with the comfort we ourselves receive from God. [5]For just as we share abundantly in the sufferings of Christ, so also our comfort abounds through Christ" (II Cor. 1:4, 5). Rendered another way, the text reads: "[3]the God of all comfort; [4]Who comforteth us in all our tribulation, that we may be able to comfort them which are in any trouble, by the comfort wherewith we ourselves are comforted of God" (3, 4; KJV). It really makes sense, doesn't it, that *only those* who have experienced *what we have* even *understand how to* help us feel better? I comprehend this now, more than ever.

Everyone cared, yes, but not everyone knew what to say. Consequently, some were hesitant to say anything at all. It was awkward when they tried, and I knew it was. But sometimes, when there is nothing to be said, "presence" is enough. It means so much to know they cared. I *really didn't* expect anything but prayer(s). And they offered them, regularly and generously.

I was grateful…just for the prayers. After all, I didn't *really* want to see *anyone, anyway.* Remember? Smile.

·　·　·　·　·　●　·　·　·　·　·

Chapter 29

My Wife's Reflections

Yep, I know you can't believe it, but my husband, Wayne, transferred his quill to me for this chapter. And, although I have never considered myself to be a good writer (like my husband), the words that follow are *actually mine,* his wife…Lou.

If you are reading *this* chapter, you have most likely read all the previous ones as well. And yes, we *both* did survive this challenging time in our lives – by God's grace and mercy, of course.

Do I remember May 17, 2006? Yes, indeed I do! And I always will! As I slept that night, I had absolutely no idea what I would face the next day and in the many months to follow. What I did know, however, was that overnight something drastic happened to my husband. His behavior, demeanor, and nature had radically changed, and I didn't understand why!

What was I going to do? How could I help him? I was alarmed, frightened, and needless to say, *worried and anxious* about our future. I felt alone, with no one to talk to or confide in. Had anyone else ever experienced this? How would I handle what was happening? Actually, what *was* happening?

How long was this going to last? Could I even survive what might lie ahead? I felt lost and abandoned!

> **I did the only thing I knew to do – ask God for His help. I needed His wisdom, guidance, understanding, and patience. I had to believe there was a light at the end of this tunnel, and therefore, I knew I could never give up or lose hope. I had to be strong for the man I loved, the one God gave me, the one to whom I said, "I will love you...*in sickness and in health!*"**

So, in the many days, weeks, even months ahead, I made my best effort to be *tender, compassionate and understanding*. I became a very *good listener*...letting Wayne express his feelings to me whenever and however he wished. And many times, it was the same thing I had heard before – that's where the "patience" came in. I couldn't say, "Wayne, I've already heard that, please quit repeating yourself." That would have been devastating and would have discouraged him further. I had to keep positive. And if need be, give him the same affirming, uplifting words in each response. (After all, He said he never got tired of hearing them anyway.)

I believe my husband has the "gift of encouragement," you know, always having just the right words to say to someone in *their time* of crisis. Saying the right things that lift others up when *they feel* dejected or hopeless. But now, the tide had turned a bit. I was the one *giving him* words of encouragement instead. I struggled, but God always helped me *remain positive and reassuring*, giving him confidence that things would eventually get better. We just had to put our trust in God and believe!

I needed to be encouraged during this season in our lives too, but for the first time, Wayne could not offer that to me – ONLY GOD COULD! And He did! All it took for *me* was a word from *Him*! If I knew God said it, I pondered it in my heart and had faith it would happen just as He said. That's all I needed to continue on from day to day…*day after day.* The words God spoke to us (cited in previous chapters) were, indeed, our hope and expectation of a brighter future. And He kept His word! This was all we needed to get us to the end of this long tunnel of darkness and out of this "deep, dark, black hole!" His grace truly was *and is* sufficient!

The only way anyone could *really understand* our journey, *feel* what we felt, or *hurt* as we hurt would be to *experience* what *we experienced.* But I *would not* wish that upon anyone! *I can say,* however, we know this happened *to us* for a reason. This crisis made us more empathetic, compassionate, and supportive toward others who *have suffered or are* suffering this kind of emotional breakdown.

My prayer is that the honest, gut-wrenching, transparent words in this book will speak to your heart and help you realize *you* are NOT alone. I pray that it will give you the assurance you need to "see the end of your tunnel," and *most importantly,* introduce you to the One who can *bring you through* this unpleasant time in your life and give you hope and a future – His name is Jesus Christ!

Chapter 30

Invitation to Eternal Life

Suffering of any sort is *never easy*...for anyone. It is my opinion that it is *even more difficult* for persons who *may not* have family, friends, *and faith,* as did I. I feel sincerest compassion for you if that is your situation.

However, I want you to know *that you* are a beautiful person, created by a loving God in His own image and likeness. And He loves you *so much* that He sent His Son, Jesus Christ, to die on the cross to pay for your sins and to give you the gift of everlasting life![124] It is God's wish for you to know Him personally and to enjoy being with Him and those you love forever!

He has a perfect plan for your life – "plans to prosper you and not to harm you, plans to give you hope and a future" (Jer. 29:11). You really ought to meet your Maker in the loving way He *always desired...personally!* And once you do, you will begin to understand your purpose in life and know what the "Inventor's" intentions for your life really are!

---

[124] "[16]For God so loved the world, that he gave his only begotten Son, that whosoever believeth in him should not perish, but have everlasting life. [17]For God sent not his Son into the world to condemn the world; but that the world through him might be saved" (Jn. 3:16, 17; KJV).

So there, you've tried just about everything else – and you are *still hurting!* Why not try Jesus?! He loves you immensely and wants you to know Him as the wonderful Savior and *really good friend* He truly is!

Let's not make it complicated…*little children* know Jesus! And He said we must become "as a little child"[125] (simply believing and accepting Jesus) to enter the kingdom of heaven.

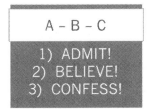

How? Easily! As easy as A-B-C!

Admit. Admit you are a sinner… don't be prudish and pious about the obvious! That keeps so many people away from a loving Savior. Just acknowledge that you need Jesus to forgive you of your sins. He's waiting…*so do it now.*[126]

Believe. Believe Jesus loves you, that He is God's Son and *can save you…*and *He graciously will!* All you have to do is ask![127] Invite Jesus Christ to come into your heart and be your

---

125 "15Verily I say unto you, Whosoever shall not receive the kingdom of God as a little child, he shall not enter therein" (Mk. 10:15; KJV).
126 "9If we confess our sins, he is faithful and just and will forgive us our sins and purify us from all unrighteousness" (I Jn. 1:9). "23For everyone has sinned; we all fall short of God's glorious standard" (Rm. 3:23; NLT).
127 "25Therefore he is able to save completely those who come to God through him, because he always lives to intercede for them" (Heb. 7:25). "6When we were utterly helpless, Christ came at just the right time and died for us sinners...8But God showed his great love for us by sending Christ to die for us while we were still sinners. 9And since we have been made right in God's sight by the blood of Christ, he will certainly save us from God's condemnation. 10For since our friendship with God was restored by the death of his Son while we were still his enemies, we will certainly be saved through the life of his Son. 11So now we can rejoice in our wonderful new relationship with God because our Lord Jesus Christ has made us friends of God" (Rm. 5:6, 8-11; NLT).

Savior. Tell Him that you are willing to give your life to Him for the higher purpose He has planned for you. Tell Him you are tired of trying and failing, stumbling and falling – see what happens when you give Him *complete control!*

Confess. Yes, your sins *first,* but your faith in Him *next.* Call Him Lord…*and let Him be!* Watch what He can do with your life when you just give Him a chance! Receive the gift of eternal life simply by inviting Christ into your heart! You will begin to notice a change *right away!*

THEN – TELL A FRIEND OR FAMILY MEMBER THAT YOU ACCEPTED JESUS INTO YOUR HEART!

You will begin to be strong in your faith as you tell others that Jesus is your Savior and Lord![128] Find a Bible [free ones online] and read it – it is God's Word to you, *and it will begin to speak to you* in your heart. You will find it full of life and hope. Reading it will build your faith in Jesus![129] The *Easy to Read Version* is a good place to start!

Finally, *find a church* in your community that believes and teaches the Bible and that loves, serves, and worships Jesus![130] Make sure they *care about others* – others than just themselves – hurting people, struggling people, imperfect people, *like you*

---

[128] "¹¹They triumphed over him [the devil] by the blood of the Lamb and by the word of their testimony; they did not love their lives so much as to shrink from death" (Rev. 12:11).

[129] "³⁹You search the Scriptures because you think they give you eternal life. But the Scriptures point to me" (Jn. 5:39; NLT)! "¹⁷So faith comes from hearing, that is, hearing the Good News about Christ" (Rm. 10:17; NLT).

[130] "²⁵…not giving up meeting together, as some are in the habit of doing, but encouraging one another – and all the more as you see the Day [of Christ's return] approaching" (Heb. 10:25).

and me. Just like Jesus does! And *if they do,* you will find a wonderful, new family who will help you become a true follower of Jesus and servant to others. They will help you find your true purpose in life…to be like Christ!

Now make the most important decision you have *ever made!* Do what your heart has *always* yearned to do – trust Jesus for your salvation and receive this gift of eternal life!

Pray this prayer with me right now, in your heart, as I lead you to Jesus with these words:

"Dear Jesus, I truly believe you are the Son of God, and that you died for my sins. I repent of my sins right now and I confess to you that I need you as my Savior *and my Lord.* I give you my life on earth, and I accept the gift of eternal life as I receive you into my heart this very moment. I believe you have answered me, and now I thank you for everlasting life and a home in heaven! Help me to live my life to please you and to bless others. In Jesus' name I pray. Amen."

Now, as a *testimony and a witness* of your faith in Christ and your love for God, sign your name below and date what just happened as you prayed this prayer!

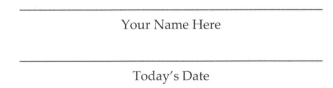

Your Name Here

Today's Date

I would be so glad to be the first person to hear about what Jesus Christ just did in your life! Email me and tell me! And I promise, I will pray for you as you begin your journey!

m.wayne.flora99@gmail.com
author@floraworkspublications.com

Chapter 31

So, "Where's the Hope?"

Oh, yeah. I don't want you to miss *that!* That's the most important part of this entire story! *Where's the hope?* Do you remember the famed commercial in 1984 that thrust Wendy's® international food chain restaurant into the spotlight? That happened only 15 years after the restaurant was founded by Dave Thomas in 1969. By the way, it increased their sales by 31% that year! Does the following 'jingle' ring a bell? "Where's the beef? *Hey! Where's the beef?!* I don't think there's anybody back there!"[131] The "diminutive and demanding octogenarian" and "gruff-talking former cosmetologist" was *supposed to say,* "Where is *all the beef?"* but Director Joe Sedelmeier says that because of her emphysema, that was too hard for her to actually say, so she quite niftily

---

[131] Burk A. Folkart, "Clara Peller (Where's the Beef?) Dies at 86," *Los Angeles Times,* Aug. 12, 1987, https://www.latimes.com/archives/la-xpm-1987-08-12-mn-440-story.html (accessed on March 17, 2020). It's really quite humorous that this little lady's "booming line" rather *incidentally* "struck the national funny bone." It even entered politics that year as Vice-President Walter Mondale used it to suggest his opponent, Gary Hart, lacked enough substance in his proposals!

improvised![132] That sweet little, old lady, Clara Peller, passed away in 1987 (a half million dollars richer).[133]

Well, that's how famous I want *these words* to be after reading this chapter, *"Where's the hope?!"* Here it is, found recorded in the words of David, the shepherd boy, the king of Israel, the ancestor of our Lord and Savior, Jesus Christ: "[4]I sought the LORD, and he heard me, and delivered me from all my fears...[6]This poor man cried, and the Lord heard him, and saved him out of all his troubles" (Ps. 34:4, 6; KJV). Read it again. Again. Again! *"There's the beef! There's the hope!"*

Could you possibly believe that *David probably suffered* depression?

After all, *almost half the psalms* are "Complaint Psalms," depending on who's counting (as many as 65 to 67)! That's why they are called "Songs of Lament!" Consider that, will you?! Why do you think the Psalms resonate so much as we read them? Mightn't it be that they "speak" to the challenges of stress in *our own lives?*

Listen to these words about David's unique and baffling life situations:

> We don't usually think about it, but there's a good chance that David battled depression. He never left God and God certainly never left him, but David struggled. David experienced the grief of losing his

---

[132] "Where's the Beef?" *Wikipedia, The Free Encyclopedia,* Updated Mar. 11, 2020, sec. "History," para. 1, https://en.wikipedia.org/wiki/Where%27s the beef%3F (accessed on March 17, 2020).
[133] Folkart, "Clara Peller..."

best friend Jonathan, his baby with Bathsheba, his older son Absalom. He probably experienced the stress of being the king of God's 'chosen people' and the spiritual pressure of being called 'a man after God's own heart.' His desperate state in [Psalm 69] may have come from having been a warrior his whole life – David fought everything from lions as a young boy to corrupt kings hunting him through the hills to other nations' armies trying to destroy him and his people. David may have just struggled in life like all of us do, but it's likely that during the most difficult times of his life, David was also depressed.[134]

Not convinced? Read David's words here:

¹Save me, O God, for the waters have come up to my neck. ²I sink in the miry depths, where there is no foothold. I have come into the deep waters; the floods engulf me. ³I am worn out calling for help; my throat is parched. My eyes fail, looking for my God. ⁴Those who hate me without reason outnumber the hairs of my head; many are my enemies without cause, those who seek to destroy me. I am forced to restore what I did not steal. ⁵You, God, know my folly; my guilt is not hidden from you (Ps. 69:1-5).

Don't take *my word* for it! Read ALL his complaint psalms and ponder this fact-of-matter for yourself! Take a look at *only a few* of these "Songs of Lament:" Psalms 3,

---

[134] Steve Sullivan, "David, a Warrior after God's Own Heart: Depressed?" *Next Sunday Resources,* May 23, 2018, para. 9, https://www.nextsunday.com/david-a-warrior-after-gods-own-heart-depressed/ (accessed on March 17, 2020). "Chaplain Steve Sullivan is a Cooperative Baptist Fellowship-endorsed chaplain and leads the VA/Clergy Partnership for Rural Veterans."

6, 12, 13, 22, 42-44, 49, 57-58, 60, 69, 74, 80, 83, 85-86, 88, 90, 137, and 139. Did you know that Psalm 88 is considered to be "the blackest of all the laments in the Psalter!"[135] Walter Bruggemann, a widely-recognized Old Testament scholar, author of over 50 books on Israel's exile (and consequent "laments"), declares of Psalm 88 that it "is an embarrassment to conventional faith."[136] Says E. Calvin Beisner of this psalm,

> Heman's psalm has nothing to do with modern
> notions of positive confession and self-esteem…
> For people tired of faking it when times get tough,
> Heman's psalm, dark and dismal as it is, should be
> a breath of fresh air! It positively reeks with honest
> misery! He makes no excuses for God. He hides none
> of his complaints. When he feels abandoned, he says
> so…he never considers that his sufferings might be the
> result of chance. He is convinced that they come from
> God. And he is more than willing to have it out with
> God over the matter. There is no
> 'possibility thinking' here.[137]

David, Elijah, Jonah, Job, Moses, Jeremiah, Paul…*even Jesus!*

So, yes, it is *highly likely*, as many scholars suppose, that *David experienced depression*, as did seven other prominent characters in the Scriptures – Elijah, Jonah, Job, Moses,

---

[135] Bill Muehlenberg, "The Lament Psalms," *CultureWatch, Bill Muehlenberg's Commentary on Issues of the Day,* Feb. 2, 2012, para. 10, https://billmuehlenberg.com/2012/02/02/the-lament-psalms/ (accessed on March 17, 2020).
[136] Muehlenberg, para. 11.
[137] Muehlenberg, para. 11, 12.

Jeremiah, Paul, and *even Jesus!*[138] Perhaps Paul's "thorn in the flesh" was just that, *depression* (my speculation)! And how possibly could Jesus, our sympathetic High Priest, be "tempted in [all] the same ways we are tempted" if He Himself never experienced depression

The point *is* the Scriptures ARE HONEST!

(Heb. 4:15; ERV)?! We needn't think that anxiety and depression *are only* modern-day phenomena, should we?! The Scriptures do not "hide" the feelings and experiences of the writers! The Holy Spirit is trying to teach us "how to complain" properly, or better stated, how to *"move from lament to laughter,"* from *"sadness to song,"* from *"pain to praise"* [emphases mine]! At some point in the believer's life, one must decide how he will handle heartache, *if and when* it happens – believe me, it *likely* will!

Therefore, it is most important for us to realize that *all complaints in Scripture* have become forms of worship, ways of expressing our "honest selves" to the Lord so that we may *reconcile ourselves* with Him in consummate confidence and eternal trust! Robert S. Smith insists the Lament Psalms are a "pathway to praise," for they teach us "to praise in the dark!"[139] I've learned to do that, my friend! Have you? You

---

[138] Debbie McDaniel, "7 Bible Figures Who Struggled with Depression," *Crosswalk.com,* June 5, 2017, https://www.crosswalk.com/faith/spiritual-life/7-bible-figures-who-struggled-with-depression.html (accessed on March 17, 2020). Elijah – I Ki. 19:4; Jonah – Jonah 4:3, 9; Job – Job 2:9, 3:11, 26, 10:1; Moses – Ex. 32:32; Jeremiah – Jer. 20:14, 18; Jesus – Is. 53:3, Mk. 14:34-36, Lk. 22:44.

[139] Robert S. Smith, "Belting Out the Blues as Believers: The Importance of Singing Lament," *Themelios* 42, no. 1 (2017), 89, sec. 5.1 and 5.2, https://themelios.thegospelcoalition.org/article/belting-out-the-blues-as-believers-the-importance-of-singing-lament/ (accessed on March 17, 2020).

need to, because you *don't know* what lies ahead? If you do not learn to *praise in the dark,* your theology will be seriously challenged *when* YOUR time of darkness ultimately comes!

Here is the problem with failure to recognize pain in the believer's life and to ignore the fact that suffering is real, as so aptly stated by Carl Trueman: "A diet of unremittingly jolly choruses and hymns inevitably creates an unrealistic horizon of expectation which sees the normative Christian life as one long triumphalist street party – a theologically incorrect and a pastorally disastrous scenario in a world of broken individuals."[140] It is NOT theologically healthy to deny *or be unwilling to deal with* suffering in a real world! So, come on, folks – get REAL! We have a whole book of *Lamentations* in the Old Testament to teach us how to worship God in the midst of pain! And, "In the NT, believers grieve and protest. To refuse to do so is often to refuse to face our pains and our losses."[141] And consequently, it equates to refusing to praise God in the "darkness of our suffering!"

You need to read this entire article! It is one of the most scholarly works available on the purpose of the "Songs of Lament" in the Scriptures!
[140] C. R. Trueman, "What Can Miserable Christians Sing?" *The Wages of Spin: Critical Writings on Historical and Contemporary Evangelicalism* (Ross-Shire: Christian Focus Publishing, 2004), 160.
[141] Muehlenberg, para. 20. As quoted by John Goldengay. He further states, "The psalms of pain and protest shock Christians who are not used to this way of talking to God. Yet they have an explicit place in the NT. Jesus uses the phraseology of Ps. 6 and/or Ps. 42 in Gethsemane, and on the cross utters the extraordinary cry that opens Ps. 22 (Mark 14:34; 15:34). Nor does Jesus pray these prayers so that we might not have to do so, for a lament such as Ps. 44 appears on the lips of Paul (Rom. 8:36)." Muehlenberg's reflections in this article are worth the read – they "normalize" the issues of pain and suffering in the lives of believers and show how they lead us to truly authentic and worshipful relationship with God. True, Paul's "thorn in the flesh," the "messenger [angel] of Satan to buffet him" (II Cor. 12:7) might have been the

Paul insists that he will worship God *in spite of* his problems (including sicknesses), *understanding that his problems compel dependency upon Christ!* Hear his words, "Most gladly therefore will I rather glory in my infirmities,[142] that the power of Christ may rest upon me" (II Cor. 12:9; KJV). Follow Paul through his gripes and complaints to his final-end resolve, "Now I take limitations in stride, and with good cheer, these limitations that cut me down to size – abuse, accidents, opposition, bad breaks. I just let Christ take over! And so the weaker I get, the stronger I become" (II Cor. 12:9, 10; MSG)!

> "Where's the beef?"
> "Where's the hope?!"

Here it is: "The LORD is close to the brokenhearted and saves those who are crushed in spirit" (Ps. 34:18)! I like *The Message* rendering of this text, "If your heart is broken, you'll find GOD right there; if you're kicked in the gut, he'll help you catch your breath." Here's Isaiah's hope in a loving and sovereign God: "'I live in the high and holy places, but also with the low-spirited, the spirit-crushed, And what I do is put new spirit in them, get them up and on their feet again'" (Is. 57:15; MSG).

Judaizers on his heels intending to slay him for making the Gospel "free" to the Gentiles. Or perhaps, it was an ophthalmological eye disease (Gal. 6:11, *as some suggest*), requiring the use of "large letters" as he wrote. Maybe it was literally a demon "let loose on him" (by God) to keep him humble. BUT, who's to say *Paul didn't suffer depression?* He surely had plenty of reason to experience depression, didn't he? See his long list of distressful trials in II Cor. 11:23-28 – plenty there to "rattle anyone's frayed nerves!"

[142] Thayer, 80. There's no way around it! The word "asthenia" here – "infirmities" – means "feebleness, malady…disease, infirmity, sickness, weakness." Further, Thayer points out that in II Cor. 11:30 and 12:9, this word specifically refers to *"the mental states in which this weakness manifests itself."* Pay close attention to the implications of this word study – *"mental states…"*

Have you ever been "kicked in the gut?" By inordinate anxiety or severe depression? I have! And the awesome God I serve who lives in the highest heavens came down to me and helped me "catch my breath!"

As stated by 21-year-old Melissa Camp to her husband of only three months in her "farewell letter," discovered *after-the-fact* of her death from ovarian cancer, *"Suffering doesn't destroy faith, it refines it."* In the face of daunting and potentially devastating odds, this young bride experienced great grace, courage, and faith to draw her final breath on earth before experiencing total healing in heaven.[143] Her inspiration gave her husband, Jeremy Camp, certified Gold and Platinum award-winning Christian singer-songwriter, the confidence to continue believing in God *even through* the valley of the shadow of death!

So, where's the hope? In the God who is present with and delivers the "low-spirited, the spirit-crushed!" And what He did for me – He'll do for you!

You need to hear me say it again –
"That's my hope...and that's
my final answer!"

---

[143] Joe Erwin and John Gunn, *I Still Believe,* Directed by Andrew Erwin and John Erwin, Santa Monica, California: Lions Gate Entertainment, Inc., 2020, https://www.lionsgate.com/movies/i-still-believe (accessed on April 11, 2020).

Chapter 32

A-OK!

I love to whistle! Oh yeah, I said that already, didn't I?! Smile! Of course, but it's important to say it again. You really oughta' hear me whistle…you know why? Well, first of all, I'm *really quite good at it!* But more importantly, I *feel like* whistling again! I was so sad when I lost my whistle. But I'm so glad I found it again. And yeah, I do it quite unconsciously nowadays, *just like before I ever got sick!* God's so good, isn't He?! He did such a wonderful job bringing me through some really tough stuff…and making me well again!

And on occasions, my kids ask me to "give 'em a break!" It seems so good to hear them say that again…like old times, "Dad, would you please give us a break?!" It's really funny now! I kind of like "unnerving them" when I whistle. It reminds me "how *good it feels* to *feel so good!*" I marvel at how awesome and gracious God is, and how precious is my family!

By the way, I'm not "boring" anymore! Ask my daughter! She and I talk almost every day, and I would say I'm probably one of her *favorite entertainers* – my grandkids think so too! I'm so silly around them, and I love cutting up with 'em. We have so much fun! Grandpa (affectionately known by one set) or Papa Wayne (affectionately known by the other) is so funny! He's a real hoot! (Just like my sister! Of course, that's genetic!) But in any event, it's been quite a while *since anyone (including Rhapsody) has said I was boring!* It's my best intention never to be boring *ever again,* if I can help it, the Lord willing!

I need to wrap this up by telling you that things are really "A-OK!" Not perfect, just A-OK! But then, they *never were* perfect, were they?! Not in my life and not in yours! They never were and *they never will be,* at least, not until we get to heaven! But that is what Christian faith is all about, isn't it?! Getting to heaven and striving *toward the perfection* we will enjoy *when we get there?!* Not perfection we achieve here on earth, but perfection *purchased by Christ for us* through the redemptive sacrifice of His life on the cross *and by* His shed blood for the forgiveness of our sins! What a relief! And what a hope we have in Him!

I *celebrate my healing,* but it may be helpful for you to know that I'm yet aware I live in a mortal frame, yes, *an aging body.* I am more self-aware than ever of

> I *celebrate my healing...*

my frailty and delicate chemistry; consequently, I pay close attention anymore to my level of stress. I know when to back off, slow down, take a break (or a nap), and get a good night's rest. I know when to turn off, turn away, turn down…say, "No!" I don't push myself as I once did, because *now I understand some of the factors* that caused my breakdown to begin with! I know that if I ignore my body's "signals," I can unnecessarily subject myself to liable lapses. That's *not at all* a lack of faith – it is simply *an abundance* of wisdom!

Hear it again: "That's *not at all* a lack of faith – it is simply *an abundance of wisdom!*"

That said, I am still on Lexapro. Disappointed in me? Don't be! I feel good *almost every day!* I give God praise for that! I take my usual 10mg dosage daily with my evening meal. It "winds me down" and helps me sleep. It keeps me quite stable day by day. Once my chemistry was corrected and my symptoms under control, Dr. Ribeiro suggested to me that I could come off the Lexapro…*gradually*, of course… *if I wanted to.*

Let me share a funny incident with you concerning that. Dr. Ribeiro happened to have an intern with him the day he made that suggestion. Almost without hesitation and certainly without thinking, I said to him, "Dr. Ribeiro, I'll bloody your nose if you even dare think about it! *I don't want to come off the Lexapro!*" You should have seen that intern's eyes! We had a good laugh together, of course, and he hasn't asked me since if I wanted to wean from the antidepressant! "It's not a problem, Pastor Flora," he responded. "The Lexapro tempers in your body and is not addictive. You can take it to the day you die if you wish, and it will never do any harm to your body's organs or systems." I was satisfied with that answer. I plan to be raptured with Lexapro in my bloodstream! Or "turn my toes" before I quit the medication!

Now then, you also need to know that *most things* I worried about were probably *never as bad* as I imagined them to really be. They seldom are. The mind is a remarkable "machine," and imagination is an amazing gift from God! But the devil enjoys using our minds *and our imaginations*[144] (when we let him)[145] to *play mean and vicious tricks* on us to disparage our faith and cheapen the sense of God's grace in our lives. He loves to make us think that God doesn't care anymore, because he knows that if we ever *come to believe that*, we're subject *to live like it!*

Oh, yes, I *was very, very sick –* *dangerously sick, in fact!*

And *because I was* very sick, it was so easy for me to conjure horrifying images of so many unfavorable outcomes. I *truly did imagine* the worst possible case scenarios that would end my life in disappointment and disaster! And *it is possible* that these things could have happened! It is simply that it wasn't *in God's plan* for my life! And I had *to realize* this fact-of-matter to be delivered and to become well again in my body…*and* in my mind.

I was so ashamed at first that, as a believer in Jesus Christ and *particularly as* a minister of the Gospel, I ever became sick to begin with, BUT especially that I became *that sick* in *"that way,"* you know – mentally, emotionally. That shouldn't

---

[144] "3For though we walk in the flesh, we do not war after the flesh: 4(For the weapons of our warfare *are* not carnal, but mighty through God to the pulling down of strong holds;) 5Casting down imaginations, and every high thing that exalteth itself against the knowledge of God, and bringing into captivity every thought to the obedience of Christ…" (II Cor. 10:3-5; KJV).

[145] "27Neither give place to the devil" (Eph. 4:27; KJV).

happen to ministers, should it? But it did, and it does! And too many, maybe, are unwilling to admit it…so they suffer "in silence," at least, perhaps, until they *no longer can. Even then,* they don't always ask for help.

So, I suppose you have concluded by now that I'm very poor, probably destitute, living out of garbage cans and sleeping on the street, maybe. Or possibly, I'm in a homeless shelter, merely surviving from day-to-day, and living on the pitiable pittance I can muster scraping pennies together to make a meal now and then. I likely gave you the impression that I would end up that way.[146] I had worried that my sickness would end my ministry, and consequently all my resources would "dry up" like an empty well and I'd have no revenue to support my family. They would be ashamed of me and embarrassed by my demise, and my wife and children would suffer for it.

But it hasn't ended up that way! In fact, I believe the most wonderful gift I can ever give my children is to live

---

[146] "Food Waste FAQs," *U.S. Department of Agriculture,* https://www.usda.gov/foodwaste/faqs (accessed on February 5, 2020). *I'm deliberately being facetious here about my situation,* yes. But I *do acknowledge, with immense sadness,* that in our country, 30-40% of retail-consumer prepared food is thrown away daily (restaurants, etc.), and yet we *really do* have hungry people living on the street and sleeping in cardboard boxes. "Hunger in America," *AmpleHarvest.org,* https://ampleharvest.org/hunger/?gclid=Cj0KCQiAhojz%20BRC3ARIsAGtNtHUUixJ5EyFTfwo U130XR 87a0LelD4n_gGfYUKzDPHvNpIvULuUTJxUaAgNXEALw_wcB (accessed on February 6, 2020). *And hungry persons in our country is an unimaginable thought (1 in 6)!* That *ought not to be* in a nation so "rich" with resources and means. Sometimes, I feel like running for politics, but I'm concerned I wouldn't survive the "rat race" (as my Mammy used to call it) that government and politics have become in our country. Surely there are ways God's Church can help end this needless suffering!

righteously before the Lord. "Righteous," that is, in Jesus Christ – not *my righteousness, no!* – but the righteousness that comes by faith in Him![147] It has absolutely nothing to do with my good deeds – they really don't count! But it has *everything* to do with Jesus taking away my sins and giving me *His righteousness.* I like the way Paul says it, "For God made Christ, who never sinned, to be the offering for our sin, so that we could be made right with God through Christ" (II Cor. 5:21; NLT). The reason *this is my greatest gift* to my children is because *it seems* there is a Scriptural precedent set in King David's statement of righteousness – that God will tend the needs of children *whose parents live righteously* before Him. King David said so, "Once I was young, and now I am old. Yet I have never seen the godly abandoned or their children begging for bread" (Ps. 37:25; NLT).

So, even though I'm a preacher, *I'm not poor!*

I'm relieved – I hope you are too! Don't mistake me, I'm not rich either (with worldly goods), but I'm not destitute. In fact, the *last personal word* the Lord spoke to me when I was very sick, I have saved to share with you here. Near the end of my crisis on a very difficult day, I was taking a very long shower. We have Rinnai instant and continuous hot water, on demand (I love it!)! I could shower all day if I wanted! One day, *I almost did,* for several hours, at least. That day, it seemed to me I shed as many tears down the drain as the number of droplets from the showerhead trickling over

---

[147] "[22]This righteousness is given through faith in Jesus Christ to all who believe" (Rm. 3:22).

my wrinkled body. I heard the Lord speak one short phrase, and it answered my *last nagging concern* for my family's well-being – *finances!* These were the words I heard in my heart, "I will recover all!" I was familiar with that language, for that's what God said to David when he asked the Lord if he should pursue His enemies who had burned the city of Ziklag and taken his army's wives and children hostage. The Lord told David, "Pursue: for thou shalt surely overtake *them*, and without fail recover *all*" (I Sam. 30:8b; KJV). That's exactly what happened! For David…*and for me!*

It quite concerns me when ministers get to the end of their journey and have little or nothing left in the way of resources to show for a full life of service to others. It also bothers me *for them* that many continue pastoring *way past* good health *simply because* they feel they have no other skills to fall back on. Or they do not have retirement resources to support them in the last, lean years of their lives. That saddens me tremendously! And most Bible and theology degrees (I have three), *even doctorates,* don't necessarily *"make money."* So, I'm training all the young ministers and students *under my guidance* how to plan for their future retirement and fiscal security at the end of their ministry.

I don't want them to end up in poverty after having served others so honorably!

My wife and I were blessed to have a really good friend, Patrick Nelson, a wonderful Christian insurance agent (*Nelson Agency*) and Gideon, to offer us very sound financial guidance 30 years ago concerning our future security needs. His proposed plan of action helped us procure five or six very attractive portfolios that have been working for us on the side all these years. IF we are thrifty, we could likely live off one portfolio until age 70, another until age 90, still another until age 110. And *if we're fortunate enough,* we can live off yet another until age 120 – Moses' age![148] Wow! *However,* I'd just as soon *not be* "ugly in my old age," and for that reason, I'm okay going to be with Jesus a bit sooner than age 120! So, frankly, *I hope* my children and grandchildren get every dime we've saved to help them with college and career startup when *their kids* begin their journey!

"Take it to the bank!"

I had apprised you earlier that when my wife, Lou, hears from the Lord, you can "take it to the bank." It's a good deposit. During the throes of my crisis, she heard the Lord speak a very specific word into her heart one day while in prayer. I've never known her to hear from the Lord and *it not happen exactly* as she heard it! I kid you not! In this instance, she heard the Lord say, "You will be completely out of debt within five years!" Listen guys, if you're not married and you're looking for the perfect wife, you need to shop for one (well, *pray for one*) just like mine! I tell you, it happened exactly as she stated it to me when the Lord spoke it! We marked the calendar, and by that very year and month, *we finalized all debt payments, and cleared the books!* Once again, God had

---

[148] Peer ministers, *please understand* that compound interest is the "eighth wonder of the world!" Why must it *always work against you?!* Start saving – a little at first – and let it *work for you* as you serve Christ and serve others! When you get to the end of your journey, there can be enough waiting for you to live comfortably within your means and not have to depend on the government, family, or friends to support you in your final years.

been personal and specific enough with us to "ease our burden" and give us hope for a brighter future yet!

I'm enjoying my journey! And I'll *always* be "Pastor Flora!" Like being President of the United States, Senator Sam or Sue, or Dr. Jones in the medical profession, once you retire (or leave office), you will always be Mr. President, Senator So and So, or Dr. "Whoever" until the day you die – *my first name* will always be "Pastor!" And that's the most endearing and sacred identity, next to "believer in Christ," ever uttered to get my attention…*especially to come to supper!*

I enjoy my family! My wife of 45 years (My goodness – that's almost half a century!) is my best friend in the whole wide world! *And* I enjoy my children and grandchildren! The Bible says, "The father of godly children has cause for joy. What a pleasure to have children who are wise" (Prov. 23:24; NLT)! Indeed, it is, and I certainly do! The Scriptures also say that, "Grandchildren are the pride and joy of old age…" (Prov. 17:6; ERV).[149] Mine certainly are! I enjoy teaching them about Jesus and answering all their many, many questions! And my, do they have a lot! I wish I had been as patient with my children (and had as much free time) as I am (and do) with my grandchildren! I'll tell you a really special secret if you don't already know it – when I'm with all of my grandchildren for one hour, *it makes me feel so young!* When I'm with them for *more* than one hour, *it makes me feel so old!* So, isn't it nice that you can *send them home* when they've worn you out?! I'm smiling!

---

[149] *The Holy Bible, Easy to Read Version* (Fort Worth, Texas: World Bible Translation Center, 1987, 1993, 2004).

So, at the end of this story, I'm wanting you to know that everything's A-OK! As far as I know, I have half-decent good sense, I'm *fairly stable* emotionally (Lou sometimes begs to differ), I'm enjoying my family and ministry, and *"the hand of God in all my life I see!"*[150]

It's important for me to tell you this – because you may need some "A-OK!" *in your life* right now too! So, I want you to know that *as you read this book,* I am praying that you will experience *your share of* "A-OK!" as well!

**Oh, by the way...I love to whistle!
Did I mention that?**

---

[150] Charles Hutchinson Gabriel, *The Singers and Their Songs: Sketches of Living Gospel Hymn Writers* (Chicago: The Rodeheaver Company, 1916). This is a lyrical phrase from the beautiful song, "He Abides," written by Herbert Buffum in 1922.

Chapter 33

Do As I Say Do, Not As I Did

Okay, this is where I get to tell you how you should live your life in a more conscientious, self-protective manner than I did. Obviously, I'm being facetious – I have no right to do that. However, as a friend once told me, "There's no need reinventing the wheel…and *square wheels are bumpy!*" That makes so much sense to me now. Why would I want to needlessly suffer *anymore if anyone* had *anything* to say to me that *might help me* prevent it?! After what I've experienced, I know *now* that I would *really rather* listen!

So, in this chapter, I would like to offer you some tips that come readily to mind that *might help you IF* you feel they resonate with you *and IF* you have it in your power *or interest* to embrace them. I will simply appeal to your "sense of need," for example, in this manner: "You may need such and such," *or* "You should consider thus and so," *or* "It would help you to understand this or that," etc. Are you ready? Okay, here we go:

- **It would help you to understand that your life has purpose!**

  Your ancestors really weren't amoebas or paramecia swimming around in a mud puddle of primordial soup! You are a "created being" and God made you with a very pristine, prophetic, and patent purpose! Purpose…remember? The "original idea for the creation of a thing? What made the Maker make it?" In fact, God delights in you, and you bring Him such wonderful pleasure![151] He *wants you* to enjoy that as well!

- **You should consider the fact that you are special!**

In fact, you are God's "one-of-a-kind" design! Your DNA says so! God "signed" His name in your being – your

> You are God's "one-of-a-kind" design!

"deoxyribonucleic acid (DNA)" is His signature. That is your chromosomal distinction that makes you so unique from everyone else! There has never been anyone else throughout all of history or in all of creation *just like you!* That makes you exceptionally special! In fact, you are the "apple of God's eye!"[152]

---

[151] "¹¹Thou art worthy, O Lord, to receive glory and honour and power: for thou hast created all things, and for thy pleasure they are and were created" (Rev. 4:11; KJV).

[152] "⁸…whoever touches you touches the apple of his eye…" (Zech. 2:8). "¹³For you created my inmost being; you knit me together in my mother's womb. ¹⁴I praise you because I am fearfully and wonderfully made; your works are wonderful, I know that full well…¹⁷How precious to me are your thoughts, God! How vast is the sum of them" (Ps. 139:13-14, 17)! "²⁹Not one sparrow (What do they cost? Two for a penny?) can fall to the ground without your Father knowing it. ³⁰And the very hairs of your head are all numbered. ³¹So don't worry! You are more valuable to him than many sparrows" (Mt. 10:29-31; TLB). "⁴What are mere mortals that you should think about them, human beings that you should care for them? ⁵Yet you made them only a little lower than God and crowned them with glory and honor. ⁶You gave them charge of everything you made, putting all things under their authority" (Ps. 8:4-6; NLT).

- **Consequently, you need to know that you matter to God!**

Repeating myself? No, not really! Beyond the fact that you are God's unique creation whose life has purpose, *God sent His Son to die for your sins!* Why? Because God wants to *be with you always!* Jesus "rebuilt the broken bridge" the weight of sin had collapsed! And it is a bridge that leads to perfect friendship and fellowship with your loving Savior forever! Wow! Ponder this fact – had you been the only person on Planet Earth who had broken fellowship with God, *Jesus would still have come to die for your sins.* Indeed, you certainly matter to Him!

- **It would help you to understand that you are not alone!**

I like the popular, freestyle paraphrase of Joshua 1:9 which reads like this: "Be strong. Be brave. Be fearless. You are never alone."[153] Remember, Jesus has assured us, "'I'll never let you down, never walk off and leave you'" (Heb. 13:5; MSG). In fact, He has promised to *always be with you,* "…to the very end of the age" (Mt. 28:20). You are never by yourself!

You are never alone! Ever!

---

[153] I also like the alternate rendering of this verse from *The Living Bible,* (Carol Stream, Illinois: Tyndale House Publishers, Inc., 1971). "⁹Yes, be bold and strong! Banish fear and doubt! For remember, the Lord your God is with you wherever you go" (Josh. 1:9; TLB).

- **You really need a strong support team of family and friends in your life!**

Hey, we *all do!* That is not to say everyone will have the *same type or extent* of support as all others, but *any support is more than none!* Okay, I acknowledge – all of us likely have *a little dysfunction* in each of our families and that may present a challenge, true. But let me invite you NOT "to burn *all* your bridges" with family and friends – you may need to cross back over them again one day. Learn to practice forgiveness...and to "make up."[154] It's really quite fun! It may "pay you back" one day when you need them most! My father-in-law, George, often says, "If we don't have family, we don't have anything!" I echo his sentiment. That said, work with *what you have!* Understand the importance of valuing those who know you best and love you most.

AND WHEN YOU *ARE WEAK*, LET THEM *BE STRONG FOR YOU!*

- **You should consider having a confidant, better still, a mentor!**

A confidant is that trusted person you can share your heart with and know it won't be on Facebook by end of day (or within the hour). In fact, no one else will ever know the things you share with your confidant! A really good friend will "step in harm's way" to protect you from danger! "A friend is always loyal, and a brother is born to help in time of need" (Prov. 17:17; NLT). That person might be your "Titus,"

---

[154] "**13**Be gentle and ready to forgive; never hold grudges. Remember, the Lord forgave you, so you must forgive others" (Col. 3:13; TLB).

perhaps, as the one Paul commended in II Cor. 7:6, "But God, who comforts the depressed, comforted us by the coming of Titus..." (NASB).[155] That

> **You *might need* a "Titus." We all do!**

good friend *might also* be your mentor, that is, someone who can "pour into you" his wisdom, knowledge, and training to help you grow and become the *best person* you can be! "Be friends with those who are wise, and you will become wise" (Prov. 13:20; ERV). That person will challenge you and *sharpen you* to your "cleanest cutting edge," for "As iron sharpens iron, so a friend sharpens a friend" (Prov. 27:17; NLT).

- **You need to consider the fact that life is not solely a destination – it is also a journey!**

Why does this matter? Well, for one thing...pace! A *healthy life* is more of a "marathon" than it is a "sprint." Running too fast for too long can be exhausting, *even enervating* – "causing one to feel drained of energy or vitality."[156] There's no need wearing yourself out prematurely! There is value in the old adage, "Stop and smell the roses!"[157] Jesus' invitation to "consider the

---

[155] *The Holy Bible, New American Standard Bible* (La Habra, CA: Foundation Publications, The Lockman Foundtion, 1960-1995).
[156] "enervating," *Lexico.com,* Powered by Oxford, https://www.lexico.com/en/definition/enervating (accessed on March 15, 2020).
[157] Kathy Keatley Garvey, "Stop and Smell the Roses," *Bug Squad, Happenings in the Insect World,* University of California, Agriculture and Natural Resources, Oct. 26, 2010, para. 4, https://ucanr.edu/blogs/blogcore/postdetail.cfm?postnum=3681 (accessed on March 15, 2020). This quote "is often attributed to golfer Walter Hagen in the 1956 book *The Walter Hagen Story*, but he didn't mention roses. His actual quote was, 'You're only here for a short visit. Don't hurry. Don't worry. And be sure to smell the flowers along the way.'"

lilies"[158] offers reason to believe that He meant for us to
ponder life's values along the way to our destination. In
fact, scientific research indicates that overall gratitude for
"meaningful things and people in our lives may play an even
larger role in our overall happiness…"[159] So it matters that
Jesus encourages us to slow down and muse the meaningful
aspects of life that are *worthy of* thoughtful consideration.

- **Therefore, you should probably begin to take
  frequent breaks!**

Learn how to "pull back, assess, regroup, and go
again." *Suck some air! Don't hyperventilate trying to keep up
with everybody else!* I'm humored to share with you that
once doing a graveside service, I looked to my left and saw
a family marker labeled, "Smith" – I looked to my right and
saw another family marker labeled, "Jones." Then I had the
amusing thought, "This is what happens when the Smiths
try to keep up with the Joneses!" I chuckled inside, but
given my pace of life *at that time*, it was quite a "wake-up
call" for me. I know you never thought you could *afford
to*, but start "getting away" more often! Listen, friend –
if you let others *use you up* (and they will!), you will be
left EMPTY-HEARTED…*and empty-handed.* Don't let that
happen! Remember? Do as I say do – not as I *did!* In fact,
you need more "recreation," more specifically, "RE-creation!"

---

[158] "28Consider the lilies of the field, how they grow; they toil not, neither do
they spin: 29And yet I say unto you, That even Solomon in all his glory was
not arrayed like one of these" (Mt. 6:28, 29; KJV).
[159] Stacey Kennelly, "A Scientific Reason to Stop and Smell the Roses,"
Greater Good Magazine, Science-Based Insights for a Meaningful Life,
Greater Good Science Center at UC Berkley, July 3, 2012, https://greatergood.
berkeley.edu/article/item/a scientific reason to stop and smell the roses
(accessed on March 15, 2020).

Jesus knows that if you don't "come apart"[160] for a while (take rest), you will *"come a-part"* (at the seams) – *after* a while! Listen to your body...it's speaking. Can you hear what it's saying? REST!

- ## You may need to ask for help!

Is that really a problem? Is it disgraceful to ask? Why? *Everybody needs somebody sometime!* Hear these words from someone who really knows! I honestly could not wish upon anyone – not even my worst enemy (*if I had one*) – what I experienced! Ever! I really wished *I had asked for help sooner!* I put off the inevitable and made matters worse, needlessly delaying my recovery. ASK! Let someone know that you need help! Your "return trip" home to health can be shorter (and less grueling) than mine, but it begins with your willingness to ask for help.[161]

- ## It would help you to understand – *to know* – that you can survive (you can get better)!

Keep that hope in your heart and keep hearing the words my caring wife spoke to me over and over again, "Everything's going to be all right!" Maybe not immediately... *but eventually.* Lean heavily on family, friends, and faith. Believe that God loves you and will help you through

---

[160] "31And he said unto them, Come ye yourselves apart into a desert place, and rest a while: for there were many coming and going, and they had no leisure so much as to eat" (Mk. 6:31; KJV).

[161] "7Ask and it will be given to you; seek and you will find; knock and the door will be opened to you" (Mt. 7:7). "11As bad as you are [in your carnal human nature, *translation mine*], you know how to give good things to your children. How much more, then, will your Father in heaven give good things to those who ask him" (Mt. 7:11; GNB)!

this difficult, perhaps, dark, dark season of your life. Keep trusting that things *will get better*. Remember that "hope" is "faith on tiptoe!" It promises a brighter tomorrow! In fact, *my definition* of hope is "the supernatural

HOPE
Hope is "forward-looking" faith!

confidence that things *will get better!*" That is what I wish for you, and that is what I pray for you as you read these words! Here is a perfect description of *hope* from *The Living Bible*: "We are saved by trusting. And trusting means looking forward to getting something we don't yet have – for a man who already has something doesn't need to hope and trust that he will get it" (Rm. 8:24; TLB). So, friend, keep trusting…keep hoping!

- **You might need a furry friend! (Or grandkids, maybe…smile!)**

Okay, *if you don't already have either*, one might be easier to come by than the other! But let me say how much my YorkiePoo,[162] "Ginger," means to me. Admittedly, I did not have her when I was very sick – I wish now that I had. I *may not have gotten as sick* had she been with me during that time. Her company with me has been so comforting and "inspiring." I'm not meaning to sound sacrilegious to use that term…*except* to say that animals are God's creation, and He made them very feeling creatures. Pets are unconditionally affectionate and so incredibly sensitive to human emotion that they quickly learn how to "please" their master and provide hours and hours

---

[162] Also variously spelled as "Yorkipoo, Yorkie-poo, and Yorkie-Poo." The YorkiePoo is a hybrid cross between the Yorkshire Terrier and a Poodle.

of cozy comfort and cheery contentment with their company. And I must say, there is something amazingly therapeutic about stroking the fur of your animal friend and sensing your anxiety level diminishing with each gentle stroke. [The pet loves it too!] Get ya' one today![163]

- ## You need a Savior!

Yes, I know…I mentioned this already. But I feel the Lord Jesus wants you to hear it again. Perhaps when you read it earlier, you weren't really sure…*or ready*, but now you are! I can't imagine you experiencing another minute of life, as difficult as it *can be* for anyone, and not knowing Jesus as your personal Savior. Invite Him into your life right now and give Him opportunity to help you through whatever it is you are presently facing. I assure you He will be with you through it all and give you courage *and grace* to face whatever tomorrow holds! Just, "Put your entire trust in the Master Jesus. Then you'll live as you were meant to live – and everyone in your house included" (Acts 16:31; MSG)! "For 'Everyone who calls on the name of the LORD will be saved'" (Rm. 10:13; NLT).

Why wait?! *Now is the best time* to trust in Jesus!

---

[163] "⁶You care for people and animals alike, O Lord" (Ps. 36:6; NLT). "⁹He gives food to the wild animals and feeds the young ravens when they cry" (Ps. 147:9; NLT). "⁹The Lord is good to everyone. He shows his mercy to everything he made" (Ps. 145:9; ERV).

Chapter 34

Why? And Where Was God?

- **THE PROBLEM**

Human suffering. *This* is the age-old question. So, why? And *where was* God? Inquiring minds want to know! Don't they?! I did! But I doubt *any answer* to this complex question will *ever satisfy* the human mind. The mind isn't capable of understanding the vast and profound wisdom of our Creator God in His providential plan for the restoration of fallen humanity.

However, *I have come to terms with* and *I am comfortable with* an answer that satisfies *my faith*. I hope, at most, it may speak encouragement to yours, and at least, be a reminder of the current reality we all face. So, hear my heart as I "unpack" this very complicated concern for all humankind.

Why suffering? Well, *why not?* Am I better than others that I should escape the horrible effects of sin upon the whole human race? When Adam fell from grace in the Garden of Eden, "...sin entered the world. Adam's sin brought death, so death spread to everyone, for everyone sinned" (Rm. 5:12; NLT). No one is exempt – not one single person...*except Jesus Christ,* the infinite "God-man" who was born sinless and lived a sinless life. He is the "second Adam" God sent to reverse the curse brought upon all humanity by Adam's failure (and ours) in the beginning of time.[164]

My mother was never a learned person in the matter of Christian theology, but she clearly understood the basics. When my wife's mother, Ruth, passed away in 2002, five years before *my mother died*, I remember Mom saying in a compassionate, but contemplative, thought-provoking manner, "I miss Ruth, and I'm sad she passed away. I'm no better than she – it could just as easily *have been me*, and one day, I *too* will pass away." Indeed, it sounds "so basic," doesn't it? Yet, I recall thinking, "How incredible her foresight, trust, and acceptance of such a biblical truism and theological reality!" Mom's self-awareness of her place in God's creation and her understanding of His redemptive plan for her life was as profound as any professor's I had ever heard "pontificate or theologize" on the subject of death!

In fact, let me help *you face and accept YOUR* current reality right now. Throughout all of history, as best as can be calculated, 108 billion human beings have lived on the face of Planet Earth. This includes the 7.5 billion people who live on earth at the present time (approx. 7 percent of all humans who ever lived).[165]

---

[164] "[20]But in fact, Christ has been raised from the dead. He is the first of a great harvest of all who have died. [21]So you see, just as death came into the world through a man, now the resurrection from the dead has begun through another man. [22]Just as everyone dies because we all belong to Adam, everyone who belongs to Christ will be given new life" (I Cor. 15:20-22; NLT).

[165] Toshiko Kaneda, "How Many People Have Ever Lived On Earth?" *PRB – Population Reference Bureau*, Jan. 23, 2020, https://www.prb.org/howmanypeoplehaveeverlivedonearth/ (accessed on March 3, 2020).

The odds of you (and me) dying are *almost exactly* one
to one (1:1). That's a pretty reliable wager, isn't it?! In other
words, throughout all of history to present-day, there has
almost concisely been one death for every human being, that
is, *except for* a few who experienced a *miraculous return from
death* (supernaturally, of course), several of these having been
recorded in the Scriptures.[166] And neither you nor I *can change
that reality*, because we were both participants *with Adam*
in the Garden of Eden when sin first happened. Unless the
Rapture of the Church occurs first,[167] it is *highly likely – NO!
entirely probable* – that you and I will pass away too.

IS THAT FAIR? WE MAY NOT *THINK* SO, BUT *IT IS A FACT!*

Fair? Is that fair of God? The Bible testifies to the
"fairness" of God, for the Scriptures declare that God "causes
his sun to rise on the evil and the good, and sends rain on the
righteous and the unrighteous" (Mt. 5:45). Yes, it is true that

---

[166] Let me invite you to research these for yourself, but let me simply
mention them here: 1) the Israelite cast in Elisha's tomb when the Moabites
raided the camp and interrupted a funeral (II Ki. 13:20, 21), 2) the widow's
son of Zarephath (I Ki. 17:17-24), 3) the Shunammite's son (II Ki. 4:18-37),
4) the widow's son of Nain (Lk. 7:11-17), 5) Jairus' daughter (Lk. 8:49-56),
6) Lazarus, Jesus' friend of Bethany (Jn. 11:1-44), 7) saints in Jerusalem
upon Jesus' death…an uncertain number (Mt. 27:50-54), 8) Tabitha or
Dorcus (Acts 9:36-42), and 9) Eutychus who "fell from the loft" while Paul
preached…smile (Acts 20:7-12). This number does not include any persons
attested to have been raised from death in anyone's contemporary
deliverance ministries.
[167] "[16]For the Lord himself will come down from heaven, with a loud
command, with the voice of the archangel and with the trumpet call of God,
and the dead in Christ will rise first. [17]After that, we who are still alive and are
left will be caught up together with them in the clouds to meet the Lord in the
air. And so we will be with the Lord forever. [18]Therefore encourage one
another with these words" (I Thes. 4:16-18).

bad things happen to good people – and good things happen to bad people! That's fair! What's more, God "...does not treat us as our sins deserve or repay us according to our iniquities" (Ps. 103:10). That's fair, *actually more than* fair! "Will not the Judge of all the earth do right?" (Gen. 18:25). Of course, He shall! Why? Because He is fair!

As rigid a proponent of Judaism and God's love for Israel as the Apostle Peter was, when he experienced the revelation of God's love *for all humanity – none excluded –* he exclaimed his remarkable surprise of *God's fairness* to everyone present when he said, "³⁴I see very clearly that God shows no favoritism. ³⁵In every nation he accepts those who fear him and do what is right" (Acts 10:34, 35; NLT). James, the half-brother of our Lord Jesus Christ, declared that God's wisdom toward human beings is "...first of all pure; then peace-loving, considerate, submissive, full of mercy and good fruit, impartial and sincere" (Jms. 3:17). James grew up with Jesus – "he oughta' know!" Let me affirm that I quite agree with the following understanding of biblical fairness, and I will invite you to personally research for yourself the *accuracy of these particular Scriptures* to resolve within your own mind how *incredibly fair* God is:

> In many people's minds, fairness is everyone receiving exactly what he or she deserves. If God were completely 'fair,' by this definition, we would all spend eternity in hell paying for our sin, which is exactly what we deserve. We have all sinned against God (Rm. 3:23) and are therefore worthy of eternal death (Rm. 6:23). If we 'fairly' received what we deserve, we would end up in the lake of fire (Rev.

20:14–15). But God is merciful and good, so He sent Jesus Christ to die on the cross in our place, taking the punishment that we deserve (II Cor. 5:21).[168]

So, there now! Let us be done with the issue of God's fairness! For after all, what *really is* fair? "For God so loved the world that he gave his one and only Son, that *whoever believes* in him shall not perish but have eternal life" (Jn. 3:16). Did you catch that? *"Whoever believes!"* God makes the same offer of salvation and eternal life *to everyone* – no one excluded!

That, my friend, *is more than fair!*

So, why *did I suffer?* Because God *knew best! Where was God when* I was suffering? He was *right there* all the time! Imminently and manifestly present with me right through the whole sordid ordeal! Okay, I admit to you, that's much easier to say *now* than it *was then!* I could neither talk about it nor rationally reflect upon it *until this time* in my life. But NOW I can! In fact, the Holy Spirit spoke to me on Sunday morning, January 26, 2020, at 5:06 am as I was offering praise to Him just before dawn of that day when He said to me, "Not before now. Not until now. But NOW!"

That message was unmistakably distinct in my heart and mind when I heard it *just as in* each of the prior instances when the Lord had been so personal with me – His voice was crystal clear! And I knew exactly what He meant! I realized that God's healing power in my life had been effective and

---

[168] "Is God Fair," *Got Questions – Your Questions. Biblical Answers.* Jan. 2, 2020, https://www.gotquestions.org/is-God-fair.html (accessed on March 2, 2020).

His purpose in my life was truly being fulfilled. I was now completely healed and at this very "kairos"[169] moment in my life, I was now ready to *share my story with you*, and the Lord knew that I was! *The time had come!* So, little by little, I began recording these words, narrating this account of my experiences to you…and as I did, it *didn't hurt anymore!*

Did I enjoy suffering? No! Was my faith challenged? You bet! Did I wobble on my "knobby spiritual knees?" Yes, I did! And did it seem I would surely derail and careen completely out of control? Actually, *I think I did!* I hit the wall – hard, really hard! And with my head spinning dizzily as I tried to regain my balance, I learned *as never before* how critically and completely dependent *I truly am* upon the God of the universe, the Creator of my very being, the Savior of my soul, the Lord of my destiny! It is absolutely true what the Apostle Paul said to the Stoic philosophers at the Areopagus on Mars Hill, "For in him we live, and move, and have our being…" (Acts 17:28; KJV).

> "For in him we live, and move, and have our being…"

Now, to close this section of *my personal convictions* about human suffering, consider this thought with me just for a moment – your favorite televangelist, *faith preacher, even* – is going to die…if he or she hasn't already. And you, his or her audience or follower, will die as well. Does it not strike you

---

[169] Thayer, 318. "kairos" – "a fixed and definite time, the time when things are brought to crisis, the decisive epoch waited for; opportune or seasonable time; the right time; a limited period of time" *as opposed to* "chronos" which implies more the *sequential passing of time*. I like to think of *kairos* as the "moment of divine instance, the divinely-timed moment" when everything is just right for God to fulfill His intention for that exact time in human history.

as odd that someone with *great faith* should die? Or for that
matter, that *anyone who was ever healed by God* will also die?!
Or anyone who was ever raised from the dead – as was
Lazarus – will die…AGAIN?! My goodness, he died twice!
"The Bible makes no promise that our present bodies,
whatever their condition, will stay healthy or last forever.
In fact, the Bible [only] promises something much more
glorious: a new body, like our present ones but also different,
a body made for eternity."[170]

Ponder this, whatever you have heard about God's will
to *always heal* one's body in *every instance* with *every prayer*
upon *every expression* of sincere faith *the very moment you pray,*
you must decide for yourself what you believe the Scriptures
accurately teach about that. And you must also determine
that *if God were* to always answer your prayer (exactly as
you "command it to be") and heal your body physically
every time you ask, *"Would you really want to live forever in
that sin-cursed sod of a clay jar you are?* A body that ages with
time, wears out with usage, finally weakens, then completely
breaks down with the normal pace of life?" The beauty
of your youth will fade,[171] and like me, you will eventually
be downright ugly – just as *ugly as dirt* (Gn. 3:19) –
smile! Can you *live with that forever?* I can't! Not
when a new body awaits me when I "fold this tent"

---

[170] J. Stephen Lang, "What Does the Bible Say About Sickness and Healing?"
CBN, 1999, para. 11, https://www1.cbn.com/what-does-bible-say-about-sickness-and-healing (accessed on March 17, 2020).
[171] "³⁰Charm is deceitful and beauty fades…" (Prov. 31:30; ISV).

on earth and lay it aside[172] for the new one God is preparing for me! No sir! Not me! I don't want to live in a ragged, worn-out vessel throughout eternity! *I want my new and glorious body!*

Yes, we are delivered from the curse of the law through faith in Jesus Christ! Ultimately *and eventually.* But *ultimate deliverance* hasn't happened until the human body is completely redeemed as Paul clearly states here:

> [18]Yet what we suffer now is nothing compared to the glory he will reveal to us later. [19]For all creation is waiting eagerly for that future day when God will reveal who his children really are. [20]Against its will, all creation was subjected to God's curse. But with eager hope, [21]the creation looks forward to the day when it will join God's children in glorious freedom from death and decay. [22]For we know that all creation has been groaning as in the pains of childbirth right up to the present time. [23]And we believers also groan, even though we have the Holy Spirit within us as a foretaste of future glory, for we long for our bodies to be released from sin and suffering. We, too, wait with eager hope for the day when God will give us our full rights as his adopted children, including the new bodies he has promised us (Rm. 8:18-23; NLT).

---

[172] "[1]For we know that when this earthly tent we live in is taken down (that is, when we die and leave this earthly body), we will have a house in heaven, an eternal body made for us by God himself and not by human hands" (II Cor. 5:1; NLT).

Until that time, my friend, we are *truly saved*[173] from our sins by the atoning sacrifice of Jesus, our Savior, through His death on the cross! And the Holy Spirit of redemption has "sealed us" for Himself until that final day of complete restoration: "Remember, he has identified you as his own, guaranteeing that you will be saved on the day of redemption" (Eph. 4:30b; NLT). But we are *also being saved* (emphasis on linear progression, *process under way*)! Notice the *tense, voice, and mood:* present passive participle – meaning that we are *being saved by His resurrection power* through His Holy Spirit living within us![174] Paul says God will complete this work in our beings (including our bodies) in *time to come…eventually:* "…being confident of this, that he who began a good work in you will carry it on to completion until the day of Christ Jesus" (Philip. 1:6).

SO, WHERE IS THE DEVIL IN ALL OF THIS? "IN THE DETAILS," THEY SAY.

While it is true that Satan is the one who was cast from heaven and then tempted human beings in the Garden of

---

[173] "⁸For it is by grace you have been saved, through faith – and this is not from yourselves, it is the gift of God – ⁹not by works, so that no one can boast" (Eph. 2:8, 9).

[174] "¹⁸For the message of the cross is foolishness to those who are perishing, but to us who are being saved it is the power of God" (I Cor. 1:18). "¹⁵For we are to God the pleasing aroma of Christ among those who are being saved and those who are perishing" (II Cor. 2:15). The word used here is "sozomenois" (present passive participle) which means "ones being saved" indicating *ongoing process* of salvation *toward eventual completion.* "¹¹And if the Spirit of him who raised Jesus from the dead is living in you, he who raised Christ from the dead will also give life to your mortal bodies because of his Spirit who lives in you" (Rm. 8:11).

Eden to sin against God, *human beings must yet take personal responsibility for their sins* by confessing them to Jesus and accepting His gift of everlasting life (and healing)! However, Satan, as I understand from Scripture, *has no more advantage against you than what you give him!* Did you hear me? Paul instructs in Eph. 4:27, "Neither give place to the devil" (KJV). The NIV renders this "foothold." It derives from the Greek "topos" from which we get the word "topography" – that is, ground or space for him to prop the bulwark of his strength against you! "Chance or opportunity," it could be read.

In other words, sickness is *not necessarily always* the devil's doings – it is the doings *of mankind himself,* stricken by the fall in the Garden. Note that in some instances when Jesus healed people – yes, He cast out devils too![175] But in other instances, He *didn't cast out devils.*[176] So, sickness is not entirely Satan's fault – it's ours! It must be noted, however, that the advantage Satan seeks (foothold, loophole, chance, opportunity) *is simply to discourage and dissuade your faith –* "steal, kill, and destroy."[177] But the Word says, "Neither give place to the devil!" So, in the end, *don't let him win!*

---

[175] "32While they were going out, a man who was demon-possessed and could not talk was brought to Jesus. 33And when the demon was driven out, the man who had been mute spoke" (Mt. 9:32, 33).
[176] "13Then he said to the man, 'Stretch out your hand.' So he stretched it out and it was completely restored, just as sound as the other" (Mt. 12:13). The following verses note *distinctions between* healing diseases and casting out devils: "34And he healed many that were sick of divers diseases, and cast out many devils; and suffered not the devils to speak, because they knew him." "1Then he called his twelve disciples together, and gave them power and authority over all devils, and to cure diseases" (Mk. 1:34; Lk. 9:1; KJV).
[177] "10The thief comes only to steal and kill and destroy; I have come that they may have life, and have it to the full" (Jn. 10:10).

Friend, my encouragement to you is this – no matter what you face or how tough it seems, *please don't bail out* in your time of suffering! Don't let Satan rob you blind and steal your future! And don't let your faith *completely lapse* because you *blame God* or *blame yourself* that what you expected didn't happen right away! The best is yet to come!

• THE POSITION

Now, before I "challenge" my own *prior* belief system, let me first restate my earlier conviction that I believe, "...divine healing is provided for all in the atonement."[178] I also believe the Scriptures teach that it is *always appropriate* to ask God for His healing of our bodies – physically, mentally, emotionally, *and to believe* that God, through His Holy Spirit, is manifesting His healing power within us as we believe. Until our *numbered days* are reached (God knows how many there are)[179] and our *appointment with death* is met,[180] it is God's providential pleasure *and provision* to *maintain, heal, and restore* our health for service to His Church and in the world. It is entirely acceptable to believe *and trust* Him to do that!

> God's pleasure is to maintain, heal, and restore...

Remember, our bodies are the temple of the Holy Spirit – it is God's will that we should *take care* of our bodies and ask

---

[178] Article 11, Declaration of Faith.
[179] "⁵A person's days are determined; you have decreed the number of his months and have set limits he cannot exceed" (Job 14:5).
[180] "²⁷Just as people are destined to die once, and after that to face judgment..." (Heb. 9:27).

for His healing touch when sickness occurs. Healing was characteristic of Christ's ministry[181] and He bore wounds in His body on the cross to pay for our healing.[182] Further, one of the very names of God ("Jehovah" – "I AM") is Jehovah-Rapha which means "I AM the God Who heals" or "I AM the Lord your healer."[183] The caution and encouragement I now observe, however, is to give God the divine prerogative that belongs to Him in His vast wisdom to heal us in the *manner and time* He knows best! *Even if it is in heaven!* I restate this personal conviction so you will clearly understand my intent for sharing it with you!

I invite you to ponder this most important consideration as you pray for healing of your body and ask God for His touch of deliverance in your life! Hear me out…PLEASE – do not *fault God* or *your own personal faith* if healing doesn't come in the time and manner you have requested! It does not mean God has no intention of answering your prayer *or* that you have not believed "strongly enough."

If *anything more* than "simple childlike faith" is required to receive healing (or you have to "muster faith" for it to

---

[181] "²³Jesus went throughout Galilee, teaching in their synagogues, proclaiming the good news of the kingdom, and healing every disease and sickness among the people" (Mt. 4:23). "³⁸…how God anointed Jesus of Nazareth with the Holy Spirit and power, and how he went around doing good and healing all who were under the power of the devil, because God was with him" (Acts 10:38).

[182] "⁵But he was wounded for our transgressions, he was bruised for our iniquities: the chastisement of our peace was upon him; and with his stripes we are healed" (Is. 53:5; KJV). "'²⁴He himself bore our sins' in his body on the cross, so that we might die to sins and live for righteousness; 'by his wounds you have been healed'" (I Pet. 2:24).

[183] "²⁶He said, 'If you listen carefully to the Lord your God and do what is right in his eyes, if you pay attention to his commands and keep all his decrees, I will not bring on you any of the diseases I brought on the Egyptians, for I am the Lord, who heals you'" (Ex. 15:26).

happen), then you have moved from the simplicity of faith in Jesus to a form of "work righteousness," which *itself* insults Christ for the completed work He has already accomplished in your behalf. So, I'm simply saying, "Be nice to yourself …an*d to your Savior* as you trust God for your healing!"

• THE PREMISES

Now, I would like to share with you *my theological perspectives* concerning what happened in my life (or *might be happening in yours*). I will not ask that you agree with me *at all if, in fact,* you cannot; but I do ask that you ponder, perhaps even acknowledge, *the possibility* that what I propose (and sincerely believe) *may be true.*

Yes, I struggled with my faith when I was very sick! Yes, I doubted myself! And yes, *it seems I doubted God* in the midst of my health crisis!

However, His Word had been soundly planted in my heart throughout the whole of my life and ministry.

Consequently, when He finally "spoke" to me, I was familiar with the sound of His voice. At long last, my faith didn't dash on the rocks because I feel what I had previously come to believe about God's Word was accurate and true.

Let me begin by premising what *I believe* are faithful theological presuppositions that *I maintain* approaching the Bible as a conservative Christian scholar:

The Bible *is* God's Word – it doesn't just *contain* God's Word. It is, in fact, God's *veritable, infallible, and inerrant* revelation of Himself to humankind, disclosing His purpose and plan of redemption for fallen humanity. In some circles of higher education, I have been asked to *"do faithful theology,"* but only after the Bible had been whittled away with the penknife of *certain forms* of historical or "higher criticism" (redaction, particularly), suggesting to me that someone smarter than I (*or they*) could actually determine *what parts* of the Bible were, indeed, *revelation from God* and what parts were *superimposed by human influence.*

I enjoy studying theology, but the starting point from which I begin *my journey* is this foundation – the Bible *is God's Word!* That said, I am unaccepting of the results rendered by any other approach to a study of Scripture that concludes otherwise.

Consequently, as the Bible is its *own witness* of integrity and authenticity, every truth it speaks concerning the *God of the Bible* revealed to us in its pages is veritable and exacting.

> Thus, the existence of God in Scripture *is never debatable*, for the Bible begins with these words, "In the beginning God..." (Gn. 1:1).

Throughout the Scriptures, every attestation of God Himself as the only eternal Creator being there is – *none like Him, above Him, or beside Him*[184] – is unequivocally declared and contended. His nature, character, and attributes are clearly revealed in Scripture, and He is described to be a God of love,

---

[184] "⁹Remember the former things, those of long ago; I am God, and there is no other; I am God, and there is none like me" (Is. 46:9). "²²How great you are, Sovereign Lord! There is no one like you, and there is no God but you, as we have heard with our own ears" (II Sam. 7:22). "¹⁶Lord Almighty, the God of Israel, enthroned between the cherubim, you alone are God over all the kingdoms of the earth. You have made heaven and earth" (Is. 37:16).

righteousness, justice, goodness, and order. While *general revelation* (nature, conscience, moral oughtness) tell us *there is* a God, the Scriptures tell us *what kind of God* He is.

As the Scriptures are reliable in their witness of God's being and nature, we learn from them that *God is good and gracious to humankind.* He is NOT the source or origin of evil. Neither does He have any wish for evil to befall anyone![185] It is God's desire that all men should be saved!

Jesus Christ is God's one and only Son, literally, the "single of its kind" (monogenes),[186] revealed from heaven prophetically in the Old Testament Scriptures and made known in the New. John says of this personage of the Godhead that Jesus was the Word "in the beginning" and that "[1]the Word was with God, and the Word was God. [2]The same was in the beginning with God. [3]All things were made by him; and without him was not anything made that was made" (Jn. 1:1-3; KJV).

---

[185] "[13]When tempted, no one should say, 'God is tempting me.' For God cannot be tempted by evil, nor does he tempt anyone" (Jms. 1:13). "[5]This is the message we have heard from him and declare to you: God is light; in him there is no darkness at all" (I Jn. 1:5). "[33]For God is not a God of disorder but of peace – as in all the congregations of the Lord's people" (I Cor. 14:33). "[12]How you have fallen from heaven, morning star, son of the dawn! You have been cast down to the earth, you who once laid low the nations! [13]You said in your heart, 'I will ascend to the heavens; I will raise my throne above the stars of God; I will sit enthroned on the mount of assembly, on the utmost heights of Mount Zaphon. [14]I will ascend above the tops of the clouds; I will make myself like the Most High'" (Is. 14:12-14). "[9]The Lord is not slow in keeping his promise, as some understand slowness. Instead he is patient with you, not wanting anyone to perish, but everyone to come to repentance" (II Pet. 3:9).

[186] Thayer, 417.

The Son of God was *always present* in eternity past and was never created; however, He *did become* "flesh, and dwelt among us," as John attests in the close of his prologue (Jn. 1:14; KJV). His identity with humanity made Him truly "empathetic" (feeling "with") for us as the writer of Hebrews states, "For we do not have a high priest who is unable to empathize with our weaknesses, but we have one who has been tempted in every way [in all points], just as we are – yet he did not sin" (Heb 4:15).

Finally, the most exhaustive and extensive expression of God's love for us was the giving of His Son, Jesus, to die on the cross for our sins (literally, taking our punishment).[187] Jesus' obedience and willingness to lay down His life in our behalf demonstrates His own personal love *for the Father* to do His will and His own personal love *for us* to redeem us back into right standing with God.[188] This He did of His own accord.[189]

I don't know how He does it – *He just does!*

Now then, in the context of our total salvation, our ultimate and complete deliverance, God by His Holy Spirit *is able to make* "all things work together for good to them that love God, to them who are the called according to his purpose" (Rm. 8:28; KJV). And He does it quite well! It's a miracle of divine providence. It is in God's

---

[187] "[16]For God so loved the world that he gave his one and only Son, that whoever believes in him shall not perish but have eternal life" (Jn. 3:16).
[188] "[7]Then I said, 'Here I am – it is written about me in the scroll – I have come to do your will, my God'" (Heb. 10:7).
[189] "[17]The reason my Father loves me is that I lay down my life – only to take it up again. [18]No one takes it from me, but I lay it down of my own accord. I have authority to lay it down and authority to take it up again" (Jn. 10:17, 18).

power to do this for those – did you *notice this?* – "who love God!" That's the clincher!

Be careful *not* to quote this verse out of context – it *does not say* He works all things for good *for anybody,* but *only* for those *who love Him!* And of course, "according to His purpose!" Remember what purpose is? "The original idea for the creation of a thing – what made the Maker make it!" So, folks, God's got it! Even when you don't think so, He really does! He's got it, and *everything's going to be okay!*

- **THE PROMISES**

I'm told there are several thousand promises of God in the Bible. Personally, I've not counted them, but apparently Dr. Everek R. Storms did – *he says* there are 7,487 promises of God to man (about 85% of all promises in the Bible)![190] Wow! That's a lot! So, it's not possible for me to cite them all to you here just now, but I personally wish to offer you the assurance of a few:

1. God has <u>promised</u> to *always love you!*

The prophet Jeremiah reminds us of this as the Lord says to us, "'I have loved you with an everlasting love; I have drawn you with unfailing kindness'" (Jer. 31:3). It's His

> IN FACT, THERE IS ABSOLUTELY NOTHING YOU CAN POSSIBLY DO TO MAKE GOD STOP LOVING YOU! HIS LOVE IS *UNCONDITIONAL!*

---

[190] R. J. Morgan, "How Many Promises in The Bible," *Nelson's Complete Book of Stories, Illustrations, & Quotes,* electronic ed., (Nashville, Tennessee: Thomas Nelson Publishers, 2000), 645-646.

nature to love you, for it is *His very essence* – "God is love" (I Jn. 4:8). That doesn't mean you can't *refuse His love,* and even decide you don't want to be with Him in heaven forever. He will be sad if you reject Him, but He *will still* love you.

2. God has <u>promised</u> to *always be with you!*

When Jesus commissioned His disciples to share the good news of salvation from sin and the gift of eternal life with others, He promised them He would be with us always, "to the very end of the age" (Mt. 28:20). In fact, God has said, "'Never will I leave you; never will I forsake you'" (Heb. 13:5). "'I will never fail you. I will never abandon you'" (NLT). The Apostle Paul understood this as he took the Gospel to the far ends of his known world, proclaiming hope in Jesus Christ:

> Heb. 13:5 (NLT)
>
> "I will never fail you. I will never abandon you."

> 7We now have this light shining in our hearts, but we ourselves are like fragile clay jars containing this great treasure. This makes it clear that our great power is from God, not from ourselves. 8We are pressed on every side by troubles, but we are not crushed. We are perplexed, but not driven to despair. 9We are hunted down, but never abandoned by God. We get knocked down, but we are not destroyed. 10Through suffering, our bodies continue to share in the death of Jesus so that the life of Jesus may also be seen in our bodies (II Cor. 4:7-10; NLT).

3. God has <u>promised</u> to *always help you!*

I like *The Living Bible* paraphrase of Heb. 2:18: "For since he himself has now been through suffering and temptation, he knows what it is like when we suffer and are tempted, and he is wonderfully able to help us" (TLB). Ps. 121 is a most beautiful "Song of Ascent" believed to have been sung by worshipers ascending the road to Jerusalem to celebrate the presence of the Lord in His holy place. I love hearing my daughter, Rhapsody, sing this song acapella, for it "lifts me up" as she sings it! How appropriate that this psalm symbolizes "ascent," a coming up out of darkness, despair, drudgery, or even the humdrum of life into the vivacious, lifegiving presence of the Lord! It is worth sharing with you here in its entirety:

> [1]I lift up my eyes to the mountains – where does my help come from? [2]My help comes from the Lord, the Maker of heaven and earth. [3]He will not let your foot slip – he who watches over you will not slumber; [4]indeed, he who watches over Israel will neither slumber nor sleep. [5]The Lord watches over you – the Lord is your shade at your right hand; [6]the sun will not harm you by day, nor the moon by night. [7]The Lord will keep you from all harm – he will watch over your life; [8]the Lord will watch over your coming and going both now and forevermore (Ps. 121:1-8).

4. God has <u>promised</u> to *always heal you!*

Can God heal your body? Yes! Will God heal your body? Yes! Is it appropriate to *always ask God for healing* in your body – mentally, emotionally, and physically? Yes, yes, it is – I have repeated this *for unquestionable clarity* in several instances so that you will understand *this is my sincerest personal conviction!* My own story of healing documented in this book is witness and attestation of it!

As I offered to you my sincerest and concisest convictions about healing earlier in this chapter ("The Position"), I encourage you to *always believe* that God *will heal you – YES!* However, I also remind you to not hold God at fault (nor disparage your own personal faith) when you pray for healing, yet it *doesn't happen right away!*

> Remember that God in His infinite wisdom may wish to heal you *HIS WAY in HIS TIME!*

Yes, it may be here on earth *while He needs you* in Christian service – *but* it may be in heaven when His purpose for your life is complete! And what could be better than heaven? God healed my mother many times before age 75, but when she passed away, I was happy for her to be with Jesus – it was her *ultimate healing*…and His perfect time!

5. God has <u>promised</u> to *give you a hopeful future!*

How powerful are these words to discouraged and dismayed persons who are weary of life! "'For I know the plans I have for you,' declares the Lord, 'plans to prosper you and not to harm you, plans to give you hope and a future'" (Jer. 29:11). Eugene Peterson's paraphrase from *The Message* expresses it so well: "'I know what I'm doing. I have it all planned out – plans to take care of you, not abandon you, plans to give you the future you hope for.'"[191] God *really does have you in His plans!* And the plans He has for you are good!

Do these promises from God imply there will never be pain or heartache, difficulty or distress? Of course not. Certainly, there *will be!* But those troubles will not *define or decide* your ultimate destiny…you know, the beautiful one God has planned for you…*except as* He may use them to refashion you…as He did me.

It wasn't easy, no, *but was it worth it?* Yes, it was! You know why? Because God makes *"every thing beautiful in his time"* (Eccl. 3:11; KJV). In fact, *He does, indeed do it – in His WAY, in His time – as* it seems *"good to the potter to make it"* (Jer. 18:4; KJV)!

I know. Because He did it for me.

---

[191] Eugene Peterson, *The Message* (Colorado Springs, Colorado: NavPress, 1993, 2002, 2018).

Chapter 35

Anthology of Comforting Words

I'd like to share with you in this closing chapter a few poems I've written through the years as well as a sermon I preached (before I got sick…smile) that spoke hope to my heart and courage to my spirit when I was very, very ill. God uses "words" to breathe life into seemingly hopeless situations: His "Word" (proper) – the Scriptures, and His "words" (prophetic) – the Holy Spirit speaking softly to the mind of the believer. He certainly did this in my life! I caution to acknowledge to you that ALL words (prophetic) *must be in complete agreement* with ALL *HIS* WRITTEN Word (proper).

In other words, I cannot (nor should anyone) honor *any words* that conflict with the divinely-inspired, infallible, inerrant, "God-breathed" Scriptures! That said, when I say these poems and messages "inspired me" during the time of my darkness, I mean that in only the *slightest sense* of the word. I *do believe* the Holy Spirit anoints poets to write, singers to sing, and preachers to preach, but not in the *"authoritative sense"* that the Scriptures themselves speak to the hearts of men! I trust these few "messages of comfort" will speak to your heart as well…as they do to me.

I DON'T UNDERSTAND, BUT GOD DOES!
© 1997 Wayne Flora

When you hurt so bad, the pain is so intense, the grief is so deep, and your heart is so heavy, *it seems it will surely break*...I don't understand, but God does!

When you've come through long, dark nights and forged toilsome trails through thick, blackened forests, and weariness overtakes you 'til you feel you may collapse...*if someone doesn't help* – I don't understand, but God does!

When you ask questions that no one can answer and ponder concerns only hurting people even consider, *and you long to know why when any logical explanation wouldn't be enough*...I don't understand, but God does!

When your valleys of sorrow deepen into canyons of despair, your hills of hurt to mountains of grief, your days of youthfulness and wonder and nights of serenity and rest *seem to turn to dreary days of desperation and endless eves of anguish*... I don't understand, but God does!

When we don't understand, God does!

When we don't know why, God does!

When we don't know *what or how* to feel, God does!

When we wonder who truly cares or if anyone does, God does! When we question whether anyone could touch our pain and heal our hurt; or offer internal strength, enduring love, and eternal hope...*when no one else can*, God does!

OPPORTUNITY KNOCKS
© 1984 Wayne Flora

Opportunity knocked and I turned it away;
Never opened the door – and I smugly did say,
"Millions more just like that! What's a few passed me by?"
    But I sensed I was wrong,
    And that this chance alone
    Now forever was gone...
I had shoved it aside.

Intently I waited longing once more to hear
Opportunity knocking as in way yesteryear.
Others came – that is true – but none like the one!
    How I grieved deep inside
    That my life I'd deprived,
    And I now realized
It would never return!

For just what the reasons opportunity missed?
Fear of failure? Distress? Or discomforting risk?
Was I cold and complacent? Or unsettled and rude?
    Why pass by the chance
    To grow and advance,
    All my dreams to enhance?
Such a sad thing to do!

Rather follow the Light...Go wherever it shines!
Abandon your fears; all regrets leave behind!
For where doors let through Light,
    There is Christ as your Guide!
    Take a step – walk on through!
    Let the Lord challenge you!
    See what God wants to do!
Opportunity knocks in your life!

HE MET US
© 1996 Wayne Flora

It was not in ivory towers,
    Distant throne rooms far removed,
That God touched us as it matters,
    And His love for us He proved.
Not in far-off light years faint,
    Some celestial glistening sphere...
So detached t'would seem but quaint
    His hope to ever heal our fears.

But He met us at the place
    Where humanity feels pain –
In a manger's tiny face,
    In the stable's quiet disdain.
Lowing oxen, bleating sheep,
    Were the child's first welcome cheer.
Lowly shepherds bowing deep,
    Humble parents bending near.

Yes, He met us in a life
    Not at all unlike our own,
Filled with suffering, toil, and strife,
    Not an anguish left unknown.
Whate're experience you'll ever know,
    Has already Jesus met;
And there's no place you can go,
    That He hasn't been there yet.

From the manger to the cross,
　　From the Babe to Dying Son,
There has no one suffered loss
　　As when war with sin was won.
For He walked with us to death,
　　Then beyond its ghastly veil,
Through its valley and its breath
　　'Til He rose again to tell.

That there's hope for every sinner,
　　And there's health for all infirmed;
And there's life where things are better,
　　And there's ease for all concerned!
There's just no one knows you best,
　　Or your loved ones here no more,
Like the Savior, I insist,
　　Who has walked this way before!

For He met us as a person,
　　Though as God and yet as man;
And His heart is filled with mercy,
　　For He cares as no one can!
How you feel about your loved one –
　　How you hurt, as love demands,
Is so felt also by Jesus...
　　No one better understands!

BACK TO THE FATHER
© 1993 Wayne Flora

How sad the day you walk away...
  A tear in the Father's eye.
A grief so deep in His broken heart
  As He quivers and begins to cry.

He knows the road you choose ahead;
  He's wiser far than you.
It's filled with spoils of plundered dead...
  None e're return, but a few.

And of those ones who make it back,
  There's pain for years to come;
For gashes, cuts, deep wounds of hurt
  Leave scars when healing's done.

Beyond the shelter of His care
  Are dangers lurking by.
The helpless, naked, wretched soul
  Is prey to Satan's eye.

He dares to steal away all hope
  And leave you faithless yet,
And crush you 'til the breath of life
  Is gone, and Death is met.

There's broken hearts and broken homes
　Outside the Father's care;
There's wasted years and wasted lives,
　And little left to spare.

But back at home where all is safe,
　The Father's waiting still...
His tear-glazed eyes still raised away
　To where you chose to live.

He has the hope and prayer within
　That one day you'll return.
Though you're convinced you'll find no place –
　Remember, you're His son.

Return, dear Friend, to home at last.
　Be done with life's dread pain.
Go back home from whence you came,
　And begin to live again!

THE WISDOM OF "WITH"
© 1993 Wayne Flora

This is a poem of the wisdom of "with,"
  The cute little word that will give you a lift!
"That's silly, now, Pastor! It's too tiny to matter!
  Why, the much bigger words would surely lift better!"

But no, this word "with" in conjunction with others
  Puts people together, like sisters and brothers,
And fathers and mothers and grandparents so sweet...
  It connects special people to the ones they should meet!

O, I know it seems small, and so shy by itself,
  But when "with's" among friends, it performs at its best!
Among people who love, why it feels right at home
  Uniting God's family, leaving no one alone!

But the most special place that I like "with" to be
  Is right next to Jesus and right next to me!
I feel so close to God knowing "with" is beside
  Bringing Jesus so near, even living inside!

So, wisdom would teach us that what matters the most –
  Not just knowing of Jesus, but to actually get close –
And the only thing ever that should come in between
  Is the little word "with" joining us to the King!

I DON'T UNDERSTAND, BUT I KNOW...
© 2001 Wayne Flora

I *don't understand* the chaos and disorder that covered the earth in the day of Creation, but I <u>know</u> God's Spirit moved upon the face of the waters, and God said, "Let there be Light!" – AND THERE WAS!

I *don't understand* the blight of sin that accosted humanity in the midst of the most beautiful garden of all time, and removed all of us from the pristine, precious fellowship of God, but I <u>know</u> God prepared a path back into His presence, and said, "Let there be a Plan!" – AND THERE WAS!

I *don't understand* the wanderings of men through the heat-scorched deserts of life and the painful toils so unnecessary to human experience, but I <u>know</u> God sent a Shepherd, a Good Shepherd, and Great Shepherd, to take us by the hand, and lead us back by the still waters, and said, "Let there be Rest!" – AND THERE WAS!

I *don't understand* the agony of the cross nor the boundless love that would motivate the Father to surrender His only Son to the tortuous penalties of sin, and liberate men from its vice-clutch bondage forever, but I <u>know</u> Jesus died there, and God said, "Let there be Help!" – AND THERE WAS!

I *don't understand* how the pressures of the depths form diamonds, and the turbulent waters of time form gems, how violent explosions in the dark night's far reaches of our universe form glistening celestial stars, nor how the death-throes of childbirth bring forth new life, and the crush of a rose petal fragrance, and the bitterness of pain the awareness of our need for God, nor how God could *possibly make some things intended for evil* EVER turn out for our good...but I know God is the Lord of Life, the Master of Restoration, the Giver of Love, and God said, "Let there be Hope!" – AND THERE WAS!

I *don't understand* the valley-deep grief you now feel, nor its untimely and senseless cause, the mysteries of the myriad unanswered questions that trouble your hearts and perplex your souls, nor the length of your journey before you and the days of sorrow you surely shall face, but I know God is with you in it, and will walk you through it, and shall lead you beyond it, and cares how you fare for the journey, and will never, ever leave you alone, and God said, "Let there be Comfort!" – AND THERE IS AND THERE ALWAYS SHALL BE!

Dealing with Discouragement
I Sam. 30:1-6, 18, 19; I Cor. 13
©2000 Wayne Flora

Introduction

1. Everybody knows doubt, discouragement, and despair.
2. None is unfamiliar with the heartsickness that comes when hopes are dashed, plans fail, or the future is dimmed by uncertain circumstances and uninvited crises.
3. But "no temptation taken you..." (I Cor. 10:13; KJV)

<u>Transition</u>: Let me take you along that all too familiar path of darkness and help you identify the <u>proper doors</u> to take to get off that self-destructive road!

Account of David's Life

1. David from a shepherd had been *anointed king, but not yet appointed king.* He had been *delegated, but not yet coronated.*
2. He was a *supposed threat* to Saul, and was now running for his life, hiding in caves.
3. Having been rejected by Israel and now by King Achish of the Philistines as the battle was set in array.
4. David is now headed home, 3 long days weary journey, disillusioned, disappointed, and disheartened. Here's what he and his weary soldiers find when they return:

I. DISASTER AND DISTRESS (1-6)

   a. (TLB) "As David and his men looked at the ruins and realized what had happened to their families" (3), "David was *seriously worried*" (6).
   b. Immediate grief! Uncertainty as to the well-being of their families!

A. Disaster

   1. Unplanned, unforeseen, unanticipated crises!
   2. Tragic *interruption and distraction* to the plans and hopes you had.

3. "Apparent" befalling of ill that *instantly* takes away a) will to live, b) heart to hope, and c) courage to dream.

B. Resulting Distress
1. Onslaught of shock and paralyzing sense of panic.
2. Horrid sense of helplessness and loss of orientation as to right and proper recourse.
3. No instinctive inclination of active response.
4. Loss of prudent initiative and lack of judgment as to what to do.

C. Some of It You Personally Brought On Yourself, David!
1. David "turned his head..." This happens when you turn your head!
2. He was fighting for the wrong causes! (context)

   a. Preoccupied with wrong ambitions.
   b. In the wrong camp.
   c. Away from his spiritual responsibilities for his own family.

3. "Amalek" – "flesh"

   a. Antagonized God's people entering Canaan.
   b. Always a distraction from the will of God.
   c. Should long ago have been conquered and overcome (Ex. 17; I Sam. 15).
   d. Cost Saul his kingdom!
   e. Now threatening to cost David his kingdom!

4. But God is still in control!

   a. Using as correction!
   b. Causing you to see yourself!
   c. Testing your faith!
   d. Protecting and preserving your family!

II. DESPAIR AND DISCOURAGEMENT (4-6)

A. Despair (4, 5)

1. Utter hopelessness, complete loss of heart!
2. Suspending overwhelming; agony of dismay!
3. Wretched embitterment for the gall of pain you now feel...AND WE ALWAYS THINK THE WORST!

    a. Are David's families safe? Yes!
    b. Has anyone been harmed? No!
    c. But WE ALWAYS THINK THE WORST!

        1) "Spouse home late?" Think what? ("Accident, hold-up, ticket")
        2) "Spouse home late often?" ("Another man/woman, affair, etc.")

    d. Your *worries escalate into fears* and *your fears into imaginations* (II Cor. 10:2ff.)

        1) Pain in chest? Think what? (Heart attack, coronary thrombosis, etc.)
        2) Dizziness? Think what? (Stroke, etc.)
        3) Teen acting strange? Think what? (Drugs, sex, gangs, etc.)

B. Resulting Discouragement

1. Negating of your "fearless (or convicting) strength of spirit."
2. The "trial of your faith" is the *testing* of all those time-worn convictions so precious to your confidence in Christ:

    a. Standards
    b. Values
    c. Principles
    d. Promises

        e.   Prophecies

        f.   Truths

        g.   Mores

    3.   "Discouragement" is *the inability to see an answer and the suspended sense of resulting dismay and protracted grief about the situation.*

        a.   Text: David was *"seriously worried"* (6; TLB)

        b.   His men are no longer rational! *They're looking for somebody to blame!* So they consider mutiny! They consider "stoning him" (6).

        c.   How Do You Get Out?!

III. DETERMINATION AND DECISION (6ff.)

A. Determination

    1.   "Strength of will"

    2.   "Volitional wisdom"

    3.   "Grace to make the right choice"

    4.   David, *"encouraged himself in the Lord,"* (KJV); (NKJV, *"strengthened* himself in the Lord").

        a.   Strengthen means, "to make yourself stronger."

        b.   ..."to build yourself up"

    5.   SOMETIMES NOBODY WILL – OR CAN!

        a.   Some roads you go alone!

        b.   Some turns you choose alone!

    6.   "Righteous determination" is the *"unwillingness to listen to the discouragements of others!"*

        a.   ...or to be swayed by the circumstances.

        b.   Refusal to be destroyed, brought down in defeat!

        c.   Eg. Bartimaeus (Mk. 10:46ff.)

B. Resulting Decision

1. Point of *volitional crisis...*

    a. You miss it, you die!
    b. You choose, you live!

2. Point of *volitional initiative...*(II Ki. 7)

    a. "Why sit we here until we die?" (II Ki. 7:3; KJV)
    b. An awakening to the right choice; "came to himself" (Lk. 15:17)

3. Point of *deliberate intention...*

    a. Critical analysis!
    b. Specific decisiveness!

4. David *decided*

    a. "This is *not* my destiny!"
    b. "This is *not* what God told me!"
    c. "This is *not* the way to die!"

C. How To Decide!

1. Recognize God!

    a. His purpose
    b. His promises
    c. His perspective

2. Renounce the Devil!

    a. His disguises
    b. His devices
    c. His deceptions

3. Rise Up!

    a. Do something! (II Ki. 7)
    b. Do it wholeheartedly! (II Chron. 25:2)
    c. Do it completely! (II Chron. 20:33)

4. Return! (to Bethel, Gn. 35; Prodigal, Lk. 15)

    a. Get up! (Lepers/Prodigal)
    b. Get out! (Israel from Egypt/Lot)
    c. Get back! (Jacob/Prodigal)

IV. DIVINE ENCOURAGEMENT AND DELIVERANCE (6ff.; 18, 19)

A. Divine Encouragement
1. Return of courage
2. Enrichment of spirit
3. Restoration of hope

    a. Your confidence not in men...
    b. not in circumstances…
    c. not in self…
    d. BUT IN GOD! (Ps. 42) Inquire of the Lord! (8) Trust His word!

4. Restoration of confidence

    a. Paradigm shift (think/see differently)
    b. Perspective adjustment
    c. Appropriation of faith!

B. Resulting Deliverance (18, 19)
1. Manifestation of God's glory in the situation!
2. Restoration of your dreams!

Conclusion: As we "strengthen" ourselves in the Lord, we will realize deliverance and restoration of hope.

Appendix

Resources, Where To Go

A prominent reason why persons suffering anxiety or depression do not seek help is because they simply *do not know where to turn or who to ask*. While *distant help* is appreciated, local *help is most urgently needed!* Hotlines can provide compassionate, safe, *distant* "ears," but *immediacy and personability* may yet be lacking when up-close, face-to-face care is desperately needed. That said, however, hotline crisis counselors *may be* well-trained and resourced to offer definitive guidance *toward local community help centers and clinics* specializing in anxiety disorder and depression.

In this section, I should simply like to offer several resources and call centers you or anyone you know could reference. If you wish to speak with someone about your experience, and inquire further as to local counseling and treatment services available to you right where you live, you may wish to consider these. Simply inform yourself of the capable, caring persons who stand by to offer help – then, "reach out" and take the hand extended and find hope and encouragement for your need!

Permit me first to ask you the most obvious questions and let's see what resource persons are already available to you:

1. Do you have *a trusted family member or friend* that you could talk to? Write his or her name and contact information here:

    _____

    Name

    _____

    Phone number

    Can you feel "safe" talking to this person? Are you "ready" *and willing* to do this, that is, ask this person for help?

2. Do you know *a pastor or associate minister* in a local church in your community that you could feel comfortable speaking with? Write his or her name and contact information here:

    _____

    Name

    _____

    Phone number

    How do you feel about talking with a minister? Consider the possibility that he or she could offer you spiritual encouragement, prayers, support, and guidance. Are you ready to schedule an appointment with this person?

3. Do you know (or *know of*) *a counseling center (or Christian counseling center) or therapist* in your community? Write the name of the center or person and contact information in the spaces provided:

_____

Name

_____

Phone number

Are you ready to make an appointment with this center? Consider calling them to schedule a visit.

4. Do you have or know *a family physician* in the community that you should visit and share with him or her the symptoms you have been experiencing? Write his or her contact information below:

_____

Name

_____

Phone number

Are you ready to make that call? Schedule an appointment with your doctor and let that person "assess" your situation – it may be more *manageable* than you think, and a treatment plan may be easily followed and help you begin to feel better. If he or she recommends referral, are you willing to consider following their advice?

5. Do you know of *a psychologist or psychiatrist* in your community you might be willing to visit? You might not be able to make an appointment *without* the referral of your family physician, but if they *do take appointments* without referral, you might consider calling them. Write the contact information below:

_____

Name

_____

Phone number

6. Finally, perhaps there is no one *locally* that you feel good about calling. But is there *a distant friend or acquaintance* you might feel comfortable to confide in? A former school teacher, perhaps, or college professor? A coach or mentor you knew in younger years? Or even a high school friend who lives in a distant state now – someone "away from home" that you could speak with and feel "safe" telling them what you are experiencing? Who is that person and what is his or her contact information?

_____

Name

_____

Phone number

Are you ready to call? Consider doing it now. Talking with *someone* will help you have "hope" and knowing that someone cares for you right now will matter. Place the call.

Now then, maybe you don't feel good speaking to *ANYONE* at all that you know personally. That's okay...I understand. Then consider calling *a trusted but anonymous help center or hotline.* I will list for you below some of the more prominent ones for you to call. Pick up your phone and call someone soon. *Or,* visit a website listed and see what resources are available to you to help you at this difficult moment in your life.

Know this – I'm praying diligently for you. You have not read this book by accident. God cares for you and I want you to know you matter to Him. He will help you though this. Keep the faith!

Call Centers

- <u>Anxiety and Depression Association of America
  (ADAA)</u> provides information on prevention, treatment
  and symptoms of anxiety, depression and related
  conditions (240-485-1001).
- <u>Children and Adults with Attention-Deficit/Hyperactivity
  Disorder (CHADD)</u> provides information and referrals on
  ADHD, including local support groups (800-233-4050).
- <u>Depression and Bipolar Support Alliance
  (DBSA)</u> provides information on bipolar disorder and
  depression, offers in-person and online support groups
  and forums (800-826-3632).
- <u>International OCD Foundation</u> provides information on
  OCD and treatment referrals (617-973-5801).
- <u>National Center of Excellence for Eating
  Disorders (NCEED)</u> provides up-to-date, reliable and
  evidence-based information about eating disorders (800-
  931-2237).
- <u>Schizophrenia and Related Disorders Alliance of America
  (SARDAA)</u> offers Schizophrenia Anonymous self-help
  groups and toll-free teleconferences (240-423-9432).
- <u>Sidran Institute</u> helps people understand, manage and
  treat trauma and dissociation; maintains a helpline for
  information and referrals (410-825-8888).
- <u>Treatment and Research Advancements for Borderline
  Personality Disorder (TARA)</u> offers a referral center for
  information, support, education and treatment options for
  BPD (888-482-7227).

- SAMHSA Treatment Locator provides referrals to low-cost/sliding scale mental health care, substance abuse and dual diagnosis treatment (800-662-4357).[192]
- Hopeline, "Hopeline – You Talk. We Listen." (Call or text: 919-231-4525 or 877-235-4525).[193]
- Families for Depression Awareness provides call or text service to assist adults suffering depression (800-273-8255 or text LISTEN to 741741).[194]
- Psychology Today Therapists, Psychiatrists, Treatment Centers, and Support Groups is not a "call center," but a nationwide directory of resource centers and professional counslors: *https://www.psychologytoday.com/us/*.

Christian Counseling Referral Services[195]

- International Association of Christian Counseling Professionals: *http://www.vision.edu/iaccp/*
- Focus on the Family – U.S. Counseling Consultation and Referrals: *https://www.focusonthefamily.com/get-help/counseling-services-and-referrals/*

---

[192] "Top Helpline Resources," *NAMI – National Alliance on Mental Health, 2020,* https://www.nami.org/Support-Education/NAMI-HelpLine/Top-HelpLine-Resources (accessed on April 20, 2020). Each of the help centers recommended above are referred by one of the most reputable institutions in our country. This list is not meant to be exhaustive, but selective.
[193] "Hopeline – You Talk. We Listen," *Hopeline,* https://www.hopeline-nc.org/?gclid=CjwKCAjwkPX0BRBKEiwA7THxiA1EqO1sGmMTMC-HP82XDyEok1qqir_0X5n1JzwZuexAMpWTxwO_NBoC4CQQAvD_BwE (accessed on April 20, 2020).
[194] Families for Depression Awareness, "Our Mission," *Families for Depression Awareness,* 2019, http://www.familyaware.org/ (accessed on April 20, 2020).
[195] Cordeiro, p. 211. Referenced from Cordeiro's *Leading On Empty, Refilling Your Tank and Renewing Your Passion.*

- American Association of Christian Counselors Referral Network: *https://www.aacc.net/referral-network/*
- Christian Care Connect, Clients, Counselors, Coaches, & Clinics: *https://connect.aacc.net/?search_type=distance*
- National Christian Counselors Association: *https://www.ncca.org/Directory/Terms.aspx?search=*
- Meier Clinics Christian Counseling Services: *https://www.meierclinics.com/*
- Better Help, Affordable Private Online Counseling: *https://www.betterhelp.com/helpme/*
- New Life Christian Counseling Network: *https://newlife.com/counselors/*
- Mental Health America, Finding Therapy: *https://www.mhanational.org/finding-therapy*
- Christian Counselor Directory Telehealth Friendly Network: *https://www.christiancounselordirectory.com/*

Share Your Copy?

Did this book speak to you? Do you know someone who might need to read it? A family member or friend? A colleague or peer? A neighbor, perhaps? Would you oblige to loan your copy to this person and let him or her read it? Or perhaps, purchase and give them their own copy of the book?

Who is that person? Write his or her name and contact information here, then be in touch to establish relationship and offer support!

_____
Name

_____
Phone number

Bibliography

"1956-1957 Boston Celtics Schedule and Results." *Basketball Reference*. n.d. https://www.basketball-reference.com/teams/BOS/1957_games.html (accessed February 2, 2020).

34 Verses About No Other is God. The Lockman Foundation. 1960-1995. https://bible.knowing-jesus.com/topics/No-Other-Is-God (accessed February 19, 2020).

"Adolescent Mental Health." *World Health Organization*. October 23, 2019. https://www.who.int/news-room/fact-sheets/detail/adolescent-mental-health (accessed January 22, 2020).

Alund, Natalie Neysa. "Pastor, Mental Health Advocate Jarrid Wilson Dies by Apparent Suicide, Wife Reports." *USA Today*. September 11, 2019. https://www.usatoday.com/story/news/2019/09/11/jarrid-wilson-suicide-apparent-death-after-mental-health-tweets/2284793001/ (accessed March 8, 2020).

"American Airlines Flight 191 ATC Recording, May 25, 1979." http://www.planecrashinfo.com/lastwords.htm and http://www.planecrashinfo.com/MP4%20AA191.htm (accessed on February 13, 2020).

Amundsen, Darrell W. "The Anguish and Agonies of Charles Haddon Spurgeon," *Christian History* 10, no. 29 (1991).

Article 11, Declaration of Faith. "Beliefs." *Church of God*. http://www.churchofgod.org/beliefs/declaration-of-faith (accessed on January 31, 2020).

Augustyn, Adam et al. "Siren, Greek Mythology." *Encyclopaedia Britannica*. Edited by revised and updated Amy Tikkanen. Dec. 19, 2017. https://www.britannica.com/topic/Siren-Greek-mythology (accessed February 11, 2020).

"AV Fistula Creation." *Azura Vascular Care*. 2017, 2020.
    https://www.azuravascularcare.com/medical-
    services/dialysis-access-management/av-fistula-creation/
    (accessed February 27, 2020).

Benzkofer, Stephan. "Worst Plane Crash in U.S. History"
    Chicago Tribune, May 25, 2014, para. 2,
    https://www.chicagotribune.com/news/ct-1979-ohare-
    crash-flashback-0525-20140525-story.html (accessed on
    February 12, 2020).

"Bethany, Bible Word Meanings." *New Christian Study Bible*.
    2019. https://newchristianbiblestudy.org/concept/bethany
    (accessed February 5, 2020).

"Biology of Depression – Neuroplasticity and Endocrinology."
    MentalHelp.net. Inc. American Addition Centers. n.d.
    (accessed February 4, 2020).

Boggs, Will. "Appetite Changes Reflect Distinct Subgroups of
    Depression." *Psychiatry and Behavioral Health Learning
    Network*. July 5, 2018. Will Boggs.
    https://www.psychcongress.com/news/appetite-changes-
    reflect-distinct-subgroups-depression (accessed February
    10, 2020).

Brown, Deaver. "Personal Finance & Investing Survival Kit."
    Simply Media, Inc. Lincoln, MA: Simply Media. Inc., 1999.

Commodores. "She's a Brick House." *Commodores, Brick
    House.* 1977. Album.

Cordeiro, Wayne. *Leading on Empty, Refilling Your Tank and
    Renewing Your Passion*. Minneapolis, Minnesota: Bethany
    Publishing House, 2009.

Cox, John. "Ask the Captain: How do pilots decide when to
    take off?" *USA Today*. Sept. 29, 2013.
    https://www.usatoday.com/story/travel/columnist/
    cox/2013/09/29/ takeoff-speed-v1-v2-rotate/2885565/
    (accessed on February 12, 2020).

Crary, David. "Stress Over Violence, Other Issues Multiply for Clergy." *The Daily Reflector.* February 2020.

"Depression." *World Health Organization.* Dec. 4, 2019. https://www.who.int/en/news-room/fact-sheets/detail/depression (accessed January 22, 2020).

"Drugs and Medications, Ativan." *WebMD.* n.d. https://www.webmd.com/drugs /2/drug-6685/ativan-oral/details (accessed February 17, 2020).

Dubin, Kaci. "Xanax." *Drugs.com.* Mar. 4, 2019. https://www.drugs.com/xanax.html (accessed February 1, 2020).

Duke Today Staff. "Clergy More Likely To Suffer From Depression Anxiety." *Duke Today.* Aug. 27, 2013. https://today.duke.edu/2013/08/clergydepressionnewsrele ase (accessed February 11, 2020).

"Enervating." *Lexico.com.* Powered by Oxford. n.d. https://www.lexico.com/en/ definition/enervating (accessed March 15, 2020).

"enthusiasm (n.)." *Online Etymology Dictionary.* Douglas Harper. 2001-2020. https://www.etymonline.com/word/enthusiasm (accessed February 20, 2020).

Erwin, Joe and John Gunn. *I Still Believe.* Directed by Andrew Erwin and John Erwin. Santa Monica, California: Lions Gate Entertainment, Inc., 2020, https://www.lionsgate.com/movies/i-still-believe (accessed on April 11, 2020).

Evans, Sara, Marcus Hummin, and Darrell Scott. "Born to Fly." *Wikipedia, The Free Encyclopedia.* CD. Prod. Sara Evans and Paul Worley. Nashville, June 26, 2000.

"Facts and Statistics." *Anxiety and Depression Association of America.* n.d. https://adaa.org/about-adaa/press-room/facts-statistics (accessed January 22, 2020).

Families for Depression Awareness, "Our Mission," *Families for Depression Awareness,* 2019, http://www.familyaware.org/ (accessed on April 20, 2020).

Flora, Wayne. "Authentic Copy of Handwritten Birth Certificate." November 19, 1956.

———. *Personal Spiritual Journal.* 2006.

Folkart, Burk A. "Clara Peller (Where's the Beef?) Dies at 86." *Los Angeles Times.* Aug. 12, 1987. https://www.latimes.com/archives/la-xpm-1987-08-12-mn-440-story.html (accessed March 17, 2020).

Food Waste FAQs. n.d. https://www.usda.gov/foodwaste/faqs (accessed February 5, 2020).

Freeborn, Donna and Chad Halderman-Englert, Reviewers. "Metanephrine (Urine)." *Health Encyclopedia.* University of Rochester Medical Center. n.d. https://www.urmc.rochester.edu/encyclopedia/content.aspx?contenttypeid=167&contentid=metanephrine_urine (accessed February 17, 2020).

Gabriel, Charles Hutchinson. *The Singers and Their Songs: Sketches of Living Gospel Hymn Writers.* Chicago, Illinois: The Rodeheaver Company, 1916.

"GAP Insurance." *Wikipedia, The Free Encyclopedia.* Nov. 2, 2019. https://en.wikipedia.org/wiki/GAP_insurance (accessed February 10, 2020).

Garvey, Kathy Keatley. "Stop and Smell the Roses." *Bug Squad, Happenings in the Insect World.* Agriculture and Natural Resources University of California. Oct. 26, 2010. https://ucanr.edu/blogs/blogcore/postdetail.cfm?postnum=3681 (accessed March 15, 2020).

"Greenville Express Care." *Donald A. Ribeiro.* 2020. https://www.ribeiromd.com/?site=Expresscare (accessed on February 25, 2020).

Groningen, Gerard Van. "Covenant." *Baker's Evangelical Dictionary of Biblical Theology.* Edited by Walter A. Elwell.

1996. https://www.biblestudytools.com/dictionary/
covenant/ (accessed February 21, 2020).

"Henry Wadsworth Longfellow Quotes." *Your Dictionary.*
LoveToKnow Corp., 1996-2020.
https://quotes.yourdictionary.com/author/henry-
wadsworth-longfellow/ (accessed on April 2, 2020).

History.com Editors. "Worst Air Crash in U.S. History."
History: This Day in History. Mar. 3, 2010. A & E Television
Networks, pub. Updated July 28, 2019.
https://www.history.com/this-day-in-history/worst-air-
crash-in-u-s-history (accessed on February 12, 2020).

Hogan, Dan, ed. "Largest, Fastest Array of Microscopic
'Traffic Cops' For Optical Communications." *ScienceDaily.*
University of California – Berkeley. April 12, 2019.
www.sciencedaily.com/releases/2019/04/190412094745.
htm (accessed February 3, 2020).

"Hopeline – You Talk. We Listen," *Hopeline,*
https://www.hopeline-
nc.org/?gclid=CjwKCAjwkPX0BRBKEiwA7THxiA1EqO1s
GmMTMC-HP82XDyEok1qqir_
0X5n1JzwZuexAMpWTxwO_NBoC4CQQAvD_BwE
(accessed on April 20, 2020).

"Hunger in America." *AmpleHarvest.org.* 2019.
https://ampleharvest.org/hunger/?gclid=Cj0KCQiAhojzBR
C3ARIsAGtNtHUUixJ5EyFTfwoU130XR87a0LelD4n_gGf
YUKzDPHvNpIvULuUTJxUaAgNXEALw_wcB (accessed
February 6, 2020).

"Is God Fair?" *Got Questions -- Your Questions. Biblical
Answers.* Jan. 2, 2020. https://www.gotquestions.org/is-
God-fair.html (accessed March 2, 2020).

Kaneda, Toshiko. "How Many People Have Ever Lived On
Earth?" *PRB – Population Reference Bureau.* Jan. 23, 2020.
https://www.prb.org/

howmanypeoplehaveeverlivedonearth/ (accessed March 3, 2020).

Kennelly, Stacey. "A Scientific Reason to Stop and Smell the Roses." *Greater Good Magazine, Science-Based Insights for a Meaningful Life.* Greater Good Science Center at UC Berkley. July 3, 2012. https://greatergood. berkeley.edu/article/item/a scientific reason to stop and smell the roses (accessed March 15, 2020).

Lang, J. Stephen. "What Does the Bible Say About Sickness and Healing?" *CBN.* 1999. https://www1.cbn.com/what-does-bible-say-about-sickness-and-healing (accessed March 17, 2020).

Lapsley, Authur Brooks, ed., *The Writings of Abraham Lincoln, Vol. 1, 1832-1843* (New York: The Knickerbocker Press, 1905), 235.

"Lexapro." *Drugs.com.* Sanjai Sinha, reviewer. Dec. 14, 2018. Sec. "What is Lexapro?" https://www.drugs.com/lexapro.html (accessed February 8, 2020).

McDaniel, Debbie. "7 Bible Figures Who Struggled with Depression." *Crosswalk.com.* June 5, 2017. https://www.crosswalk.com/faith/spiritual-life/7-bible-figures-who-struggled-with-depression.html (accessed March 17, 2020).

McFly, Marty. "Insider Series: A Day in the Life of a Pilot – During the Flight." *The Points Guys.* Oct. 1, 2017. https://thepointsguy.com/ 2017/10/what-pilots-do-during-the-flight/ (accessed on February 12, 2020).

McGavran, Donald A. *Understanding Church Growth.* 1st ed. Grand Rapids: Eerdmans Publishing Company, 1970.

"Mental Health Care by the Numbers." *National Alliance on Mental Health.* 2019. https://www.nami.org/learn-more/mental-health-by-the-numbers (accessed January 31, 2020).

Morgan, R. J. "How Many Promises In The Bible." In *Nelson's Complete Book of Stories, Illustrations, & Quotes*, 645-646. Nashville, Tennessee: Thomas Nelson Publishers, 2000.

Muehlenberg, Bill. "The Lament Psalms." *CultureWatch, Bill Muehlenberg's Commentary on Issues of the Day.* Feb. 2, 2012. https://billmuehlenberg.com/2012/02/02/the-lament-psalms/ (accessed March 17, 2020).

Neighborhood Psychiatry. "Why 75% of Anxiety Sufferers Fail to get Proper Care." *Psychology Today.* Aug. 13, 2018. https://www.psychologytoday.com/us/blog/psychiatry-the-people/201808/why-75-percent-anxiety-sufferers-fail-get-proper-care (accessed January 31, 2020).

Nicholls, Emma. "What Causes Disorientation?" *Healthline.* MD Reviewed by Seunggu Han. Aug. 22, 2019. https://www.healthline.com/health/disorientation (accessed January 28, 2020).

"Number of Combinations." *The Rubik Zone.* n.d. https://www.therubikzone.com/number-of-combinations/ (accessed January 26, 2020).

"Passion." *Merriam-Webster Dictionary.* 1828, 2020. https://www.merriam-webster.com/dictionary/passion#h1 (accessed March 13, 2020).

"REM Sleep and Our Dreaming Lives." *ResMed.* 2015. https://sleep.mysplus.com/library/category3/REM_Sleep_and_Our_Dreaming_Lives.html (accessed February 21, 2020).

Robertson, Archibald T. *Word Pictures in the New Testament.* Grand Rapids: Chistian Classics Ethereal Library, 1930-1933.

Shakespeare, William. "Hamlet, Act III, Scene I [To be, or not to be]." 1564-1616. *Poets.org.* https://poets.org/poem/hamlet-act-iii-scene-i-be-or-not-be (accessed February 12, 2020).

Shiel, William C., Jr. "Medical Definition of REM Sleep."
    MedicineNet. Dec. 27, 2018.
    https://www.medicinenet.com/script/
    main/art.asp?articlekey=8677 (accessed February 21, 2020).

Sifferlin, Alexandra. "Divorce More Likely When Wife Falls
    Ill." May 1, 2014. https://time.com/83486/divorce-is-more-
    likely-if-the-wife-not-the-husband-gets-sick/ (accessed
    February 14, 2020).

Smith, Robert S. "Belting Out the Blues as Believers: The
    Importance of Singing Lament." *Themelios,* 2017: 89, Sec.
    5.1 and 5.2.

Smith, Yolanda B. "What Is the Half-Life of a Drug?" *News-
    Medical, Life Sciences.* Aug. 23, 2018. https://www.news-
    medical.net/health/What-is-the-Half-Life-of-a-Drug.aspx
    (accessed February 1, 2020).

Spurgeon, Charles. *The Minister's Fainting Fits,* Lecture XL,
    retrieved from www.the-highway.com/articleSept99.html.

Stancill, Susan. "In His Will On His Wheel." nd.

Strong, James. "4834 – sumpatheo." In *Strong's Exhaustive
    Concordance of the Bible,* by James Strong. Nashville,
    Tennessee: Abingdon Press, 1890.

"Suicide claims more lives than war, murder, and natural
    disasters combined." *American Foundation for Suicide
    Prevention.* 2015.
    https://www.theovernight.org/?fuseaction=cms.page&id=
    1034 (accessed February 20, 2020).

Sullivan, Steve. "David, a Warrior after God's Own Heart:
    Depressed?" *Next Sunday Resources.* May 23, 2018.
    https://www.nextsunday.com/david-a-warrior-after-gods-
    own-heart-depressed/ (accessed March 17, 2020).

Teresa, Mother and Rev. Brian Kolodiejchuk. *Mother Teresa:
    Come Be My Light.* New York: Doubleday, 2007.

Thayer, Joseph Henry. *A Greek-English Lexicon of the New Testament.* Translated by Thayer. New York: Harper and Brothers, 1889.

"The Endocrine System and Glands of the Human Body." *WebMD.* Sec. "What Is a Gland?" https://www.webmd.com/diabetes/endocrine-system-facts#1 (accessed on February 4, 2020).

"The State of Mental Health in America." *Mental Health America.* 2020. https://www.mhanational.org/issues/state-mental-health-america (accessed January 31, 2020).

_____. https://www.mhanational.org/issues/mental-health-america-adult-data#six (accessed on January 31, 2020).

Thomas, Gilbert. *William Cowper and the Eighteenth Century.* London: Ivor Nicholson and Watson Ltd., 1935.

"Thoughts On The Business of Life." *Forbes Quotes.* Forbes Quotes.com LLCTM. 2015. https://www.forbes.com/quotes/2656/ (accessed January 27, 2020).

"Top Helpline Resources," *NAMI – National Alliance on Mental Health, 2020,* https://www.nami.org/Support-Education/NAMI-HelpLine/Top-HelpLine-Resources (accessed on April 20, 2020).

Trueman, C. R. "What Can Miserable Christians Sing?" *The Wages of Spin: Critical Writings on Historical and Contemporary Evangelicalism.* Ross-Shire: Christian Focus Publishing, 2004.

Underhill, Evelyn. *Mysticism.* New York: New American Library, 1974 [1930].

"V Speeds." *Wikipedia, The Free Encyclopedia.* Updated Jan. 9, 2020. https://en.wikipedia.org/wiki/V speeds (accessed on February 12, 2020).

Wagner, Karen Dineen. "Anxiety Disorders in Children and Adolescents: New Findings." *Psychiatric Times* 36 (Feb. 2019).

"Welcome to the Rubik Zone." *The Rubik Zone.* n.d. https://www.therubikzone.com/ (accessed January 26, 2020).

"Where's the Beef?" *Wikipedia, The Free Encyclopedia.* Updated Mar. 11, 2020. https://en.wikipedia.org/wiki/Where%27s the beef%3F (accessed March 17, 2020).

Wierzbicka, Anna. *What Did Jesus Mean? Explaining the Sermon on the Mount and the Parables in Simple and Universal Human Concepts.* New York: Oxford University Press, 2001.

Winerman, Lea. "By the Numbers: Antidepressant Use On the Rise." *American Psychological Association.* November 2017. https://www.apa.org/monitor/2017/11/numbers (accessed February 11, 2020).

Zumbach, Laura. "The Legacy of Flight 191: When An Engine Ripped Off A DC-10 At O'Hare It Killed 273 People, And Changed Air Travel Forever." May 23, 2019. *Chicago Tribune.* http://graphics.chicagotribune.com/flight-191-anniversary/ (accessed on February 13, 2020).

Made in the USA
Columbia, SC
19 June 2020

11475351R00178